GREAT BRITISH
RIDGE WALKS

Bill Birkett

David & Charles

To mountain people everywhere –
a race apart

Page 1: Looking to the pinnacles at the end of the Crib Goch ridge, with the summit of Snowdon seen beyond

Page 2 and 3: A sublime snowy scene – over tranquil Little Langdale Tarn to the Greenburn Horseshoe arrayed above. Wetherlam stands to the left with Swirl How and Carrs at the head and Wet Side Edge sweeping down to the right

This page: Above the clouds on the Five Sisters of Kintail: the dramatic result of temperature inversion

DISCLAIMER

Hill walking and mountains are potentially dangerous and each individual following the routes described within this book is responsible for their own safety and actions – neither the author nor publisher accept any responsibility for the individual safety or actions of anyone using this book. Although the author encountered no difficulty with access on the routes described, and while considerable effort has been made to avoid any such problems, the inclusion of a route does not imply that a right of way or right of access exists in every case or in all circumstances. Readers are also advised that changes can occur to the landscape that may effect the contents of this book. The author welcomes notification of any such changes.

Contents

Introduction

Ridges, the long narrow elevated crests which run between peaks or from the mountain top to its base, offer the most aesthetic and challenging form of hill walking. From the grandeur of the high mountains of Snowdon, Scafell Pike and Ben Nevis and the rugged knife-edged spectacle of Tryfan, Blencathra and Sgurr nan Gillean to the wilds of the Arans, the Crinkle Crags and Suilven, this book explores in detail fifty of Britain's greatest ridge walks. Over the most compelling mountains of Welsh Snowdonia, the English Lake District and the Highlands and Islands of Scotland, these walks are planned to capture the spirit of excellence and the wide-ranging diversity of our magnificent hills.

The ten routes in Wales all lie within the wonderful Snowdonia National Park and in England the selection of fourteen walks has been made exclusively from the beautiful Lake District National Park. Those from Scotland, however, range over the vast area of the Highlands, including the Cairngorm massif, and out to the islands of Arran and Skye. While the quality and diversity of each mountain walk is impressive enough, that of the whole, from the regal Cadair Idris in the south to the Arkle/Foinaven traverse in the distant north, is simply breathtaking.

Primarily the routes I have selected have been chosen for their outstanding quality. In terms of being manageable walks, easily accomplished within a single day or less, they are undoubtedly amongst the finest mountain walks to be had anywhere in the world. Each is unique, and while the nature and difficulty of the majority of the routes have been pitched at the 'average hill walker' there are outings here which range through all degrees of difficulty.

At the top end of the scale the Pinnacle Ridge of Sgurr nan Gillean (Scrambling Grade 3 and an average time of 6 hours) takes an inspired and dramatic line up one of the Black Cuillin's most evocative peaks. This route, often greatly exposed, demands basic technical rock climbing ability. At the easier end, Lakeland's Dow Crag and Coniston Old Man provide a straightforward though infinitely sublime outing (no technical difficulty and an average time of 4 hours). Between these extremes will be found a kaleidoscope of difficulty and experience.

While this is not designed to be a field book carried *en route*, it will serve as both a practical and inspirational source of reference for those who aspire to tackle the challenge of Britain's greatest ridge walks. The text on each route includes a fact sheet that gives details of location, length and duration, the ascent, seasonal considerations, access, accommodation and useful field notes on geology, flora and fauna, and a comment on the reason for the walk's inclusion. The main body of the text not only describes the route in detail but endeavours to portray the essential spirit of the walk. It examines the overall mountain scene whilst focussing on specific points of interest, the natural world and on man's involvement in the landscape. It is accompanied by a map, presenting a three-dimensional impression of the ridges and tops, and awe-inspiring colour photographs chosen to be both evocative and informative.

The fact sheets enable the reader to make a quick appraisal of the walk. Most of the items covered are self-explanatory but some need further clarification. These are:

Time: This is not an absolute value, but rather an approximation of the minimum time a hill walker of average fitness and competency could expect to take to complete the route. It is based on actual experience – not on the theoretical Naismith's Rule – and includes an allowance for rest and refreshment stops.

Difficulty: I have used two different grading systems which are currently in general use – for summer conditions these are a Scrambling Grade from 1 to 3, and when under snow and ice, a Winter Mountaineering Grade from I to III (all routes classified thus become *bona fide* mountaineering/climbing expeditions under winter conditions and require skills beyond those of hill walking). They are defined thus:

Scrambling Grade 1 is a straightforward scramble (use of hands required) with little route-finding difficulty. The described route takes the most interesting line, which can usually be varied or avoided. Generally, exposure is not

Ben Cruachan seen over the head of Loch Etive with the shapely western top of Stob Dearg (Taynuilt Peak) to its right

great though care must always be exercised to avoid a slip.
Scrambling Grade 2 contains longer and more difficult sections of scrambling. A rope may be useful for safety in particularly exposed places. Some skill in route finding is necessary and some sections may be inescapable.
Scrambling Grade 3 is a serious undertaking only to be attempted by those with proven basic climbing and ropework skills. A rope may be advisable for safety on exposed sections and it may be necessary to abseil or to scale pitches of technically easy rock climbing.
Winter Grade I represents easy angled ridges or snow gullies around 45 degrees. Cornices may be encountered.
Winter Grade II steep snow or short ice pitches may be encountered, and also more difficult and involved ridges (usually classed as a summer Scrambling Grade 1 upwards).
Winter Grade III difficulties are more sustained than on a grade II route and there may be significant ice pitches or technical ridge or buttress sections.
The Tops: Based on three principal languages (though not exclusively), Welsh Gaelic, Old Norse and the Gaelic of Scotland, the pronunciation and meaning of the mountain names is a combination of painstaking academic reference and in-depth mountain knowledge. It is open to hugely different interpretation.

On a personal note I believe the mountains are god-given (whomsoever your particular god may or may not be) and it is the right of everyone to explore and enjoy them. To my mind climbing mountains is all about doing your own thing, about freedom of self expression. Any mountain climbed, any ridge walked – irrespective of grade, conditions and time of ascent – is a considerable achievement. Of course with that freedom comes great responsibility, to yourself, to others and to the natural world. One should strive to take only photographs and leave only light footprints. It is assumed that everyone using this book will have some mountain walking experience and be familiar with all safety techniques and procedures (for detailed information I recommend *The Hillwalker's Manual,* Cicerone Press). Know beyond any doubt that the mountains give and the mountains take.

Finally I would like to say that this book is born of love for the mountains and steep places. There have been times when its completion seemed all but impossible; the going hard, the way long and the obstacles formidable. To cover the length and breadth of the Great British Ridge Walks in one volume was a monumental undertaking. Well, now the tops have been crested and the routes completed, I feel particularly good about the result – and hope you do to. Should it impart to you just a little of the wonder of these special places, it will have indeed been a worthy exercise.

BILL BIRKETT
Little Langdale, March 1999

1: Snowdon Horseshoe by Crib Goch and descent via Lliwedd Edge

2: Tryfan's North Ridge and Bristly Ridge to Glyder Fach descending via Y Gribin – Cwm Bochlwyd Horseshoe

3: Y Garn's North-East Ridge descending via The Devil's Kitchen

4: A Traverse of the Carneddau – Pen yr Ole Wen via the Lloer Ridge, Carnedd Dafydd, Carnedd Llewelyn and descent via Y Braich

5: Carnedd Moel Siabod by Daear Ddu and descent via the North-East Ridge

6: Cnicht and Moelwyn Mawr – The Cwm Croesor Horseshoe

7: Moel Hebog by the North-East Ridge and a Traverse of the North Ridge over Moels Yr Ogof and Lefn

8: The Nantlle Ridge – from Craig Cwm Silyn to Y Garn

9: The Aran Ridge

10: Cadair Idris – Complete Traverse

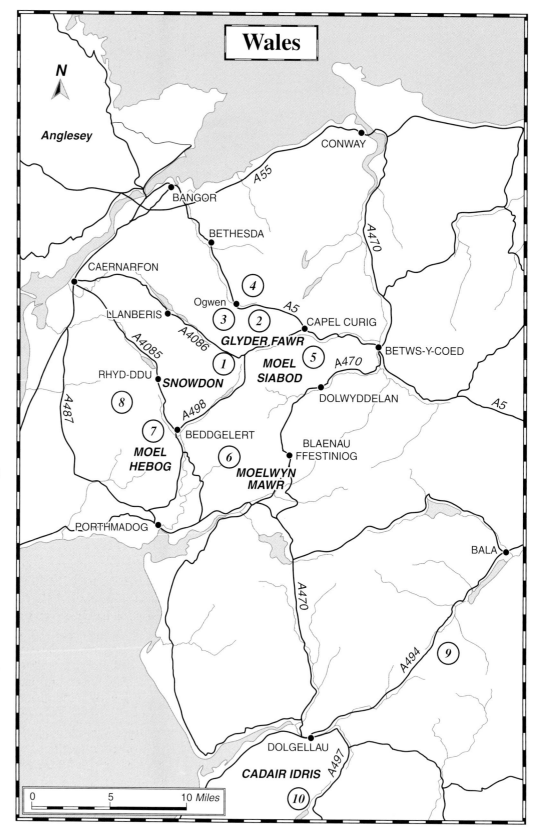

Wales

All ten of the tremendous mountain ridge walks described here are located within the Snowdonia National Park, an area most associated with the rugged grandeur of Snowdon – the highest mountain in Wales and higher than any in England – and the intense wildness of its deep-cut valleys and high passes. In point of fact Snowdonia, occupying a good part of north-west Wales, is an extremely diverse and rich mountain area, one which on exploration displays a huge range of character.

Of the ten national parks of England and Wales, Snowdonia is the second largest, by a mere whisker to the English Lake District, with an area of some 2171 sq km. It stretches from Conwy Bay on the North Wales coast some 85km to Aberdovey (Aberdyfi) on the estuary of the River Dovey (Afon Dyfi) in mid-Wales, and from the neck of the Lleyn Peninsula in the west some 50km to the flanks of the Berwyn Hills in the east.

On Crib Goch with Snowdon beyond

taking approximately four hours, it is of striking form and includes the charms of Twll Du (the Devil's Kitchen) and lovely Llyn Idwal.

The most northerly mountain massif in Snowdonia, the mighty Carneddau and its great burial cairns of pre-history, is traversed by Walk 4. This circular route across huge broad shoulders and knife edges dominates the North Wales coast. It stretches for some 16km and provides an expansive outlook, ranging as far as the distant fells of Lakeland. On the eastern fringe of the main mountain groups which surround Snowdon, Moel Siabod, Walk 5, provides a fine outing with unrestricted views. The Welsh Matterhorn of Cnicht and Moelwyn Mawr, Walk 6, overlook quiet Cwm Croesor and the forlorn remnants of a once-great industry, the scars of slate quarrying adding a social dimension to this wonderful landscape.

Above bustling Beddgelert the extinct volcanic mass of Moel Hebog and the northern satellites of Moels

The geographical order of the walks begins with the Snowdon Horseshoe, Walk 1, to make a clockwise journey through the different areas surrounding Snowdon to reach the most westerly walk, Walk 8, the Nantlle Ridge. It then spirals southwards to include Walk 9, The Aran Ridge and Walk 10, Cadair Idris. There are seven walks of a circular nature, and three linear walks which require pre-arranged transport or two cars. Individually each walk is outstanding, and as a whole there is considerable diversity.

The eagles may have left Eryri (Snowdon), yet Walk 1 lacks positively nothing in terms of wild rugged mountain grandeur: it is undoubtedly one of the finest and most exciting mountain expeditions in the whole of Britain. Walk 2, including Tryfan's famous North Ridge which rises above the Ogwen Valley, traverses perhaps the most dramatic skyline in Wales. Y Garn is the subject of Walk 3 and whilst it is the shortest outing, on average

yr Ogof and Lefn, Walk 7, offer an outing which contrasts high mountains with sylvan splendour. And so to the open west, above the neck of the Lleyn Peninsula, looking over The Brothers, and over Holyhead Mountain to the distant faraway hills of Ireland. This, the long spine of the Nantlle Ridge, Walk 8, is a linear route of sustained interest and outstanding quality.

The spiral southwards includes The Arans, Walk 9, in the south-eastern corner of the National Park. This high upland ridge provides exemplary hill walking at the northerly end of the Cambrian Mountains of mid-Wales. Superbly different, it is now free from access problems due to the tremendous work of the Snowdonia National Park Authority. Finally Walk 10, Cadair Idris: of legendary stature, it is one of the big three mountains of Wales. Walk in space across a lost world plateau, a walk where red kite wheel though the air.

SNOWDON HORSESHOE by CRIB GOCH and descent via LLIWEDD EDGE

Highest mountain in Wales, sensational exposure

Fact Sheet

Location: Snowdonia National Park, North Wales

Length: 12km (7½ml)

Ascent: 2000m (6560ft)

Time: 7 hours

Difficulty: In summer a long and potentially serious mountain walk, involving sections of easy though exposed scrambling (Scrambling Grade 1); the exposure is particulary acute along the crest of Crib Goch. A mountain expedition in winter (Winter Grade I)

Seasons: Summer conditions can generally be expected between May and October; with winter conditions from November to April

Map: OS Outdoor Leisure 17, Snowdon and Conwy Valley

Start & Finish: Pen-y-pass car park (SH 647 557); fills quickly in summer

Access: Follow the A4086 east from Caernarfon, or the A5 and then A4086 (from Capel Curig) west from Betws-y-coed

Tourist Information: Office in Llanberis (Tel: 01286 870765)

Accommodation: Youth Hostel at Pen-y-pass; the traditional climbing inn is the Pen-y-Gwryd Hotel, east of the pass. Campsites, B&Bs, self-catering and bunkhouse facilities stretch down the pass to Llanberis, where there are a number of hotels and shops.

Geology: Of volcanic origin the rock mass is solid rhyolite, which contains bands of smoother more easily fragmented slate. On the whole both rock types are a joy to walk and scramble over

Flora & Fauna: A number of rare plants can be found here, including the Snowdon lily and purple saxifrage. Raven and the rare chough can be seen. Feral goats occupy the ridges and big-eared mice the summit

Comment: Though the technical difficulties are fairly low and short-lived the going is spectacularly exposed in many places, the crux being the spectacular traverse of Crib Goch. The way is long, steep cliffs abound and strenuous ascent or descent predominates. It is best to pick good weather conditions. In terms of quality this tremendous outing has few peers, despite man's rape of Snowdon's summit by the intrusion of a railway and hotel

The Tops

Crib Goch	923m (3026ft)	(crib gok = red ridge)
Crib y Ddysgl	1065m (3494ft)	(crib-i-thes-gul = saucer-shaped ridge)
Snowdon/Eryri/ Yr Wyddfa	1085m (3560ft)	(snowdon/er-ree-ree/ir wuth-va = snow-capped peak/lair of the eagles/burial place)
Y Lliwedd West Peak	898m (2946ft)	(ii clue-eth = grey peak)
Y Lliwedd East Peak	893m (2930ft)	(ii clue-eth = grey peak)
Lliwedd Bach	818m (2684ft)	(clue-eth bak = little grey peak)

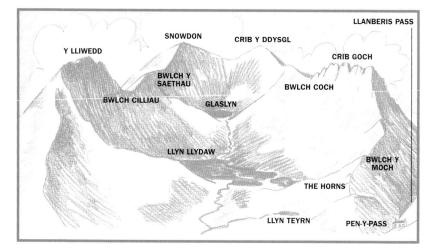

■ A most influential mountain, and the highest south of the Western Highlands of Scotland, mighty Snowdon lends its name to the whole of this wild and rugged National Park. From the summit an array of fine ridges reach out through all four points of the compass. Hidden within their secretive cwms are dark llyns and huge cliffs of black rock. The lesser peaks cluster around its bulk. In all, plunging to the dark rocky rift of Llanberis Pass to the north, and the valleys of Nantgwynant to the south-east and Nant Colwyn to the south-west, the Snowdon massif occupies a huge 70km square.

Of all Snowdon's ridges this combination provides the finest outing. Starting from Pen-y-pass, already conveniently situated at an altitude of 359m, this horseshoe of high tops, encircling Cwm Dyli and the mountain lakes of Llyn Llydaw and Glaslyn,

Viewed from Y Lliwedd's West Peak a lone figure stands atop the East Peak, beyond which the ridge descends over Lliwedd Bach. Moel Siabod seen in the distance

culminates in the summit of Snowdon itself. Tackling the walk anti-clockwise leads to Crib Goch first, with its incredibly exposed knife-edge ridge and pinnacles, and leaves the aesthetic West and East Peaks of Y Lliwedd until last. Finally the Miner's Track makes easy descent from Llyn Llydaw.

Looking over the stark rocky grandeur of Llanberis Pass below, and up to the pyramidal heights of Crib Goch ahead, the well-constructed Pyg Track rises up to the right from the car park. Rocks of purple-black-blue slate are strewn everywhere. The old miners' track utilises these natural materials to good effect; great slabs bridge the streamlets whilst rectangular blocks form the steps to take you rapidly from valley head to the heights. The notch in the ridge is named Bwlch y Moch ('pass of the pigs', hence Pyg Track), and marks the start of the ridge to Crib Goch. It is worth noting that once started there is no easy escape from the ridge (save retracing the route described) between this col and the summit of Crib y Ddysgl, which lies some considerable distance ahead. Opposite, the

awsome sweep of the black cliffs of Y Lliwedd rise soberingly above the waters of Llyn Llydaw. The distant summit of Crib Goch lies 305m above.

Bear right off the main Pyg Track to climb the ever-steepening ridge above. Craggy rocks, though looking formidable from below, provide straightforward scrambling. Fine views north to the Glyders and south to Lliwedd always provide an excuse for a rest. Finally the sharpening arête leads more easily to the summit of Crib Goch. Should there be snow, the scene ahead can look Alpine: a razor's edge of rock leads across to a cirque of rock pinnacles and buttresses. To the right the precipice drops vertically into bottomless black; to the left the ground appears only marginally less steep. Beyond, mighty Snowdon watches in anticipation.

The famous ridge of Crib Goch, the most mentally demanding section of the whole route, requires a cool approach and a head for heights. Traverse the knife-edged ridge, with great exposure though little technical difficulty, to reach the rocky pinnacles. These are circumnavigated to the left, until at a gap in the crest on the right easier scrambling leads in a few hundred metres to the relative security of the col Bwlch Coch.

The ridge continues with considerable elegance though is now much easier. After traversing the initial narrow section the ridge broadens before reaching a broken rocky wall. This can be taken directly, or more easily to the left. A little distance beyond, the ridge narrows again. The scrambly crest provides the best views, though alternatively the right flank is easier, and leads to the concrete trig point marking the summit commonly known as Crib y Ddysgl. Perhaps more accurately this name refers to the summit ridge only, the whole peak being named Garnedd Ugain. A broad easy shoulder dips to the col of Bwlch Glas at which point, marked by a stone monolith, the Pyg Track joins from the left. Other stones could be the remains of ancient burial chambers and so provide the origin of the name Yr Wyddfa ('burial place'). Join the rails of the iron horse, first used in 1896, to ascend to the summit of Snowdon. Purists may keep to the left edge, as far as practical from the railway. This has the added bonus of providing impressive views down to and over the green waters of Glaslyn cradled far below. Topped by a stone pillar, the views from Snowdon are sufficiently rewarding to ignore the station and hotel down to the west. Apparently you can get the highest pint of beer in Britain here, though it must be close call with the ski developments of Cairngorm. I must admit I've never tried; the free spirit of these Welsh mountains has always been intoxication enough.

Though the long descent to the horizontal haven of Bwlch y Saethau can be taken directly from the summit, down the east nose of Clogwyn y Garnedd, this is not recommended. It is made awkward, if not dangerous, by moving scree, craggy outcrops and loose rock. It is preferable and safer to find the Watkin Path which lies a little way down the south west shoulder. The path is topped by a large conspicuous finger of rock, a useful marker in poor weather, and though eroded in places it leads more easily to the col. A large cairn, Carnedd Arthur, once adorned this point – one of the many supposed burial sites of the fabled King Arthur.

The almost horizontal path, a luxury on this demanding outing, is followed for 500m to a large cairn at Bwlch Ciliau. The Watkin Path drops rightwards to Nantgwynant at this point. The horseshoe, however, departs to make steep ascent to gain the twin

With Snowdon standing to the left, the view west through the rocky steeps of Llanberis Pass

peaks of Lliwedd. Easy scrambling in a spectacular position with steep ground plunging below to your left leads first up and then along the edge of the cliffs. First the higher West Peak and then the lesser East Peak are topped. The cliffs below fall sheer for 100m and were, in the early days of rock climbing the most important in Wales, likened, if rather fancifully, to the Alpine faces around Chamonix. The West Peak was first climbed (directly from below) in 1883 and the East Peak in 1903. A photograph of O.G. Jones, one of the greatest early rock climbing pioneers, by the Abraham brothers of Keswick, hangs in the Pen-y-pass cafeteria to this day. George Mallory of Everest fame also cut his teeth here.

Descend to the lower heights of Lliwedd Bach and continue to a prominent cairn. Here the path swoops down left to gain the Miner's Track alongside the shore of Llyn Llydaw. Divided by a causeway the two sections of the llyn intriguingly dipslay quite different colouring. The larger most westerly is typically black-blue reflecting the surrounding slates and derelict mine buildings. The smaller is copper green, matching that of Glaslyn high above. Presumably a phenomena influenced by the mineral content of the surrounding rocks. Warmed with a justifiable sense of achievement this a tranquil place to pause awhile and reflect. Snowdon seems distant now, a great deal of effort away. The demands of Crib Goch, a golden memory. Simple descent of the track, although hard on tired legs, leads easily back to Pen-y-pass and completion of the great Snowdon Horseshoe.

TRYFAN'S NORTH RIDGE and BRISTLY RIDGE to GLYDER FACH descending via Y GRIBIN – CWM BOCHLWYD HORSESHOE

Classic ridge climbing, Adam and Eve, the Cantilever, Castle of the Winds

Fact Sheet

Location: Ogwen Valley (Nant y Benglog), Snowdonia National Park, North Wales

Length: 6km (3¾ml)

Ascent: 910m (2985ft)

Time: 8 hours

Difficulty: All the routes up Tryfan's North Ridge, and Bristly Ridge beyond, offer steep and unavoidably strenuous going. In dry summer conditions the scrambling comprises short, steep, rocky sections separated by frequent ledges (Scrambling Grade 1). The topmost part of Y Gribin is also steep and exposed and provides scrambling directly down the crest (Scrambling Grade 0.75). However, should one prefer a hill walk, the beauty of this spectacular route is that all difficulties can be avoided by taking well worn paths to the side (generally to the right of the crest). In winter conditions, particularly if the rocks are covered in verglas without a build up of snow, the route becomes a full climbing expedition (Winter Grade I to II).

Seasons: Summer conditions can be expected between May and November; with winter conditions from December to April

Map: OS Outdoor Leisure 17, Snowdon and Conwy Valley

Start & Finish: Recessed car park on the south side of the A5 (SH 659 602). Numerous alternative free car-parking areas either side of the A5 beneath the nose of Tryfan

Access: The route lies just above the main A5 trunk road, 15km west of Betws-y-coed and 15km east of Bangor

Tourist Information: Office by Ogwen Cottage (Tel: 01248 600683)

Accommodation: Youth Hostel by Ogwen Cottage. Camping at Gwern-y-Gof-Isaf farm 2km east. The nearest little centre is Capel Curig, 7km east

Geology: The rock is volcanic rhyolite, generally rough and sound, but frequently offering substantial, sharp-edged, flake handholds. Lovely in dry conditions; unfortunately rather slippery and greasy when wet or damp

Flora & Fauna: Ring ousels flit beneath the rocks of Tryfan's North Ridge. The tiny jewel flowers of starry saxifrage may also be spotted on the round

The Tops

Tryfan	915m (3020ft)	(*tri-van* = three peaks)
Glyder Fach	994m (3262ft)	(*glidd-er vark* = small heap)
Castell y Gwynt	972m (3189ft)	(*cas-tell ii gwint* = fortress of the wind)

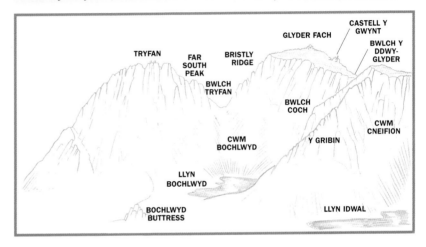

Comment: The ascent of Tryfan's North Ridge, one of the most popular mountain challenges in North Wales, continuing by Bristly Ridge to top Glyder Fach and Castell Gwynt, provides one of the classic mountain outings of Britain. The steep descent of the Y Gribin ridge offers a logical finish. A big day, strenuous and sustained. Dry, clear conditions should be sought

■ The shark's-fin blade of Tryfan plunges directly north towards the A5 and the Ogwen Valley (Nant y Benglog). The naked rock crest is topped by three distinct peaks, and the highest of these, the central peak, is in turn topped by two stone monoliths (seen from the road) with their own persona, Adam and Eve. Behind Tryfan rises the great bulk of the Glyders. To the Romans, building their road from London to Holyhead, Tryfan must have been an impressive symbol of wild, troublesome, untamed, mountainous Wales.

The Glyders, Glyder Fach and Glyder Fawr, run east to west between Llanberis Pass to the south and

Adam and Eve, the twin stone pillars of Central Peak, form the highest points on Tryfan; a good place to pause for those with a degree of climbing ability and a head for heights

Ogwen Valley to the north. Third in altitude to, and sandwiched between, Snowdon and the Carneddau, their tops comprise a great scattering of stones and splintered blocks, exemplified on our route over Glyder Fach by the summit pile, the nearby Cantilever and the rock tower of Castell y Gwynt.

In effect, Tryfan forms a northern spur leading off the high spine of the rocky Glyders, with the distinct outline of Bristly Ridge falling from the shoulder of Glyder Fach's summit plateau to Bwlch Tryfan before the ridge rises again, first to Tryfan's Far South Peak and then on to the three peaks themselves. To the west, on the far wall of the basin of Cwm Bochlwyd, the impressive airy ridge of Y Gribin falls from the Glyders to the Ogwen Valley.

These days the North Ridge of Tryfan offers one of the most dramatic mountain courses in Wales. Combined with Bristly Ridge leading to Glyder Fach and Castell y Gwynt and taking the fine steep descent down Y Gribin you have a mountain route of classic stature, but one on which, despite its fear-

The classic view of Tryfan from Nant y Benglog – the profiled North Ridge falls rightwards to the valley, whilst Bristly Ridge rises to the left

Left: Scrambling the crest of Tryfan's challenging North Ridge

some appearance, all technical difficulties can be bypassed. The route is equally attractive to the hill walker or scrambler. However, a word of caution: whilst proximity to the road ensures great popularity, bringing the rock in places to a state of high polish, this route should not be underestimated. Whether scrambled or walked, steep ascent must be made, exposure can be considerable, and the full round is both strenuous and demanding. Allow considerably more time than the application of Naismith's Rule would suggest.

The first objective is the deep-cut rift to the west of the toe of Tryfan's North Ridge (Milestone Buttress, a favourite haunt for rock climbers, lies just to its right). Leave the car park and follow the path which rises to a stile over the stone wall to gain the base of the rift. Another well worn path follows the line of the wall to reach the same point. Make zigzags up the steep eroded scree of the gully until the going levels and a traverse left can be made to gain the crest

Looking from the summit, Central Peak, over the rocky aspect of Tryfan's North Peak

of the ridge. (Note, at the head of the gully an alternative route moves up and right to provide a path avoiding the main scrambling difficulties.) The most interesting route follows the crest reasonably faithfully, though many variations are possible.

Ledges of vivid white quartz are crossed before the 'first shoulder' is marked by a 7m finger of rock protruding from the back wall: The Cannon. To this point the ridge has been relatively wide, but it now begins to narrow, and further rocky scrambling up little rock walls and past further large rock splinters leads to the 'second shoulder'. The rocky crest continues steeply until the angle slackens and the top of a gully is crossed, followed by another more deeply cut gully; the latter is topped unmistakably by a large chockstone. Above this the rocks steepen, and a short scramble – easier ground may be found to the right – leads to the first top: Tryfan's North Peak. A little way beyond this point the two stone pillars of Adam and Eve mark the Central Peak.

To reach the highest point (making the summit of Tryfan 917m in altitude?) you must of course climb either Adam or Eve (which is which I don't know). They aren't easy, particularly when slippery and wet, and the exposure is considerable; the resolute (or slightly insane) may wish to complete the 'step' (looks more of a jump, actually) between them. Most will be content to unfurl the sandwiches, savour the position, admire the magnificent panorama, and contemplate whether Adam and Eve were placed so strategically and precisely by human hand or by an act of even greater power.

The rather insignificant South Peak lies only a little further along the crest before the descent leads to a stone wall (unmarked on the 1998 OS map) which crosses a little col. The Heather Terrace ascends from the east flank to this point, and ladder stiles provide access. Follow the wall and ascend to the rocky top of Tryfan's Far South Peak. Descend to the right (westwards) and skirt around the rocky flank of the peak to regain the ridge where a stone wall crosses the larger col of Bwlch Tryfan. This forms a crossroads of paths with safe descent possible to Cwm Bochlwyd (right) or Cwm Tryfan (left).

Above the col the spiky rock outline presents a fine challenge. Those wishing to pass it by will find a path to the right; those wishing to seek out its intricacies should take the last ladder stile left over the wall and ascend to the base of the ridge. Traverse left beneath the rocks until a V chimney groove is reached. Climb this (Scrambling Grade 1.25) to a well defined route following the crest, before deviating slightly to the right flank. Regaining the crest as soon as possible leads to a small notch which is crossed to follow steeper ground above. A larger notch is crossed by first descending to the left, then exited by climbing out rightward behind a great finger flake. The crest of the ridge leads airily, though with no great difficulty, to the shoulder plateau of Glyder Fach.

The cairned path trends rightwards to a pile of rocks supporting the famous Cantilever, a huge slab some 5m in length, balanced on a rocky pillar. Standing on its tip is an unmissable photo opportunity. A little way beyond will be found the summit mound, a great collection of huge rock slabs scattered and piled like tumbled giant playing cards. The actual summit point is formed by a great tilted block slab lying across a ridge of solid rock, and

makes a pleasant scramble. Descend and continue along the path near the north edge of the plateau to find the evocatively named Castell y Gwynt; a turret of slabby spires, it certainly lives up to its name. Tackled directly it provides a short scramble (Scrambling Grade 0.5).

Descend directly at first, and then trend rightwards to cross the hollow of Bwlch y Ddwy-Glyder, to gain the edge and traverse along to the flat top, strewn with small slatey stones, of Y Gribin (ii gribin = the small crest of the hill) ridge. There are traces of a small, ruined circular shelter. Steep rocky scrambling down the crest follows (Scrambling Grade 0.75), avoidable by a path to the left. The ridge flattens and 'greens' to provide a profiled view over to Bristly Ridge and down to 'Australia Lake' – Llyn Bochlwyd. The ridge takes rocky form again, and is followed along the crest until the path leads down and across a col to descend until a point at which it bears right to the foot of the llyn.

Don't cross the issuing stream at this point, but descend the path on its left bank until a point where the waterfalls end and the Bochlwyd Buttress can be seen profiled to the right. Cross the stream here and traverse rightwards under the buttress, descending slightly on a narrow boggy path to intercept a well defined path which ascends directly from the car park.

Defying gravity on Glyder Fach's famous Cantilever

Right: Lovely Cym Idwal viewed from the east shore of the Llyn to the black basalt rocks of Twll Du (black cavern)/Devil's Kitchen; the shelf coming in from the left, feeding the largest tumble of boulders, marks the line of descent

Y GARN'S NORTH-EAST RIDGE
descending via THE DEVIL'S KITCHEN

Quarry canyon, curving arm of North-East Ridge, Devil's Kitchen (Twll Du), Llyn Idwal

Fact Sheet

Location: Ogwen Cottage, Snowdonia National Park, North Wales

Length: 7km (4½ml)

Ascent: 650m

Time: 4 hours

Difficulty: Straightforward, strenuous hill walking

Seasons: Summer conditions can be expected between May and November; winter conditions from December to April

Map: OS Outdoor Leisure 17, Snowdon and Conwy Valley

Start & Finish: Ogwen Cottage car park (SH 650 604). It is often full, and unfortunately rather expensive; an alternative larger free car park can be found 600m east along the A5

Access: The route lies just above Ogwen Cottage found on the main A5 trunk road, 17km west of Betws-y-coed and 13km east of Bangor

Tourist Information: Office by Ogwen Cottage (Tel: 012248 600683)

Accommodation: Idwal Youth Hostel by Ogwen Cottage. Camping at Gwern-y-Gof-Isaf farm 4km east. Nearest little centre is Capel Curig 9km east

Geology: The rocks encountered are slate/shale (quarried at the start), volcanic rhyolite on the summit of Y Garn, and basalt (the cliffs of Twll Du). They take the form of scree near the summit of Y Garn, and large boulders descending into Twll Du/Devil's Kitchen

Flora & Fauna: Ravens and herring gulls are frequent visitors to the summit feeding grounds. Most famously, Cwm Idwal is very special for its arctic/alpine plants, particularly the Snowdon lily (or mountain spiderwort). More commonly, hairbells offer patches of blue amongst the dark rocks of Twll Du (*tuth-the* = black cavern). Feral goats cling to the rocky slopes

Comment: Cwm Idwal is a National Nature Reserve. Strenuous beginnings lead to reasonably amiable descents on this aesthetic and intriguing hill walk

The Top

Y Garn   947m (3106ft)   (*ii-garn* = the prominent peak)

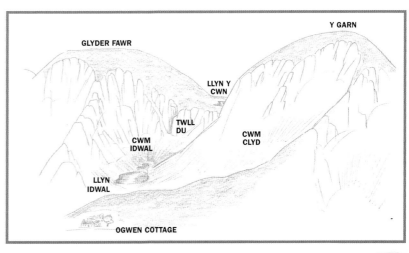

■ Like a cloaked ghoul-like figure, Y Garn rises above Ogwen Cottage with two arms encircling the basin of Cwm Clyd. Two tiny llyns, unseen from below, lie entrapped within. Her most powerful arm, visually striking from any angle, extends beyond. This, the north-east ridge of Y Garn, offers a tremendous ridge walk directly from Cwm Idwal to the summit of the mountain: strenuous though straightforward, ascent is followed by an easier descent down the other arm, then a path falling down the shoulder first to Llyn y Cwn, leads into the Devil's Kitchen and on to traverse the shore of lovely Llyn Idwal.

The Devil's Kitchen is a Victorian English label

for what is more correctly and accurately called Twll Du (*tuth-the* = black cavern). Whatever name may be used, it is a spectacular and atmospheric location not to be missed. Rocks of black basalt, mottled white with lichen, drip and ooze water to form a wonderful plant habitat.

Raven and peregrine make home amongst the heights. The cliff is rent by a huge chasm, and a pile of great boulders fall to the floor of the cwm below.

Remarkably a good path, recently structured and reinforced by the National Park's team, their work facilitated by a large natural shelf sloping in diagonally from the top left of the cirque (as looked upon from below), provides straightforward descent down to, and through, the boulders.

The main footpath leaves directly behind the Information Centre and café, to split immediately. Go right, up into the rift quarried directly through the solid rock; apparently the slatey shaley rock from here was once prized as a whetstone material for sharpening steel. Despite appearances this canyon is the footpath, and a ladder stile leads over the stone wall to continue the passage. The path rises rightwards out of the rift over another ladder stile and, with the pyramidal top of Y Garn in view, follows a vague grassy path along the shoulder. A tumbledown stile crosses the fence with the path leading along the shoulder until ascent leads up to the right to a gap in the stone wall.

The going steepens immediately, though the path is clear and the ascent straightforward. On a level with the base of Cwm Clyd the angle eases and the line of the ridge curves over to the right. To the left there are two areas of water separated by a wall of moraine: the furthest away, and the largest, is Llyn Clyd, and the nearest, virtually a puddle, is unnamed. Gain the crest of the ridge and follow it as it curves gracefully upwards to the summit plateau. Near the top it is fun to stick to the crest itself, necessitating easy scrambling (Scrambling Grade 0.25), though the main path lies to the left. A dip and a short section of ascent lead to the true summit, airy and open with tremendous views extending west to the sea. Best, however, is the view eastwards along the Glyders and over Tryfan.

From any angle, Y Garn's north-west ridge cuts a fine line above the Ogwen Valley, here admired from the rocks of Pen yr Ole Wen opposite

With the National Nature Reserve of Cwm Idwal to its left, Y Garn rises powerfully above Llyn Ogwen and the Ogwen Valley

Right: A westward glance from the rugged rhyolite summit rocks of Y Garn as the cloud begins to roll away. The head of the north-west ridge lies unseen just beyond

Whilst the main path plunges directly down the back shoulder towards the col and Llyn y Cwn, it is more interesting to skirt along the left edge until you reach a terminus cairn which stops short of the descent of the steep craggy ground falling to Cwm Clyd and Cwm Idwal; here a path leads down to the right to join the main trod just before a ladder stile leads over a fence. Continue by crossing the stream and skirting the rocky base of the little llyn to find, a short way beyond, the well marked path leading down the shelf into the basin of Twll Du.

The path, a constructed staircase of rock slabs, leads down, then left along the shelf, eventually to steepen and descend into the boulder field. Despite the size of the rocks and the apparent chaos, it continues to weave a clear way down until it splits by a particularly large boulder. Which way you go is your choice.

To traverse the west shore of Llyn Idwal you can either go left, passing in front of a huge overhanging boulder complete with a walled bivouac site beneath; or you can go right, to pass directly beneath the famous Idwal Slabs, popular with many generations of rock climbers, to follow the east shore. Should it be winter and the llyn frozen, with ice perhaps masked by snow, beware taking a direct course across it. A well known climbing friend of mine once broke through the ice under such conditions and was very lucky to be rescued. At the base of the llyn, beyond a ladder stile, a well constructed and popular footpath curls back down to Ogwen Cottage.

A TRAVERSE OF THE CARNEDDAU – PEN YR OLE WEN via the LLOER RIDGE, CARNEDD DAFYDD, CARNEDD LLEWELYN and descent via Y BRAICH

Tumbling waterfalls, ancient burial cairns, high mountains, broad shoulders, narrow ridges

Fact Sheet

Location: Ogwen Valley (Nant y Benglog), Snowdonia National Park, North Wales.

Length: 16km (10ml)

Ascent: 1035m (3400ft)

Time: 9 hours

Difficulty: Hill walking throughout; there are no real technical difficulties save for a short, easy, scrambly descent from Carnedd Llewelyn to the col of Bwlch Eryl Farchog, and the ascent from there to Pen yr Helgi Du (Scrambling Grade 0.25)

Seasons: Summer conditions may be expected between May and November; winter conditions from December to April. This is a hill-walking route for all seasons

Map: OS Outdoor Leisure 17, Snowdon and Conwy Valley

Start & Finish: Plentiful wide verge parking mainly on the south side of the A5 opposite the cottage at Glan Dena (SH 668 605)

Access: The route lies just above the main A5 trunk road, 14km west of Betws-y-coed and 16km east of Bangor

Tourist Information: Office by Ogwen Cottage (Tel: 01248 600683)

Accommodation: Youth Hostel by Ogwen Cottage. Camping at Gwern-y-Gof-Isaf farm 2km east. Nearest little centre is Capel Curig, 7km east

Geology: A mixture of slaty shales and rhyolites offers pleasant walking

Flora & Fauna: Ravens nest on Ysgolion Duon; alpine club moss may be seen, and also the red fox

Comment: A delightful, airy round over Snowdon's second-highest mountain group. The greatest consideration must be the relatively isolated position (distance to valley base) and the length of the expedition. Due to the broad shoulders of the Carneddau and the scarcity of distinctive rock architecture, navigation in poor visibility can be demanding. The grassy descent down Y Braich couldn't be easier on tired legs

The Tops

Pen yr Ole Wen	978m (3210ft)	(*pen ear olloy wen* = hilltop of the white light)
Carnedd Dafydd	1044m (3426ft)	(*carn-eth daf-eth* = David's cairn)
Carnedd Llewelyn	1064m (3490ft)	(*carn-eth lew-elin* = Llewelyn's cairn)
Pen yr Helgi Du	833m (2732ft)	(*pen ea helgi the* = the hilltop of the black hunting dog)

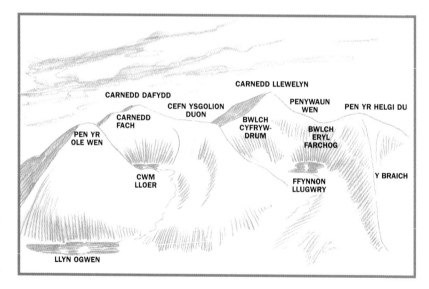

■ Looking down upon the strategically important towns of Bangor and Conwy, the Carneddau dominate the skyline above the western seaboard. Despite their comparative lack of rugged splendour they have an amazing power. They occupy more land space than any other group of hills within the Snowdonia National Park, they are the most northerly mountain massif, and their distant rolling shoulders reach an altitude second only to Snowdon.

The ancients of prehistory, perhaps 5,000 years ago, knew their worth. Along the spine of the Carneddau they buried their greats within huge stone chambers: the carns or cairns of the Carneddau were a symbol of power to be obeyed, a

Looking from the path, above the great cliff of Craig yr Ysfa, across Bwlch Eryl Farchog to the heights of Pen Yr Helgi Du, from whence the easy grassy nose of Y Braich descends to the valley

deity to be worshipped. Later in history the individual tops received their present names. The highest top, Carnedd Llewelyn, most probably derived its name from 'Llewelyn the Great', a figure of written history, one of the last native princes of Wales (1194–1240). The cairns remain, although today, thankfully, we can walk by them in freedom and without fear.

The Ogwen Valley, to the south, separates the Carneddau from her neighbours and provides a convenient starting point from which to launch an assault. Our route makes a considerable and graceful horseshoe, taking in the highest tops of the Carneddau above Cwn Lloer and Cwm Llugwy before closing the loop down the long ridge of Penywaun Wen and Y Braich, above the Fynnon Llugwy Reservoir, back to the valley. (Despite its delightful name, Pen Llithrig y Wrach – hilltop of the slippery witch – lies beyond the scope of this round.)

Follow the track, leaving the main road to cross the bridge, enter the trees, past a cottage and head for the archetypal Welsh hill farm of Tal y Llyn Ogwen. Bear right (signed) off the track before the farm to follow a stone wall to a ladder stile. Climb up the hillside until the patch makes a crossing over the stream of Afon Lloer to ascend by its left side to a kissing gate in the hill wall. The tumbling waterfalls of crystal-clear water, and the rough rhyolite rocks amongst the pasture and dwarf juniper, make this ascent to open hillside a great delight.

At the distinct fork in the path, before Llyn Lloer, go left to take a natural little corridor through the rocks and onto the broad ridge. The well pathed Lloer Ridge provides a marvellously easy ascent directly to the domes summit of Pen yr Ole Wen. Beyond the dip of Bwlch yr Ole Wen, a broad elegant ridge of ever-whitening rocks makes an ascending curve to Carnedd Dafydd.

The walking is easy and open, with the waters of Ffynnon Loer down to the right and the Isle of

Anglesey and the sea stretching out to the left. A gentle ascent soon brings Carnedd Fach to heel. Of considerable proportions, a tumble of rocks some 10m high and 15m in diameter around its top, whilst it may perhaps be just a pile of stones to the uninitiated, is in fact a burial chamber of classic Bronze Age configuration. A pathway of dazzlingly white, flaky little rocks leads on up the shoulder. It is now only a short way to the summit of Carnedd Dafydd. But before it is reached a flat area appears to the right, an oasis of green grass and heather amongst a stony desert. Careful observation will reveal the outlines of burial cists sunk into the ground.

Carnedd Dafydd has a special atmosphere, perhaps retaining something of the power of the ancients despite the fact that modern shelters have been constructed by the plundering of stone from more ancient structures. The shoulder takes a turn to the right and the main path leads to the right of the craggy outcrop of Cefn Ysgolion Duoun. Those traversing above the rim will glimpse impressive rock architecture. Far below lies the massive cliff of Ysgolion Duon (Black Ladder), a vertical height of 300m and a strong winter challenge for those seeking the cold thrill of snow and ice climbing.

Just past the craggy outcrop and by the remains of an old stone wall, the route veers to the left to traverse the narrow, rock-slab ridge of Bwlch Cyfryw – drum. The most fun can be had by sticking resolutely to the crest. At its end, among the piles of rocks of the next hill, a little stone structure framed by rock lintels may be discerned. Could it be an ancient burial cist? Carnedd Llewelyn looms above, and its ascent is best described as short but strenuous, with the path zigzagging through the scree in an attempt to break the grade. A circular shelter adorns the summit. Whilst it looks tempting to continue northwards to Foel Grach, our way lies to the right.

An open descent follows down the crest of Penywaun Wen, then slightly to the right down the grassy shoulder. A cluster of stones to the left appears to have been the work of man and resembles a neolithic burial chamber. Natural or man-made, who knows? The rocky edge is regained above the great cliff of Craig yr Ysfa. Take care not to stray, as considerable steeps lie below. The deserted slate quarries of lonely Cwm Eigiau, to the left, now lie quiet and forlorn and somehow seem to fit the landscape.

Peregrine falcons nest on these cliffs, and if dis-

turbed will often betray their presence by a screaming alarm call. Climbing folklore records that Craig yr Ysfa was first seen by the Abraham brothers, Ashley and George – famous mountain and climbing photographers from Keswick – by telescope from the summit of Scafell, and that they promptly left for Wales to record the first ascent of a rock climb called Amphitheatre Buttress. It is certainly fact that they climbed the route in 1905, but whether or not they did see the crag from Scafell, or made the story up to antagonise the regular Welsh rock-climbing pioneers, I wouldn't like to say (it does appear technically possible).

The going steepens and a short, easy scramble reaches the narrow rim of Bwlch Eryl Farchog. Traverse the edge, resisting the temptation to take the well worn path that drops towards the reservoir, to make the exciting ascent to the grassy top of Pen yr Helgi Du (Scrambling Grade 0.25). An easy, soft grassy path leads luxuriously down the nose of Y Braich, first to a ruined stone wall then to a ladder stile giving access to the bridge over the concrete water leat. Bear right along the path, then down diagonally; the path disappears and it becomes a little boggy, but you will find a ladder stile over the stone wall just above a sheepfold. Carry on along the same line, rather rough and boggy, to intercept a track just above the main A5. Continue to the road and either walk by this, a shorter route, or cross it to take the track over the river to find a footpath running parallel to the road to rejoin the road precisely at the start point. This is more tiring, though much pleasanter.

Carnedd Fach, the huge pile of stones astride the ridge between Pen yr Ole Wen and Carnedd Dafydd, displays the classic characteristics of an ancient burial mound of prehistory

Looking back southwest from the final slopes of Carnedd Dafydd to Pen yr Ole Wen, with Y Garn, Snowdon and The Brothers of the Lleyn Peninsula arranged beyond

CARNEDD MOEL SIABOD by DAEAR DDU and descent via THE NORTH-EAST RIDGE

Fine ridge scrambling, ancient cairn, extensive open views

Fact Sheet

Location: Overlooking and south of Capel Curig, Snowdonia National Park, North Wales

Length: 9km (5½ml)

Ascent: 725m (2375ft)

Time: 4.5 hours

Difficulty: A good track leads to the 500m contour and thereafter provides interesting hill walking; the ascent of the crest of Daear Ddu gives easy scrambling with little exposure (Scrambling Grade 0.75), and is easily avoided on the left. The going along the broad north ridge is rocky, and a little easy scrambling may be found. In full winter conditions it may be considered a mild climb (Winter Grade 0.5)

Seasons: Summer conditions can generally be expected between May and November; winter conditions from December to April

Map: OS Outdoor Leisure 17, Snowdon and Conwy Valley and OS OL 18, Harlech, Portmadog & Bala. Unfortunately the route is split between the two and both are required. Alternatively OS Landranger 115, Snowdon

Start & Finish: Limited parking before the houses on the Pont Cyfyng lane just beyond the bridge (SH 734 571). Otherwise in Capel Curig

Access: The route lies just above the main A5 trunk road, 6km west of Betws-y-coed and 23km east of Bangor

Tourist Information: Betws-y-coed (Tel: 01690 710426)

Accommodation: Youth Hostel, camping and most other types of accommodation and facilities at Capel Curig

Geology: Rhyolites and slates; the scrambling up Daear Ddu is on sound rough rock and the slabby north ridge is wonderfully rough and grainy

Flora & Fauna: Peregrines occupy the eastern cwm. Ling and bell heather grow in abundance

Comment: Despite a bland, grassy appearance from the A4086 above Llynnau Mymbyr, Moel Siabod is a fine independent mountain with hidden quality best appreciated by first-hand experience

The Top

Carnedd Moel Siabod 872m (2375ft) (*carn-eth mowal shabod* = cairned dwelling place of the bare hill)

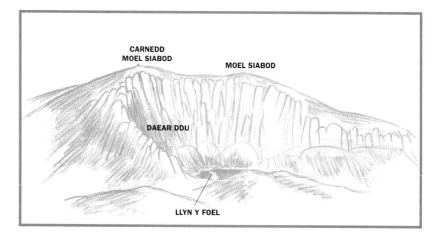

■   Surrounded by deep-cut valleys on all sides, Moel Siabod and the high area of rugged moor that falls south-west to the rest of her group, Cnicht and the Moelwyns, stands independently on the north-eastern edge of Snowdonia. This allows a panoramic view of considerable range, sweeping across the open east, on to The Arans and Cadair Idris in the distant south, to Snowdon and The Glyders commanding the westerly skyline, and to the powerful Carneddau in the north. Despite an introvert appearance from the west, where bland grassy slopes rise to a seemingly unexciting crest, look forward to a character full of vibrancy and surprise. The route as described here rises speedily to the quiet eastern cwm of Llyn y Foel, tackles the steeply curving rock ridge of Daear Ddu, and traverses the wonderful north-eastern shoulder ridge in descent, bringing out her considerable qualities to the full.

Under the pont (bridge), the Cyfyng Falls of the Afon Llugwy offer a famous natural spectacle worthy of attention, though I recommend that you view them after the walk. Our way lies up the surfaced lane above the houses. Cross a cattle grid to rise

Sunrise illuminating Moel Siabod's north-east ridge falling into the mists of Llynnau Mymbyr

Left: Sections of easy scrambling make pleasant ascent of Daear Ddu and lead to summit of Moel Siabod

steeply through the trees; as the pace slackens, a constructed path rises off to the left. This avoids the farm of Rhos to rejoin the quarry track just above it. Pass through a gate/ladder stile with a deserted, almost derelict cottage to the left. Stick to the track – scruffy notices warning you to keep out are fixed to any gates to the side – until it levels and bears left to pass the little dammed reservoir. Deteriorating, it rises from here to pass ruined quarry buildings, which tell a tale of ingenuity and enterprise. Above the stone ruins the path runs round the edge of a water-filled quarry hole, first to its left and then right across its top protected by a wire fence. A good, though stony path continues to a little shoulder on the edge of the Llyn y Foel basin.

Enclosed by grey rocky bluffs, its llyn reflects the blueness of the sky; its floor is carpeted purple with heather, interspaced by cotton grass; a high ring of crags encircles it above to the right; and the elegant, curving profile of the sharp-edged Daear Ddu ridge

rises in front. This is a lovely little cwm. Crossing above the llyn to gain the base of the ridge provides the most direct route, though it is fearfully boggy (it may be better to traverse below).

Keeping to the crest of the ridge as much as possible provides a series of amusing scrambles up short walls and corners. Although the crag drops steeply away to the right, the position is open without ever being too seriously exposed. Easier alternatives can be found to the left. At about half height, descend into a little col. For a while, above, the angle eases, but it steepens again near the top to provide an invigorating final scramble directly to the edge of the summit plateau. Pass the remains of a large circular cairn on the right, an ancient burial chamber, sited amongst a great scattering of rocks and boulders. Bear left and surmount the summit rocks, which at the time of writing are topped by a masonry triangulation tower.

The view is quite stunning, and the general

ambience of the mountain's position and its feeling of well being, with much of Snowdonia arrayed before you, must go far to explain the origins of the name Carnedd Moel Siabod. Such a commanding site, above the afforested valleys and with a view to Tremadoc Bay, must have indeed proved attractive to those in prehistory who made it their dwelling place (Siabod). Perhaps separated by thousands of years of history, another race were minded to build their imposing carnedd (burial mound or cairn).

Descend from the summit dome and strike across the plateau to gain the slabby broad rock crest of the north-east ridge. Flat slabs of rock, occasionally punctured by craggy bedrock, lie at all angles, flags of superb hue and micro texture placed perfectly to provide adventurous walking along a gently descending astral highway. About half way along, an easy scramble leads down into a cleft in the crest. This may be easily left by detouring left beneath the continuation crest for a short distance, or by simply climbing up a craggy buttress. All of the rocky crest may be passed by a straightforward path to the left.

All too soon the crest ends and the path leads down into an eroded gully on the left. After a little scree, a straightforward descent leads into a natural grassy corridor formed by fins of bedded slates on each side. (The fins themselves may be used, though they end in craggy drops which must be avoided.) Continue to a ruined stone wall, cross this and on to a ladder stile which leads back to the quarry track taken in ascent. At the going down of the sun, with the broad rock crest of the north-east ridge illuminated by golden light, the cliffs to the east plunged dark in shadow, and the stark outline of Snowdon's most rugged mountain architecture detailed to the west, there can be few pleasanter places than the heights of Moel Siabod.

Moel Siabod with Daear Ddu falling rightwards from the summit, viewed over Dolwyddelan from Crimea Pass to the south

Left: Wonderful slabs of rock are traversed along the crest of Moel Siabod's north-east ridge

MOEL HEBOG by the NORTH-EAST RIDGE and a TRAVERSE of the NORTH RIDGE over MOELS YR OGOF and LEFN

Bands of volcanic lava, Owain Glyndwr's cave, Princess Quarry, Beddgelert Forest

Fact Sheet

Location: Immediately south-west of Beddgelert, Snowdonia National Park, North Wales

Length: 12km (7½ml)

Ascent: 980m (3200ft)

Time: 6 hours

Difficulty: Straightforward hill walking, reasonably amiable after a strenuous start. Mild scrambling (rough scree walking) leads up Y Grisiau a little below the summit of Moel Hebog. Route finding between tracks in Beddgelert Forest can be confusing

Seasons: Summer conditions can generally be expected between April and November; winter conditions from December to March

Map: OS Outdoor Leisure 17, Snowdon and Conwy Valley

Start & Finish: Beddgelert car park – fee charged (SH 588 481)

Access: Beddgelert lies at the junction of the A4085, 23km south east from Caernarfon, and the A498, 30km west of Betwys-y-coed

Tourist Information: At Llanberis (Tel: 01286 870765) and Porthmadog (Tel: 01766 512981)

Accommodation: Camping and a variety of accommodation in Beddgelert. The nearest Youth Hostel is Bryn Gwynant

Geology: Rhyolites, bands of lava, and slates (reputedly there is also an outcropping of fossil-bearing limestone) provide interesting walking

Flora & Fauna: Kestrels nest on the crags, and buzzards within the forest. There are foxgloves and woodland flowers on the lower slopes. Grey squirrels are plentiful in the woods, having ousted the lovely red

Comment: There are no sharply defined knife edges on this ridge walk; however, Moel Hebog and her satellites, arrayed along the northern spine, provide an outing full of interest. Navigation over the forestry tracks near the end of the walk requires a sense of calm and overall direction. Note that a small section of the public right of way map reference 572492 to 582481, as marked on the 1998 OS map, is, at the time of writing, a mess; fortunately it is easily avoided on pleasant tracks by the campsite

The Tops

Moel Hebog	782m (2566ft)	(*mowl heb-og* = bare mountain of the hawk)
Moel Yr Ogof	655m (2150ft)	(*mowl ear og-of* = bare mountain hillside of the cave)
Moel Lefn	638m (2094ft)	(*mowl lefen* = smooth hillside)

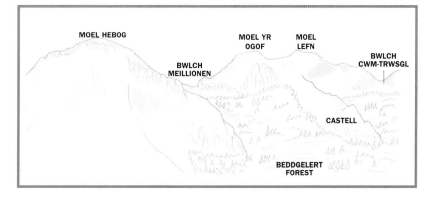

■ The bulk of Moel Hebog may have been bashed about a bit by the occasional ice age since it first erupted millions of years ago, but seen topped by snow, particularly from along the Nantgwynant Valley, you could be forgiven for thinking that you are looking at a still active, high volcano situated somewhere along the Pacific Rim. The satellites of Moel Yr Ogof and Moel Lefn still retain their classical cone-like structure. With Moel Hebog itself rising directly from little Beddgelert, the group as a whole runs north between the valleys of Cwm Pennant to the west and Nant Colwyn to the east.

Starting from Bedgelert, this intriguing round passes through wooded vale, then into the open to make steep ascent of the north-west ridge to gain the summit of Moel Hebog. To the north the great length of the Nantlle Ridge dominates the skyline (our next walk) and to the south-west, Cnicht and the Moelwyns are seen to fine advantage. A grassy descent leads to Bwlch Meillionen where a natural rift leads through the volcanic band of cliffs and provides

By the summit trig point of Moel Hebog, Roy Garner thrills to the prospect of finding Owain Glyndwr's cave somewhere on the next objective – Moel Yr Ogof

the key to traverse the northern spine and satellites of Moels Ogof and Lefn. Bwlch Cwm-trwsgl lies at their end and provides access to Beddgelert Forest. This is a walk of considerable quality which contrasts sylvan valley with expansive mountain architecture.

Today the little town of Beddgelert bustles with tourists, yet retains a tremendous dignity of character. Nestling amidst the mountains with the confluence of the Afon Glaslyn and Afon Colwyn at its heart, the town stands strategically at the meeting of three valleys: Nant Colwyn, Nantgwynant and the Pass of Aberglaslyn. Much legend and folklore are attached to this little community: for instance, the

Augustinians built their priory by the river, and the troublesome – to the Norman English and their monks – Welsh freedom fighter Owain Glyndwr escaped to his cave from here. Lately it was the centre for copper mining and slate quarrying, which was served by the Welsh Highland Railway. The disused line is crossed by this walk.

Go to the right of the Royal Goat Hotel (stifling the desire to giggle at the name) then turn right, up the lane between the houses. Then go left – this is a public footpath signed Llwybr Cyhoeddus, if the signpost hasn't been interfered with – to find a footbridge over the tree-filled and overgrown railway

The upturned hulk of Moel Hebog seen rising beyond Llyn Gwynant. The north-east ridge rises centrally, and the northern spine traverses rightwards

cutting of the now defunct Welsh Highland Railway (at the time of writing there is some talk that this line may be restored). Go immediately right, along a walled, grass-covered track; the railway line runs parallel over the wall to the right. A ladder stile, then a footbridge over the stream lead to a track. Bear left past the buildings and through a wooded plantation of tall Scots Pine (point of return). A cottage stands to the left and a barn to the right.

A path bears off right by the end of the barn and crosses a field, boggy in places, to a ladder stile over a stone wall. The ascent now begins in earnest. Climb the field, a myriad of foxgloves in June, to cross a ruined wall and gain the broad crest of the north-west ridge of Moel Hebog. Ascent leads to a locked iron gate in a stone wall, crossed by a ladder stile. White quartz marks a steepening in the ascent, though the gradient eases again beneath the banded lava cliffs Y Diffwys. Pass these on the left, to tackle the next steep ascent. Various ways are possible: whilst the technically easiest routes follow runnels of steep scree, it is more attractive – though technically slightly more difficult, making easy scrambling necessary – to pick a line through the rock bluffs to the right.

The rock bluffs also display very interesting volcanic features in that distinct and differing bands of lava may be identified. Thus lower down, pillow lavas are found, in which the rock actually takes the shape of a pillow – this is a characteristic of molten material extruded under water, suggesting that they erupted into a crater lake. Higher, the material forms a matrix of large circular spheres like footballs; this is characteristic of airborne pyroclastic bombs – that is, globules of molten lava blown out of the volcano, which take this shape after landing in water.

Whichever route is followed, a natural escape to the right, with steeper ground above, leads along a natural shelf. This zigzags upwards to pass another lava band of tennis-ball size 'bombs' before emerging onto the shoulder of Y Grisiau. Climb the steep rocky nose on the left, where there is considerable exposure to the east, then traverse along to the summit trig point of Moel Hebog. A strenuous approach but the prize is worthy, and there are fine open views in all directions. To the north an examination of Moel yr Ogof reveals several craggy bands of which the base layer is the most formidable. Various dark areas hint at the promise of the hidden cave retreat of Owain Glyndwr. More importantly, note the rift of brown scree running through the cliffs above the col of Bwlch Meillionen, the safe line of ascent to gain the next summit: Moel yr Ogof.

From the trig point the stone wall falls very steeply down grassy flanks to the col, and rises again

Looking from Moel Hebog along the north spine to Moels Yr Ogof and Lefn. Can you see Owain Glyndwr's cave? The Nantlle Ridge is profiled behind

to the rift which is ascended without difficulty, save for the loose scree. Continue along the line of the wall to find a secretive hidden vale of cotton grass which holds a tiny llyn. Cross alongside the wall to find a grassy path splitting off to the right; follow this for 50m or so to a weakness in the broken band of crags above. A path climbs directly up through the broken rocks, then bears slightly right near the top. The shoulder continues easily at first, steepening to climb a subsidiary rocky knoll, and then along again to the final cone of hard grey rock. Ascend this directly to gain the summit of Moel Yr Ogof.

On the 1998 OS map 'Ogof Owain Glyndwr (Cave)' lies written large right across this shoulder. I couldn't find any sign of it hereabouts (others confirm this); it must lie beneath the end of the name (obvious really) in the cliffs of the first lava band, but below and to the east of the shoulder – beyond the scope of this round, I'm afraid. Descent leads through some beautiful, pudding-stone grey ryholites, before passing the wall/fence to a low point on the shoulder. Continue across an easy, grassy traverse (there is a large stone cairn over to the left), before moving right to make a short scrambly rock ascent and along the rock ridge to the summit of Moel Lefn.

A path leads down the grassy centre of the shoulder until steep ground falls away in front. Move diagonally right and down, following the curving path to pass beneath the steeps. The pace slackens at Bwlch Sais, then the gradient steepens again to descend to the old workings of Princess Quarry. An improvised stile allows the path by the stone wall to be gained; follow this down to the little col of Bwlch Cwm-trswsgl. A stile leads to the right, into the possessive gloom and mire of the ranked pines. At a track go left for 50m, and you will find a path disappearing once more into the trees down to the right: follow this. Bear right at the slight junction and take the stile onto open ground. Traverse above the wall – Llyn Llewelyn can be seen to the left through the trees – following a good path through the heather and bracken. A stile leads back into the forest.

The path now attempts to descend straight down the hillside, taking a course which cuts across various forestry tracks, until level going is established. Intercept a forestry track and go left for 25m until a path cuts off right. Regain the track above the bend, go round this bend, then take the path off right, to regain the track again. Follow the path off left to pass by

Hafod Ruffydd Uchaf and gain another track. Follow the track to the right to intercept a main surfaced track. Go right along this – do not ascend the lesser track rising off to the right. The track curves round eastwards to follow a line parallel to the Afon Meillionen. Do not branch right to cross the iron gated first bridge just below the meeting of the two streams. Despite the fact that the 1998 OS map green marks a right of way, the route beyond this point is very confusing. Continue along the main track for 200m until a bridge bears off right, directly into the campsite. Take the high track through the campsite, following the gated/ladder-stile lane through the woods and out into the open, and so into the Scots Pine plantation; thus you will intercept the original track taken in ascent.

Looking up Moel Yr Ogof, the deep natural rift of brown scree passes through the volcanic cliffs above Bwlch Meillionen

THE NANTLLE RIDGE – from CRAIG CWM SILYN to Y GARN

Cwm Silyn, the Great Slab, obelisk, faces of rock

Fact Sheet

Location: Western fringe of the Snowdonia National Park, North Wales

Length: 10km (6¼ml)

Ascent: 800m (2625ft)

Time: 5.5 hours

Difficulty: Generally of moderate difficulty and relatively unstrenuous, there are nevertheless a few sections of descent and ascent, including two short sections of scrambling (Just about Scrambling Grade 1): the final section of descent from Craig Cwm Silyn to Bwlch Dros-bern, and the descent north from Mynydd Drws-y-coed (Winter Grade 0.5)

Seasons: Summer conditions may be expected from March to November; winter conditions from December to February

Map: OS Outdoor Leisure 17, Snowdon and Conwy Valley

Start: Small parking area in a field (National Park agreement) at the end of the surfaced road above Llanllyfni (SH 496 511). Please respect the farmers access and do not block the gate or track

Finish: Wide verge parking above the right-angled bend by the side of the B4418, 400m south-west of Rhyd-Ddu (on the A4085)

Access: the start: A minor road leads from the Nantlle Valley B4418 through the hamlets of Tanyrallt and Dolfelin to Llanllyfni on the A487(T). Some 800m west of Tanyrallt, a minor road ascends towards Cwm Silyn, passes through a gate where it becomes unsurfaced; this is found 15km south of Caernarfon. It is rightly regarded as one of the great ridge walks of Snowdonia

The finish: Some 6.5km north of Beddgelert

Tourist Information: Caernarfon (Tel: 01286 672232)

Accommodation: There is a variety of accommodation within the area. The nearest campsite is at Llyn Nantlle Uchaf, and the nearest Youth Hostel is the Snowdon Ranger by Llyn Cwellyn

Geology: An assorted mix of rhyolites, slates and shales. The scrambly sections are on generally sound rock, though some flakes are detached. There is a presence of loose scree, and caution should be exercised

Flora & Fauna: There are ravens and peregrine falcons;

The Tops

Craig Cwm Silyn	734m (2408ft)	(*craige coom silin* = crag of the mountain basin spawning ground)
Mynydd Tal-y-mignedd	653m (2142ft)	(*min-uth tal-ii-mig-neth* = boggy end of mountain)
Trum y Ddysgl	709m (2326ft)	(*trum ii thys-gal* = dish shaped ridge)
Mynydd Drws-y-coed	695m (2280ft)	(*min-uth droos-ii-coyd* = mountain door to the wood)
Y Garn	633m (2077ft)	(*ii-garn* = prominent peak)

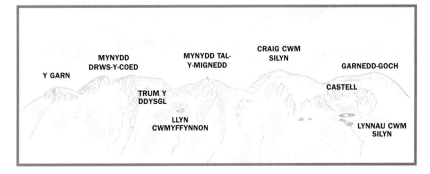

amongst flowers, northern bedstraw and mountain sorrel

Comment: A linear route requiring two cars or pre-arranged transport. Once the heights have been gained the going is generally straightforward and the path good, though the ridge is by no means horizontal. The route is described from south-west to north-east, the least strenuous way. It can, of course, be done in either direction

■ Looking to Cwm Silyn from the village of Talysarn, or to Mynydd Tal-y-mignedd over the Pennant Valley, there are hints of the character of the distant Nantlle Ridge, but from below it is difficult to appreciate its full flavour. For whilst the spine remains straight overall, it is individually fashioned from collective vertebrae: each is scalloped by deep cwm, and each supports an individual protruding rib to form a switchback series of 'S'-like curves connecting the tops. In isolation each section is fascinating; together they fuse naturally to produce a high mountain traverse of exceptional quality.

The ridge runs in a south-westerly to north-easterly direction between the Nantlle Valley to the

Where now? Poor visibility at the point where scrambling begins on the descent from Craig Cwm Silyn to Bwlch Dros-bern

north and Cwm Pennant to the south. This walk begins up Craig Cwm Silyn and finishes over Y Garn. Initially it offers unsurpassed open views westwards, down the Lleyn Peninsula and over the distinctive hills commonly known as The Rivals (though more correctly translated from the Welsh as The Brothers) and up across the Isle of Anglesey to Holyhead Mountain, extending on a clear day over the sea to the emerald hills of Ireland. At its far end, before it descends towards Rhyd-Ddu, it allows the most complete visual examination of Snowdon's western flanks, including the Snowdon Ranger path.

Easy walking leads up the track, through a gate, to pass a locked gate to the right. The second gate on the right is an opening through the stone wall for the old quarryman's track which leads to the workings above Llynau Cwm Silyn. Go right to quit the track and climb up to the crest of the shoulder. Follow the shoulder along the worn grass path that

runs parallel to the wire fence line, until the end of the fence is passed and the ground steepens. The path makes a curving ascent leftwards to follow around the rim of cliffs encircling lovely Cwm Silyn. Observe the seemingly vertical buttress known as the Great Slab, the site of some classic rock climbs – experts only. (The more direct ascent from the shoulder leads straight to the summit of Garnedd-Goch, the south-western end of this ridge; however, this route lengthens the walk and bypasses the dramatic rock scenery of Cwm Silyn. The most popular route goes by Cwm Silyn, as described above.)

Beyond this the path begins to climb towards a stone wall running along the crest of the ridge. Follow this until at a corner junction it is crossed by a stile. The path leads on easily across the broad back of Craig Cwm Silyn to make a rough ascent over finely textured, grey-white banded rocks. Pass a ruined shelter, then a stunted rectangular tower, and at last gain the circular cairned top sited amongst the boulders.

The Nantlle Ridge seen from the south above Cwm Pennant Valley. To the left, Mynydd Tal-y-mignedd. Right is Trum Yddysgl, and far right the sharp-edged outline of Mynydd Drws-y-coed

Right: A rock climber tackles the great slab of Cwm Silyn the rim of which is traversed by the Nantlle Ridge walk. Llynnau Cwm Silyn and Menai Strait beyond

The path drops down to the left to reach a green flat area before joining the rugged rock edge of Craig Pennant. A stone wall guides the way until, with the wall balanced on the end of a crag, some 20m of scrambling are necessary to reach easier ground (Scrambling Grade 1 if tackled directly, easier to the left). The wall is replaced by a ruinous fence line (large cast-iron straining posts bear the proud name 'Liverpool' on their side) which leads to the col of Bwlch Dros-bern (some 220m of descent).

The initial ascent leads to a ruined circular 'shelter' of flat slabs on a little top. Beyond, it is a steep, slippery ascent up the exposed crest. Eroded grass proves to be muddy when wet, and the vertically bedded, shaly slates offer little comfort. Soon, however, the angle slackens to a straightforward ascent up the grassy shoulder directly to the approximately 8m high masonry obelisk adorning the summit of Mynydd Tal-y-mignedd. Built by the local quarrymen, it is a fitting tribute to Queen Victoria's Jubilee.

The wall leads the way. Marked by an indestructible 'Liverpool' iron straining post, the remnants of a wire fence then begins. A knife-edged ridge leads enthusiastically to a minor top, from where a long subsidiary 'rib' falls south-east down to the head of Cwm Pennant. Curve left to make a long, rather laborious grass ascent to the summit of Trum y Ddysgl. A clean-cut summit edge is defined by virtue of its easy, grassy south-west slopes, which are suddenly sliced away by its vertical north-east face. The subsidiary ridge from here descends north-west towards the Nantlle Valley. With an awakened sense of exposure, descend the aesthetic knife-edge arête, steep grass on each side, heading west.

With an increasingly dramatic rocky profile to the left, ascend to the north. Glances over the left edge reveal the sickeningly undercut cliffs to be perched on impossibly steep grassy hillside – even the grass appears to be vertical. How do those sweet-looking white-wool Welsh sheep roam in such carefree manner on this terrain? Have they no fear? The top of Mynydd Drws-y-coed is located ignominiously by a stile leading over the fence.

Cross the stile and continue along the exposed edge. The fence ends after 30m, whilst the cliff, Clogwyn Marchnad, continues unbroken in spectacular fashion to make the descent of the now rocky ridge, a very exposed affair. Piles of rock slabs litter the way and scrambling is necessary (Scrambling

Grade 0.5 to 0.75 depending on the line taken). It seems particularly greasy here when wet; however, difficulties are short-lived and the col is soon gained.

With the impressive outlines of 'faces' crag on your left (monkey and organ grinder can be seen from the col, and other personalities appear as you progress) make your ascent negotiating around the precipitous rim to a rocky knoll topped by a stone wall. This first dips, then ascends to pass two large burial cairns, and finally on to the smaller summit cairn of Y Garn.

The downward path leads eastwards through the summit rocks to a stile over a another stone wall: it is a straightforward, though steep descent down the grassy shoulder of Y Garn. Perhaps it is something to do with the output of energy necessary to reach this point, but this descent, straightforward or no, seems awfully long (it is a real slog in ascent). The going levels off before a ladder stile leads over the fence, then a kissing gate and gate lead onto a track. Take this leftwards (the track lies a little way below the farm of Drwsycoed Uchaf) to find a little iron gate onto the road.

This is a walk which deserves its reputation for outstanding quality, though most will require a little time to recuperate before setting off again in the opposite direction.

The magnificent aspect of Cwm Silyn with Llynnau Cwm Silyn seen below the cliffs to the left

THE ARAN RIDGE

Triumph of access, remote atmosphere, solitude, memorial cairn

Fact Sheet

Location: South of Bala, south-east corner of Snowdonia National Park

Length: 15km (9ml)

Ascent: 800m (2625ft)

Time: 7 hours

Difficulty: Straightforward, easy hill walking with no technical difficulty; however, escape would be difficult

Seasons: Summer conditions may be expected from March to November; winter conditions from December to February

Map: OS Outdoor Leisure 23, Snowdonia Cadair Idris Area; unfortunately this omits the start and the first kilometre, and OS Landranger 124 Dolgellau is necessary for the whole picture

Start: In the car park by the bridge, over Afon Twrch, in Llanuwchllyn (SH 880 298)

Finish: There is ample parking at the end of the surfaced road up the Cwm Cywarch valley (SH 854 185)

Access: the start: Found 10km south of Bala along the A494(T), then along through the village of Llanuwchllyn on the B4403. The finish: A minor road leads south from the start over the pass of Bwlch y Groes to turn north at Aber Cowarch into the valley of Cwm Cowarch – 23km. It is a similar distance west of Dolgellau along the A470(T): turn left onto a minor road at Dinas Mawddwy, and left again into Cwm Cowarch at Aber Cowarch

Tourist Information: Bala (Tel: 01678 521021) and Dolgellau (Tel: 01341 422888)

Accommodation: There is a variety of accommodation within the area. The nearest campsite to the start is at Brynculed, and for the end it is at Dinas Mawddwy. The nearest Youth Hostels are Rhos y gwaliau (Bala) and Minllyn

Geology: A mixture of rhyolites, slates and shales; where they are exposed they always provide pleasant, easy walking

Flora & Fauna: Classic hen harrier country, and skylarks fill the ridge with song in summer. There is also golden sedge, hawthorn and huge ash

Comment: A linear route requiring two cars or pre-arranged transport. This long, generally grassy ridge, standing proud above the surrounding countryside, forms the northerly end of the chain of the Cambrian Mountains of mid-Wales. A superb outing

The Tops

Aran Benllyn	885m (2901ft)	(*aran ben-thlin* = lake at the head of the high mountain)
Aran Fawddwy	905m (2969ft)	(*aran fa-thuwi* = high mountain source of the Dyfi – Afon Dyfi/River Dovey)
Drws Bach	762m (2500ft)	(*droos bakh* = small door/gateway)
Drysgol	745m (2444ft)	(*dris-gol* = rough hill)

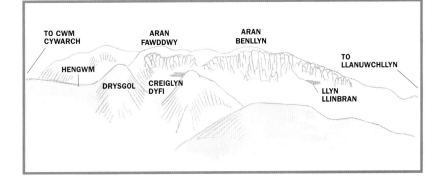

■ Pushed against the south-east margin of the Snowdonia National Park the linear spine of The Arans runs due north–south from Llanuwchllyn at the end of Bala Lake (more properly called Llyn Tegid) to the head of Cwm Cowarch. They are seen at their best when viewed southwards over Bala Lake. Two majestic summits, Aran Benllyn and Aran Fawddwy, raise their heads above a formidable east face, a wall of virtually unbroken crag.

Beneath the eastern cliffs a quiet upland area of rolling hill and peat moor stretches beyond the park boundary. The west flanks fall rather sedately to the Afon Wnion, a deep broad valley which effectively separates them from the rest of Snowdonia. A gradually ascending high shoulder gains, and links, the summits to form a broad-backed ridge running for some 10km. Gentle in nature and straightforward in execution, The Arans stand aloof, one of the most beguiling ridge walks in the whole of Wales.

Other influences to those that shaped Snowdonia have been at play here, and the quiet landscape is quite different. It has an Austrian or even a Swiss

The descent from Drysgol down by Hengwm to Cwm Cywarch at the southern end of the walk is gloriously easy. Crossing the stile on the flank of Waun Goch

quality – and what is more, it is comparatively little trod. Access problems between landowners and walkers dogged The Arans until comparatively recent times. Finally in the early 1980s Snowdonia National Park Authority triumphed, successfully negotiating an access agreement which covers the whole length of this route.

Tackled as described here, north to south, it is a gradual ascent; with your objectives dead ahead the route leads intriguingly over Aran Benllyn and along the ridge to Aran Fawddwy. Finally it falls delightfully down spongy turf in a curving grassy descent over Drws Bach and Drysgol, with the beauty of the Cwm Cowarch valley all the time drawing you on. It would be quite a different story the other way round!

In the early stages, until the real heights are gained, there are numerous waymarked ladder stiles and I will not describe these individually. The signing and path is kept in very good order by the National Parks Authority, and it is imperative to

keep to the route as marked, in order to avoid future access problems in this still sensitive area. Opposite the car park a lane, waymarked and signed, leads in about 800m to a track which leads off right up the field (large sign). Follow this until it splits, and then go left. Generally in ascent the path follows the western flank of the crest of the ridge. It is pleasantly open, with the Rhinogs profiled to the west and Bala Lake looking splendid behind; in summer the air is full of birdsong.

The pyramidal profile of Aran Benllyn begins to dominate the forward horizon in most dramatic fashion. A steep ascent leads to a col, and then continues to the left (a number of stiles offer different points of access) to the rocky Aran shoulder. White-streaked rocky knolls abound, and in poor visibilty it is exceedingly difficult to recognise the highest top of Benllyn. With the fence line to your right, a number of tiny llyns are passed before you reach a substantial cairn with an old stone wall running just

Looking south over Bala Lake to the majestic twin peaks of The Arans: Aran Benllyn and Aran Fawddwy

Heading south along the final section of the main spine of The Arans from Aran Fawddwy

beyond: this marks the top of Aran Benllyn.

A ladder stile (there must be more stiles on The Arans than on any other mountain in Wales) crosses the fence by tiny twin llyns; the path continues along a hollow in the shoulder. Undulations lead to an open shoulder of spongy turf and slate rocks; here there is a great feeling of openness and space. Views leftwards extend down to the peat bogs and lonely Creiglyn Dyfi (the source of the River Dovey). A short descent leads to a col (twin ladder stiles allow two-way traffic, in the unlikely event that this should ever arise!) and a steep rocky ascent soon brings you to the highest top of The Arans. Aran Fawddwy is marked by a trig point.

A little way on, a cairned upstanding knoll, an outlier of the main peak, marks the end of the ridge and the point from which to begin the descent to Drws Bach. Pick the best way through the rocky outcrops to follow down the right side of a fence line leading along the grassy shoulder, and then up

to the top of Drws Bach. A plaque on the summit cairn commemorates Mike Aspain who was killed by lightning near this spot whilst on duty with the RAF Mountain Rescue team on 5 June 1960; a sobering reminder of the dangers of the hills.

A long grassy arm leads over Drysgol and down to the col beneath Waun Goch before the path falls to the right above the subsidiary valley of Hengwm. As you get closer to the valley floor of Cwm Cywarch the way is clearly waymarked: it leads through a hawthorn lane, past tumbled farm buildings and ash trees of stupendous girth, to reach a footbridge over the river; apparently when the heavy snows of the winter of 1947 thawed, the original bridge here was washed away. Go left on the track to reach the head of the surfaced road, and the open common land parking. Time now to study the remarkable beauty of this unspoilt mountain valley and mentally tick off a route that should be on the list of every serious ridge walker.

CADAIR IDRIS – COMPLETE TRAVERSE

Wildest cwm in Wales, mountain shelter, lost world plateau, red kites

Fact Sheet

Location: South of Dolgellau, in the south-west corner of Snowdonia National Park

Length: 13km (8ml)

Ascent: 985m (3250ft)

Time: 6 hours

Difficulty: There are no technical difficulties, but this is a big walk along a high mountain plateau beginning with a strenuous ascent

Seasons: Summer conditions may be expected from March to November; winter conditions from December to February

Map: OS Outdoor Leisure 23, Snowdonia Cadair Idris area

Start & Finish: Large car park at Minffordd (SH 732 116)

Access: Some 15km south of Dolgellau on the A487(T) and B4405. Also 60km north-west of Newtown on the A470(T), A489(T), A487(T) and the B4405

Tourist Information: Dolgellau (Tel: 01341 422888) and Corris (Tel: 01654 761224)

Accommodation: There is a variety of accommodation within the area. The nearest campsites (both within a few hundred metres) are at Doleinion and Cwmrhwyddfor Farm; the nearest Youth Hostel is at Abercorris

Geology: A mixture of volcanics, slates and shales provides straightforward walking, although there are fields of boulders and scree on the summits of Craig Cau and Pen y Gadair

Flora & Fauna: Red kite, buzzard, kestrel and peregrine are regulars here. The beautiful purple saxifrage flowers in April or May, and lady's mantle can also be seen. Grey squirrels are resident in the sequoias and oaks

Comment: In terms of influence, Cadair Idris is commonly regarded as one of the big three mountains of Wales (the other two being Snowdon and Plynlimon); it is a National Nature Reserve. This clockwise round walks the full length of its high ridge and makes a splendid exploration of its many faceted character

The Tops

Craig Cau	791m (2595ft)	(*crayg cowl* = crag above the hollow)
Cadair Idris/ Pen y Gadair	893m (2929ft)	(*cad-er id-ris/pen ii gad-er* = seat of Idris/mountain head of the seat of Idris)
Mynydd Moel	863m (2831ft)	(*mun-eth mowl* = bare mountain)
Gau Craig	683m (2240ft)	(*gowl crayg* = crag above the hollow)

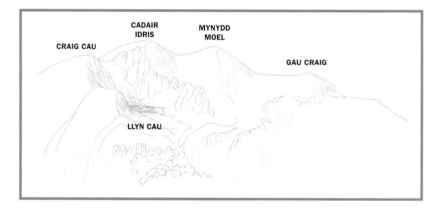

■ Occupying high ground above Dolgellau and the Barmouth estuary, Cadair Idris has long been a favourite mountain. The mythical giant Idris supposedly reclined here even before the railway brought a great outpouring of Victorians onto her flanks and tops. For Cadair is of intriguing shape and impressive size: just short of the 914m mark, she stretches herself for 10km to form a long, high plateau flanked by precipitous cliffs – a distinctive 'lost world' mountain of compelling attraction.

Although there are many routes of ascent, most of which are easier than the one I have chosen, I feel the most rewarding of all is the path which rises from Minffordd. Leaving woods and waterfall it rises to Cwm Cau – some say this is the wildest mountain cwm in the whole of Wales – then climbs in clockwise direction to make a striking arc around the rim of the cwm and so to the top of Pen y Gadair, the summit of Cadair Idris. A westwards traverse leads along the plateau to cross Mynydd Moel and the extended shoulder of Gau Craig, then the route finally descends down Mynydd Gwerngraig

One of most stunning mountain vistas in Wales, over Llyn Cau to the precipitous Craig Cau, the first top reached on the Minffordd path to Cadair Idris

(Mountain Crag of the Elder Coppice) and returns by the Cwm Rhwyddfor Valley. This achieves a complete traverse of the high ridge of Cadair Idris.

Step from the car park and take the 'Minffordd Path' – it is well signed – into the avenue of chestnut trees, and follow it to bear left, passing what is now an information centre. Impressive exotic trees are a reminder that these grounds were once part of the estate of the Idris family, who prospered making soft drinks and who very generously left their land in the safe keeping of the National Park Authority. A wooden bridge crosses the rushing stream, and steep steps lead up through the wonderful oakwoods to the roaring accompaniment of the falls. A gate through the wall leads to open hillside, and the well worn path winds upwards to the edge of Cwm Cau.

By a great whaleback outcrop of rhyolite the path veers left to climb steeply up the hillside and so to

the crest of the ridge. However, few will be able to resist the lure of Llyn Cau beckoning in front, and it is well worth walking on to get a complete view of the llyn and of the spectacular cliffs which rear up from the water's right-side edge to the summit of Craig Cau, 320m above. Said by some to be the wildest mountain cwm in Wales, it is incontrovertibly a scene of striking grandeur and beauty. A direct route left up the hillside leads back to the main path.

Traverse the broad crest around the knolls of rock until the path leads steeply up boulders and scree (better by the right edge) to gain the summit of Craig Cau, a rock knoll just beyond the fence. The edge of the cliff gives a spectacular view, though it is unfenced and caution must be exercised. Descend into the col of rocky knolls, and continue, to begin the steep ascent of Cadair Idris. Steep, loose, bouldery scree passes outcrops of volcanic rock and a small plateau. Finally pass through the remnants of a ruined stone building and climb – steps to the north – to the summit trig platform of Pen y Gadair. It is truly a tremendous panorama from this open and unrestricted summit, with Plynlimon to the south, Ireland to the west, Snowdon to the north and Worcestershire to the east.

Apparently the remnants of the aforementioned building were once, in fairly recent times, a tea house. Was it political correctness that brought about its demise – this is, after all, a National Nature Reserve – or the fact that staff became increasingly fractious? Just to the north, on the shoulder immediately below, is a roofed shelter. Bring your own refreshments but it is in very good condition, and may save someone's life in bad weather. It is all credit to the National Park staff and helpers, and to the good behaviour of mountain people, that on my visit in 1998 there wasn't a single piece of litter or rubbish in the whole hut.

Initially the descent from the summit cone leads east along the shoulder; in clear conditions, however, it is worth making a detour to the northern edge of

the plateau by a small rocky knoll, to follow the edge: steep cwms and cliffs plunge away below, and the scenery is most dramatic. After the col, the route ascends to a subsidiary fin of grey rock, then crosses a fence and gains the circular shelter that marks the true top, Mynydd Moel.

A section of steep, though straightforward descent traverses the long grassy shoulder which leads to the top of Cau Craig. It is probably best to keep to the left of the central fence line which runs along the crest (though it is boggy on both sides) to take the ladder stile to the right at the final summit mound. Follow the fence to the right to the edge of the cliffs – take care, for a substantial drop lies directly below – until the path bears off to the left. Follow this until it begins to zigzag down through steep ground, a little scrambly but really no more than a rough walk. The going levels again and the path traverses rightwards back to the crest to regain the line of the fence. Follow this down through a deep runnel until the going slackens. At this point you might wish to shorten the walk and miss the short section along the A487(T). Although there is

Left: A great stone pile marks the top of Mynydd Moel before the route descends to the grassy far eastern shoulder of Cadair Idris

Above: Looking west back along Cadair Idris's high shoulder to the summit; Craig Cau can be seen to the left

no longer a trace of a stile, many people cross the fence to follow a faint path down through the grass and bracken, keeping to the left of a stone-walled hill pasture (ffridd). Directly gain the track along the floor of the Cwm Rhwyddfor Valley. Alternatively you can keep along the grassy crest of Mynydd Gwerngraig, by the fence line, until it falls to join the main road.

If the latter course is taken, head west along the road over the crest to pass the lay-by car park until, in 1km, a stile by a gate gives access to the old track on the right. Follow this, delightfully, until forced again to join the main road. Walk the road with care for 500m, passing Minffordd Hotel, and finally enter the car park, rather grandly, through great wrought-iron gates.

11: Dow Crag and Coniston Old Man

12: The Greenburn Horseshoe: Wetherlam via the Little Langdale Edge, Swirl How via the Prison Band and descent over Carrs and down Wet Side Edge

13: Langdale Pikes via Jack's Rake

14: Over the Crinkles – The Oxendale Horseshoe rising by Browney Gill and descending via The Band

15: The Scafells from Eskdale

16: The Mosedale Horseshoe – by Black Sail to Pillar Mountain continuing over Red Pike to Yewbarrow

17: The High Stile Ridge

18: The Little Dale Horseshoe by Scope End to Hindscarth and the Littledale Edge to Robinson descending via High Snab Bank

19: The High Ridges around Coledale

20: Skiddaw by Ullock Pike and descent via Birkett's Edge

21: Blencathra by Sharp Edge and descent via Hallsfell Ridge

22: Helvellyn by Striding Edge and descent via Swirral Edge (starting up The Nab and finishing down Catstycam North-West Ridge)

23: A Deepdale Circuit – Fairfield via Hartsop above How Ridge and descent via Cofa Pike and St Sunday Crag

24: The Mardale Horseshoe – High Street via Riggindale Ridge descending Harter Fell via Gatescarth Pass

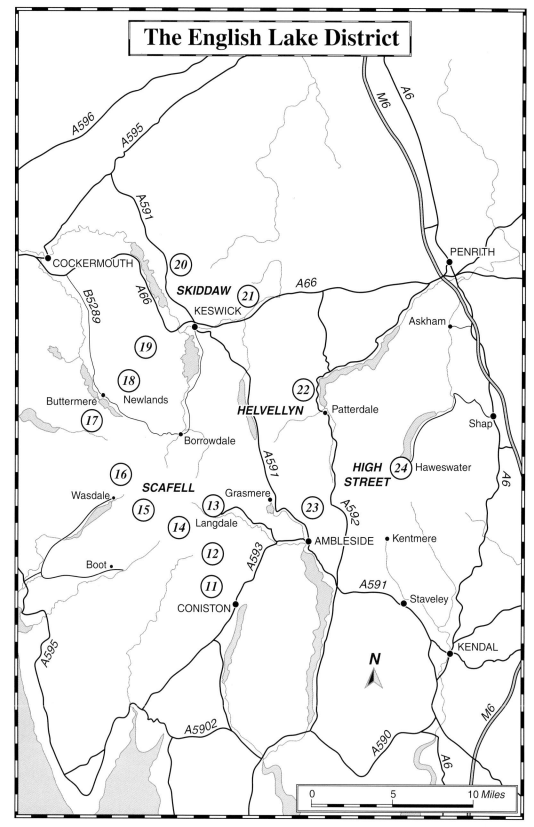

The English Lake District

The Lakes

Fourteen ridge walks range over the wonderful fells of the English Lake District. Above an area noted for its outstanding beauty and perfection of scale, the high fells and fine ridges are in perfect balance with the sylvan slopes, lakes and little stone farms of the deep dales. There is high adventure here, and a kaleidoscope of changing form and colour makes this one of the best loved mountain areas.

This is the largest National Park in Britain, with an area of some 2,280sq km. Roughly circular in plan, its 55km diameter stretches from Ravenglass on the west coast to Shap Abbey on the east, from Caldbeck in the north to Lindale in the south. Within its boundaries are six distinct areas of fells (see *Complete Lakeland Fells* by the author for full details): the Southern Fells, the Western Fells, the North Western Fells, the Northern Fells, the Central Fells and the Eastern Fells.

The walks are selected from all six areas of fells, and are spread throughout the region: thus from Dow Crag and Coniston Old Man, Walk 11, in the Southern Fells, they proceed in a clockwise rotation, ending with the Mardale Horseshoe, Walk 24, in the Eastern Fells. There are two walks within the Southern Fells, six in the Western Fells, two in the North Western Fells, two in the Central Fells and one in the Eastern Fells. For convenience, all the walks are of a circular nature, and start and finish at the same point. They are spread over a wide range of difficulty and length, from the straightforward Dow Crag and Coniston Old Man Round (Walk 11) to the technically difficult and demanding Scafells from Eskdale (Walk 15).

A crisp, frosty winter's morn at the head of Great Langdale, with the Crinkle Crags seen spanning the skyline above Oxendale

DOW CRAG and CONISTON OLD MAN

Walna Scar Road, Blind Tarn, Coniston Old Man, Low Water, Coppermines Valley

Fact Sheet

Location: Above Coniston, Coniston massif, Southern Fells, Southern Fells, Lake District National Park, north west England

Length: 9km (5.6 miles)

Ascent: 700m (2300ft)

Time: 4 hours

Difficulty: A high mountain ridge, rough and stony in places, though there are no technical difficulties and the going is generally straightforward

Seasons: Summer conditions can be expected from April to November; winter conditions from December to March

Map: OS Outdoor Leisure 6, The English Lake District – South West

Start & Finish: There is ample parking by the side of the start of the Walna Scar Road track (SD 289 970)

Access: The Walna Scar Road track is gained by following a steep surfaced road rising from the centre of Coniston; after a while you reach a gate, where the track begins. Coniston lies 10km (6.2 miles) south west of Ambleside along the A593, and 23km (14.3 miles) north of Ulverston along the A590/A5084/A593

Tourist Information: Ambleside (Tel: 015394 32582). Also the National Park Information Centre at Coniston (Tel: 015394 41533)

Accommodation: Coniston has it all, including a campsite and two Youth Hostels (Coppermines House and Holly How)

Geology: A mixture of rough rhyolite and smooth slate provides pleasant walking, though the going is very rough and stony in places

Flora & Fauna: Birds that may be sighted include the raven, the kestrel and the peregrine. Crowberry, wild thyme and starry saxifrage grow in this area; and amongst animals the red fox is common, though seldom seen

Comment: A delightful round including the major top of the Southern Fells, Coniston Old Man. It contrasts a fine open aspect to the south west with the craggy confines of the Coppermines Valley.

The Tops

Brown Pike	682m (2237ft)	(brown pike = brown rocky pointed top)
Buck Pike	744m (2441ft)	(buck pike = male rabbit rocky pointed top)
Dow/Doe Crag	778m (2554ft)	(dow/doe crag = dark crag/female deer crag)
Coniston Old Man	803m (2633ft)	(cun-is-tun olwd man = enclosed rabbit farmstead of old man mined mountain)

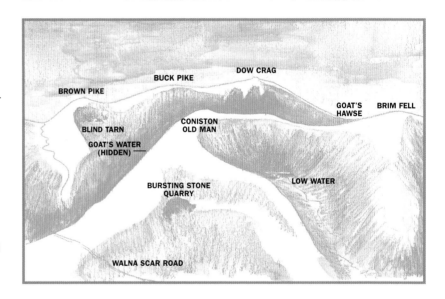

■ Rising some 750m above the little town of Coniston and deep, dark Coniston Water, the massif known as Coniston Old Man is the visually dominant mountain of Lakeland's Southern Fells. Moreover, not only is it the foremost mountain in a delectable group of fells, but for thousands of years it has been the great provider for, and the economic lifeblood of the region. Since the Bronze Age, from perhaps 3000 years BC, it has provided slate and copper in abundance, so much so that when 'modern' copper mining started in the 1560s – the Elizabethan era – under the expert guidance of German miners led by the remarkable master miner Daniel Hochstetter, they discovered so many 'old men' workings (ancient mines of unknown antiquity and unwritten history) that they referred to this copper mountain as Coniston Old Man.

Snow-clad Coniston Old Man stands above Coniston Water and Coniston Village. The summit point lies on the left edge of the plateau with its eastern edge falling rightwards to the Coppermines Valley

Left: Breathtaking views extend in every direction from the summit of Coniston Old Man; seen here from the trig point the view to the north east extends over the Coppermines Valley and Wetherlam's Lad Stones ridge as far as the Central Fells

In this round, the open expanses lie in effective juxtaposition to the wild craggy grandeur within the massif itself. The route includes the Dow Crag ridge from the high mountain pass between Coniston and the Duddon Valley, the Walna Scar Road (a rough track unsuitable for vehicles), and then it encircles the rugged mountain basin of Goat's Water before rising to the summit of Coniston Old Man. The descent falls rapidly down the eastern ridge of the mountain: this must be the most popular path in the Coniston Fells, skirting the Coppermines Valley and its dark craggy countenance and complexity of mines and quarries, to follow the quarry track back to the starting point. Much of the route was once walked daily by the quarrymen and copperminers of Coniston. John Ruskin admired it from his Brantwood mansion across the lake, and today it is one of the best loved mountain walks in the Lake District.

Parking at the end of the Walna Scar Road gains a good deal of altitude. Be thankful, because in days gone by the quarrymen *walked* all the way from Coniston to reach this point before continuing to the summit quarries of the Old Man. The going along the track is easy, though beware of quarry traffic; keep left at the fork (the right road climbs alarmingly to the still working quarry of Brossen Stones – named Bursting Stone on the OS map). Pass tiny Boo Tarn on the left of the track; here, though unseen from the track itself, are a number of Bronze Age earthworks on the moor. Follow the deteriorating track, cut through solid rock in two places; keep on the level, ignoring the path that forks off right, and then climb the steep, grassy fellside – this route leads to Goat's Water and, for rock climbers, the incomparable face of Dow Crag. A short way ahead a stone-arched bridge crosses Cove Beck, and from here the ascent to the summit col of the Walna Scar Pass is increasingly rugged.

Make a stony ascent to the right, first to gain Brown Pike and then along the shoulder, with Blind Tarn below to the right and the wonderful aspect of the Scafell Range to the north west (left). Little Blind Tarn has no visible stream either feeding into it or exiting from it, but on a still May evening the surface can be ringed by trout jumping to the fly. Icelandic char, remnants of the last ice age, have also been caught here on fly by local fishermen. Continue over Buck Pike to the rocky outcrops marking the top of the mighty Dow Crag. Below – and in fact best viewed from the flanks of Coniston Old Man on the opposite side of the basin – the magnificent rock architecture of the great precipice of Dow Crag (some rock climbers still refer to it as Doe Crag, though more popularly it is now known as Dow) falls for some one hundred vertical metres to steep scree which cascades into the copper blue of Goat's Water.

Over one hundred years ago, on 14 April 1898, the rock-climbing pioneer O.G. ('only genuine') Jones arrived by train at Coniston Station (the line is now defunct, having been axed in the 1960s); in the morning he completed an amazing climb known as Central Chimney to arrive at these summit rocks. He then continued by a high-level route to Scafell to make another rock climb, before descending to Wasdale Head for his supper.

Make a straightforward descent to the col of Goat's Hawse and the view to Goat's Water; here there is a crossroad of paths with ways north to the head of Seathwaite Tarn or south to Goat's Water. Ascend to the right on the curving, zigzag path that leads first to the shoulder, with Brim Fell and the high ridge running to Swirl How on the left, then right past the trig point and on to the summit platform and cairn of Coniston Old Man – a commanding position with an extensive view in all directions.

The well worn descent track, which originally served the extensive summit slate quarries, leads east initially and then plunges northwards towards the edge of Low Water (the OS name – it should, of course, be High Water!), a tarn nestling in a formidable mountain setting, particularly striking when the white snows of winter contrast sharply with the blackness of the encircling crags. From here the track leads east again, making a slaty descent through a number of now deserted quarry levels. This was the route taken by quarryman George Coward and his rescue team on the appalling night of 14 December 1937.

It had snowed heavily all through the day of 13 December, cutting off the roads to Coniston. Nevertheless, despite the continuing heavy snow, the quarrymen walked back up to the Old Man Quarries the next day; one team even went to Spion Cop, the

highest of all the quarries. However, as conditions deteriorated further, most workers took stock and returned home early – though two lads in particular who were working inside the confines of the 'closehead' (underground chamber) stayed on, delaying their exit until around 2pm. And disaster struck, because as they descended the mountainside the whole slope avalanched: one lad managed to extricate himself, but the other was buried. In the lower quarries George Coward and some of his men were also about to depart, but rushed up the mountainside to help. After searching for 1.5 hours there was still no sign of the missing quarryman, so George returned to Coniston to organise lights and men, and the assembled team mobilised at 7.30pm. They finally returned to Coniston at 6.30am the next day, having rescued the missing quarryman.

Looking across the Coppermines Valley, the jumble of buildings and deserted mining relics of Red Dell can be seen; these lead up to Wetherlam, a powerful and inspirational mountain scene, albeit a landscape extensively ravaged by man. Indeed, though hard to believe now, at the height of the mining activity in 1855 some 600 men were employed here, and workings extended for 500m (255 fathoms) below the surface, some 250m below sea level!

Continue the stony descent until the track levels and strikes out right to contour the flank of the mountain. At this point a grassed rocky knoll, The Bell, stands above to the left. Although off route and usually bypassed, a short, scrambling ascent reveals it to be a worthy viewpoint. The track, notoriously swathed in ice in winter, leads easily back to the beginning of the Walna Scar Road.

Looking over the Coppermines Valley from The Bell, reached by a short scramble from the main track. Above right stands Wetherlam and on the left the top of Swirl How. The white building bottom right is now the youth hostel. Little is left today to indicate that 600 men once worked the mines here

THE GREENBURN HORSESHOE – WETHERLAM via the LITTLE LANGDALE EDGE, SWIRL HOW via the PRISON BAND and descent over CARRS and down WET SIDE EDGE

Slater's Bridge, expansive view over Lakeland, Halifax 'S' for Sugar, easy descent

Fact Sheet

Location: Above Little Langdale, Coniston massif, Southern Fells, Lake District National Park, north west England

Length: 14km (8.75 miles)

Ascent: 975m (3200ft)

Time: 5.5 hours

Difficulty: Good paths prevail, though the going is often rough and stony; this is a high mountain walk which shouldn't be underestimated. The ascent of the Little Langdale Edge of Wetherlam steepens at the top and involves a few small rocky steps (possibly Scrambling Grade 0.25 if tackled head-on)

Seasons: Summer conditions may be expected from April to November; winter conditions from December to March

Map: OS Outdoor Leisure 6, The English Lake District – South West

Start & Finish: At Little Langdale village, where there is extremely limited parking by the side of the road above the telephone kiosk (NY 316034). Do not block the road or any entrances

Access: Some 8km (5 miles) west of Ambleside along the A593 Coniston road, and then along the minor road leading to Wrynose Pass

Tourist Information: Ambleside (Tel: 015394 32582). Also the National Park Information Centre at Ambleside (Tel: 015394 32729)

Accommodation: There is self-catering and 'B&B', and also the Three Shires Inn within Little Langdale. The nearest campsites and Youth Hostels are in Great Langdale

Geology: Rhyolites provide pleasant walking, though the going is rough and stony in places

Flora & Fauna: Birds that may be seen include the raven, heron and kestrel. Flora include the elder buckthorn and parsley fern. The increasingly rare red squirrel can still be seen – fleetingly – in Little Langdale

Comment: A classic horseshoe with wonderful vistas.

The Tops

Birk Fell Man	525m (1722ft)	(birk fell man = craggy top of the birch hill)
Wetherlam	672m (2502ft)	(wether-lum = hardy [castrated] sheep high pasture)
Swirl How	802m (2630ft)	(swirl how = encircling hill mound/ burial hill)
Great Carrs	785m (2575ft)	(girt cars = big/high rocks)
Little Carrs	692m (2270ft)	(la-lle cars = lile cars = small rocks)

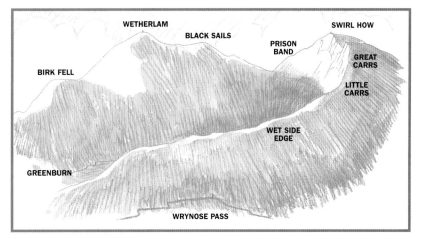

■ Particularly regal when clad white with snow, Wetherlam – fair in face, fair in nature – is undoubtedly queen of the Southern Fells and has captured many a heart. The most north-easterly mountain of the Coniston massif, she looks down upon Little Langdale Tarn and presents a noble aspect to all points south and east. Beneath her northern flank, scalloped from the mountain by glacier, lies the great hanging basin of Greenburn, a wild, secretive mountain cove backed by high crags falling to Wet Side Edge.

This mountain round follows the high crest which encircles Greenburn, and provides a walk of exceptional quality. Rising from Little Langdale over Birk Fell Man, it ascends the Little Langdale Edge of Wetherlam before traversing the flank of Black Sail into the col separating the coves of Greenburn and

White rhyolite rocks mark the summit of Great Carrs with steep ground tumbling into Greenburn far below

Levers Water. Climb up Prison Band, a steep ascent leading to the highest summit, Swirl How, then follow the curving line of descent over Carrs and down Wet Side Edge back to the Greenburn basin.

Ascend to the crossroads astride the hill above Little Langdale village, and go left along the High Birk How Farm lonin (drive). A gate on the right, found at the point of entry to the farm, leads across the field, with wonderful views across Little Langdale Tarn right into the Greenburn Horseshoe; descend to Slater's Bridge – which has two main spans, one of flat slate and one a stone arch – leading across the river. Turn right along the track; this runs uphill through the buildings of Low and High Hall Garth to a gate. Continue along the track, keeping right at the first junction; the track then splits again, and you take the left fork which rises to Greenburn.

Cross the stile by the locked gate some way before the old mine workings, to ascend left by the side of the stone wall. Nearing the top of the rise, the path veers right and ascends to a fence. Keep right, then take the ladder stile over the fence, rising until a further ladder stile leads over to the right to the craggy flanks of Birk Fell. Follow a vague path up a grassy incline; in a little while it becomes better defined and weaves a route through the craglets, first right, then left. The top of Birk Fell is crested by two cairned rocky knolls known as Birk Fell Man. The shoulder of Birk Fell Hawse leads to the steepening ascent of the Little Langdale/Wetherlam Edge of Wetherlam.

Nearing the top, little crags present very mild scrambling, and all can be avoided. Take care in winter, because even in the absence of any snow covering, this path can become very icy. Suddenly the going flattens, and the summit of Wetherlam can be seen, marked by a little rocky knoll to the left. The view is expansive, the rugged splendour of the fells to the north complemented by the open silvery splendour of the shining lakes to the east and south. It is easy to understand why, for many, Wetherlam is a favourite mountain.

The path leads right off the summit plateau to descend to Red Dell Head Moss, then traverses the Greenburn flanks of Black Sail. Straightforward in most conditions, this north-facing slope, with the steeps of Keld Gill Head lurking below, can be particularly tricky under snow and ice, when an ice axe becomes essential and crampons highly desirable.

At the end of the traverse a short descent falls to the col of Swirl Hawse; fierce winds often blow through here, making it no place to linger. It does, however, provide the one escape route back to Little Langdale should that option be prudent. If this route is taken, after the initial descent it is best to traverse fairly high across the flanks of Wetherlam before dropping down to the old mine buildings below the reservoir – the way down by the valley bottom is now most unpleasant, with no real path and lots of troublesome and boggy going.

Above rises Prison Band, a jagged rocky ridge, though in fact not as bad as the name may suggest. Sections of steep scrambling (no technical difficulty) ascent are interspersed with horizontal stretches, which provide some respite in the effort required. The band finishes abruptly by the distinctive beehive cairn of Swirl How, the highest point of the horseshoe. Leave the marble-veined, white summit rocks to make an easy descent to the rim of the cove named Top of Broad Slack.

After a short section of ascent the sad remains of 'Halifax Bomber, LL 505 - 'S' For Sugar, RCAF, October 22 1944' can be seen to the left; this is only the undercarriage section, as most of the plane was scattered down the scree of Broad Slack below. Some long-time residents of Little Langdale can still recall the explosion. The crash occurred during a terrible night, with heavy rain and gale-force winds, so extreme that it wasn't until first light the next day that anyone could attempt a rescue. In vain,

Two walkers pause on the steep ascent of Wetherlam's Little Langdale Edge, to be rewarded by expansive views over Little Langdale, Lake Windermere to the Eastern Fells and beyond to the hills of the distant Yorkshire Dales

because tragically, all the crew were killed.

Soon the summit rocks of Great Carrs are reached, Scafell and Crinkle Crags presenting a superb backcloth to the north west. The main path lies slightly to the left of the crest, although an exposed way can be picked along the rim of the crags, until a little section of steep descent leads to a col. A slight rise leads to the top of Little Carrs, though this summit is hardly discernible. Again the main path keeps to the left side of the ridge until the angle slackens and the shoulder becomes increasingly grassy; this change heralds the beginning of the delightful grassy shoulder of Wet Side Edge.

Keep to the crest of Wet Side Edge, ignoring the well blazoned paths which veer off left, and so descend to the summit of Wrynose Pass. With Pike O'Blisco standing proud over Wrynose Pass and the Three Shires Stone to the left, and the great flank of Wetherlam over Greenburn to the right, the way lies straight ahead (the Three Shires Stone marks the meeting of the old counties of Lancashire, Westmorland and Cumberland that are now called Cumbria). With the 'Hobbit'-like charm of Little

The Greenburn Horseshoe above Little Langdale Tarn

Langdale beckoning, the path falls with delightful ease. At a point just preceding the rocky terminus it is best to follow a vague path leading down to the right to the easier grassy flanks below. Once these are reached, continue easterly, traversing the high ground and following the path along the rounded shoulder. Even at these lowly heights the view over Little Langdale Tarn extends to the distant Central Fells. Continue, over rather boggy ground in places, until at a point above the fell wall it becomes expedient to descend to the right to Greenburn Beck.

A recently constructed bridge situated just upstream of the fell wall provides safe passage across the Greenburn Beck as it charges noisily through the confines of the little rocky ravine. Below, where the flow spreads and deep pools form beneath the silver birch, oak, holly and rowan, with brown trout gliding in their still waters, it is easier to see the clear, mint-green, copper carbonate colouring that gave this beck its name. A short climb regains the Greenburn track at a point just above the stile. Turn and make your way back to lovely Little Langdale and, should you wish it, to the welcome of the Three Shires Inn.

LANGDALE PIKES via JACK'S RAKE

Stickle Tarn, Jack's Rake, neolithic stone axe factory, Dungeon Ghyll

Fact Sheet

Location: Great Langdale, Langdale Fells, Western Fells, Lake District National Park, north west England

Length: 6.5km (4 miles)

Ascent: 875m (2875ft)

Time: 4 hours

Difficulty: Whilst good paths prevail, the going is mostly rough and rocky, and there are strenuous sections of ascent. Using Jack's Rake to climb Pavey Ark is exposed, though this often goes unnoticed as it follows a well defined trough for much of the ascent, and involves sections of scrambling interspaced by easier ground (Scrambling Grade 1). Under snow and ice conditions it should be considered a winter climb (Winter Grade I)

Seasons: Summer conditions can generally be expected from April to November, and winter conditions from December to March

Map: OS Outdoor Leisure 6, The English Lake District – South West

Start & Finish: The large car park (it fills quickly) behind The Stickle Barn, just beyond the New Dungeon Ghyll Hotel (NY 295 064)

Access: Some 8km (5 miles) west of Ambleside along the A593 Coniston road, and then along the B5343 Great Langdale road through Chapel Stile

Tourist Information: Ambleside (Tel: 015394 32582). Also the National Park Information Centre at Ambleside (Tel: 015394 32729)

Accommodation: All types of accommodation can be found within the valley: there is a campsite at the head of the valley, two Youth Hostels – Elterwater and High Close – and a bunkhouse attached to the Stickle Barn

Geology: A predominance of rhyolite means stony ground; deposits of silica-rich tuffs (volcanic ash) were once a source of material for the neolithic axe factories

Flora & Fauna: Birds include raven and peregrine; amongst the flowers, yellow mountain saxifrage and rose-root can be seen. Pavey Ark is inaccessible to sheep and is therefore a bilberry heaven in August

Comment: A fine mountain adventure over Britain's best known skyline. Missing out Jack's Rake considerably lowers the standard of difficulty.

The Tops

Pavey Ark	697m (2288ft)	(pavey ark = dark/mysterious large steep-sided mountain mass)
Harrison Stickle	736m (2414ft)	(harrison stickle = Harrison's sharp point)
Pike O'Stickle	709m (2324ft)	(pike O stickle = THE rocky point of the sharp points)
Loft Crag	682m (2238ft)	(loft crag = top crag)

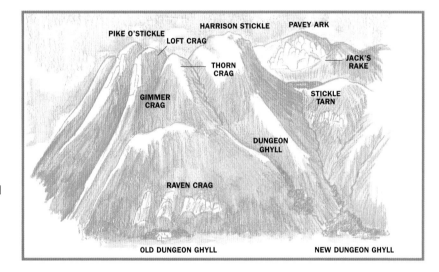

■ Viewed across Windermere Lake or from the lower reaches of Great Langdale, the silhouette presented by the Langdale Pikes looks remarkably like a reclining lion ready to pounce. Indeed from most points south, the craggy skyline is nothing less than superb: from left to right we see Pike O'Stickle and Loft Crag, with the great rock bastion of Gimmer Crag beneath, and cleft from Harrison Stickle and Pavey Ark by the depths of the Dungeon Ghyll – to feel their power, to live in their shadow, who could want for more?

There are many possible routes over these popular fells, but I consider that the one selected here has the most to offer. Direct in ascent via Stickle Ghyll and beneath Tarn Crag, it rounds Stickle Tarn to gain and follow the remarkable

The lofty Langdale Pikes towering above Great Langdale. In the foreground stand the Langdale Boulders, whilst the snow-clad Pikes include (from centre left to right) Pike O'Stickle (just discernible above Loft Crag and Thorn Crag), and Harrison Stickle (the highest – seen centrally), followed by the dark rock face of Pavey Ark

diagonal break of Jack's Rake across the face of Pavey Ark. The heights are gained quickly, and Harrison Stickle, Pike O'Stickle and Loft Crag follow with a minimum of further effort. The path down follows a natural and easy passage through crags and steeps to make an easy crossing of the Dungeon Ghyll beneath its waterfalls.

The path leaves the head of the car park and follows the left side (the true right bank) of Stickle Ghyll until a footbridge crosses the stream; it leads on over a stile and by an old sheep fold, and then ascends steeply up the true left bank of Stickle Ghyll by cascading waterfalls. Nearing the head of the highest fall, a path branches off right, climbing by ascending zigzags until it breaks grade to traverse left beneath the rocks of Tarn Crag. At the end of the crag a scrambly ascent gains a shoulder. Rejoin the main path above Stickle Ghyll, and emerge by the dam on the east shore of Stickle Tarn.

This delightful mountain tarn frames the impressive great face of Pavey Ark. Some 150m in

height, this extensive cliff of steep rock broken by ledges of heather and bilberry looks impossible to all but the accomplished mountaineer – but look more carefully, and a tantalising line of weakness will be seen running diagonally across the cliff from the bottom right, by the start of the deep East Gully, to the top left. With a little scrambling it lies within the capabilities of most hill walkers.

To reach it, it is best to bear right and follow the path which traverses above the east shore. At the head of the tarn bear left and cross Bright Beck – there are usually enough exposed stones to enable a dry passage – to follow a good path into bouldery scree below the deep rift of East Gully. Ascend the scree and boulders as best you can until you are level with the base of the gully. The start of Jack's Rake lies just to the left. Do not ascend East Gully: it is better to descend again should you not wish to proceed at this point, because over recent years there has been some movement of the large boulder scree and it is very unstable and unsafe.

Those wishing to avoid Jack's Rake should begin their detour at Bright Beck. Do not cross the stream, but follow the path up its right side (the true left bank) until it swings across and makes a straightforward ascent of Pavey Ark's east ridge. The route is well marked, and leads through a series of little rocky steps to the summit plateau of Pavey Ark. The rocky knoll-top lies just to the left.

Those wishing to follow Jack's Rake should make their ascent to the left, with the cliffs looming above and gathering below. Keep a steady head, and remember your responsibility not only to yourself but to others: despite heavy traffic, a good deal of loose stone remains on the ledges and easier angled sections, and it is important to try not to dislodge any because there may be other climbers below, in particular rock climbers. An easy initial section is followed by a trough-like rift just beyond a deep chimney which splits the rock wall above – Rake End Chimney. You will have to use hands as well as feet to ascend the rift, as it is now very polished; after perhaps 50m a ledge is reached and the going eases. You may be thankful to learn that you have just accomplished the hardest section – but do not

let your guard slip yet, however.

After an easier section, a horizontal ledge is gained at about half height; traverse left to pass beneath Gwynne's Chimney which cuts through the rocks above. Beyond this there is a very exposed section which climbs a short, polished corner; a slip here would be serious. Thereafter the going is easier and climbs to a large rift known as Great Chimney. Ascend this for a short way until the path traverses left, to wind its way to the top of the crag; the summit knoll of Pavey Ark lies just over to the right. Well done!

A circular path traverses south-westwards around the rim of the cliffs to make a steep and scrambly, though easy, ascent of Harrison Stickle, the highest point of the Langdale Pikes. The far extremity of the pike offers the fairest prospect, although you will have to return the same way because steep crags lie below: over Great Langdale to Blea Tarn twixt the two Langdales Little and Great, and over Side Pike and Lingmoor to lovely Wetherlam and distant Windermere Lake. The way to Pike O'Stickle can be clearly seen from here.

As you descend, before gaining the boggy hollow

Standing on the edge of Harrison Stickle – the highest of the famous Langdale Pikes at 736m (2414ft) – to look over the Great Langdale Valley to Side Pike and the idyllic Blea Tarn, at the head of Little Langdale, beyond

Seen from the heights the clouds have lifted to reveal the smoking cone of Pike O'Stickle. The top, once marking the centre of stone age axe manufacture, is reached by a short scramble

between Harrison Stickle and Pike O'Stickle, the banding of the rhyolite rocks is most noticeable. Smoother rocks lie littered on the slope, these weathered to a white skin with a glassy, dark blue composition revealed beneath, where the skin is broken: these are the silica-rich tuffs whose properties put Langdale at the forefront of technology and made the Pikes a very important site of prehistory. Hit this rock with the correct technique and it chips with a concoidal fracture, leaving an edge as sharp as a razor. Stone axes from Langdale have been found all around Britain. (NOTE: If you find one, please leave it.)

Specially constructed paths take you on across the hollow and over to the free-standing knoll of Pike O'Stickle, perhaps not the highest, yet in terms of individuality certainly the most distinguished of the Langdale Pikes. A steep scramble leads to the top. The unbroken view west across Mickleden provides a fine aspect of Bowfell and further, beyond Allen Crags and Glaramara, to Scafell's Great End and the dome of

Great Gable. The view south-east, however, over the white-red rhyolite rock of the north-west face of Gimmer Crag, is for me one of the finest of mountain scenes – perhaps because, like my father before me, I have climbed these rocks and know their worth.

From Pike O'Stickle it is necessary to descend by the same route taken in ascent; then the path bears right and traverses east. The broad main path lies down to the left of the crest; however, I recommend that you keep right and crest the top of Loft Crag before making your way down the broad scree gully which runs by the side of Thorn Crag. Beyond a grassy shoulder the path narrows again, to follow an intriguing route across and down the hillside to the base of the Dungeon Ghyll. Cross the Ghyll and take the stile on the right; follow down by the wall, and then go left over a stile to take the track, and then the path right – this leads straight back to the car park. Now is the time to reflect on this relatively short mountain excursion, but truly in God's own country.

OVER THE CRINKLES – THE OXENDALE HORSESHOE rising by BROWNEY GILL and descending via THE BAND

Red Tarn haematite, Crinkle Crags, Three Tarns, The Band

Fact Sheet

Location: Great Langdale, Langdale Fells, Western Fells, Lake District National Park, north west England

Length: 11km (6.8 miles)

Ascent: 825m (2700ft)

Time: 4.5 hours

Difficulty: A demanding walk in a high mountain setting, although the technical difficulties are low and the immediate exposure slight, except for the Bad Step: this is located on the south end of Long Top (the Second Crinkle) and requires a short (10m) scramble (Scrambling Grade 1), although this can be avoided. Beyond the path there are many crags and much steep ground

Seasons: Summer conditions may be expected from April to November, and winter conditions from December to March

Map: OS Outdoor Leisure 6, The English Lake District – South West

Start & Finish: At the Old Dungeon Ghyll car park (it fills very quickly) at the head of the valley (NY 286 062)

Access: Some 8.5km (5 miles) west of Ambleside along the A593 Coniston road, and then along the B5343 Great Langdale road through Chapel Stile

Tourist Information: Ambleside (Tel: 015394 32582). Also the National Park Information Centre at Ambleside (Tel: 015394 32729)

Accommodation: All types of accommodation can be found within the valley. There is a campsite at the head of the valley, there are two Youth Hostels – Elterwater and High Close – and a bunkhouse attached to the Stickle Barn

Geology: Rhyolite means that the ground is stony; deposits of haematite (iron ore) occasionally add a deep red colour

Flora & Fauna: Birds to be seen include the raven and the kestrel. Amongst flowers, purple saxifrage and lady's mantle can be found; and the weasel and the rabbit are quite common

Comment: The rugged outline of The Crinkles, at the head of Great Langdale and the basin of Oxendale, is a much celebrated skyline. This is an exposed, rocky mountain ridge walk of high calibre.

The Tops

Great Knott	696m (2283ft)	(great not = great rocky knoll)
First Crinkle		
Long Top –	833m (2733ft)	(crinkle = wrinkle)
Second Crinkle	859m (2816ft)	(ditto)
Third Crinkle	840m (2754ft)	(ditto)
Fourth Crinkle	832m (2730ft)	(ditto)
Fifth Crinkle –		
Gunson Knott	815m (2674ft)	(gunson knot = Gunson's rocky knoll)
Shelter Crags	815m (2674ft)	(shelter crags = shelter crags)

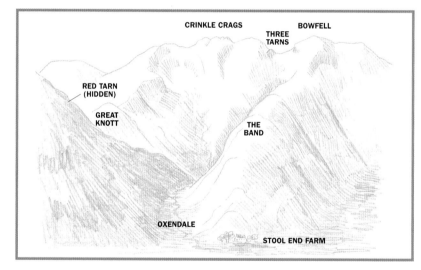

■ The long valley of Great Langdale, with its two villages of Elterwater and Chapel Stile, snakes into the surrounding mountains. At its head, just beyond the Old Dungeon Ghyll Hotel, it splits, each branch probing even deeper: Mickleden stretches north-westwards between Pike O'Stickle and Bowfell to Rossett Gill. Oxendale, the most prominent, lies to the south west, a compact, steep-sided bowl, its flanks gouged by deep ravines and hidden waterfalls, and its rim, with Pike O'Blisco to the left and The Band to the right, dominated by a complex of up-and-down knolls running like the teeth of a battered saw-blade straight across the skyline.

Crinkle Crags seen from the Blea Tarn road across the head of Oxendale. From left to right all five Crinkles can be seen, ending with Shelter Crags, before the ridge dips to the Three Tarns col

Winter solstice between the first Crinkle and Long Top with a watery sun setting over Eskdale

The serrated rocks of the Crinkle Crags instantly grip the imagination, and with Great Langdale on one side and the remote regions of Mosedale, Lingcove and Upper Eskdale on the other, they provide a fine, challenging, high mountain ridge walk in a remarkable setting. Many routes are possible, but the one chosen here follows the purest horseshoe around Oxendale; traditionally it starts from, and finishes at, the Old Dungeon Ghyll Hotel.

Join the main road, following it to the right-angled bend. Continue straight on through the gate and up the track, to pass through Stool End Farm which nestles at the toe of The Band. Beyond the farm, take the rising path for a little way until a track bears off to the left (the route up The Band continues rising to the right). Follow this path, well signed, to pass around a sheep fold and continue with open ground and Oxendale Beck to your left. In about 100m a footbridge crosses the beck. Take this, and climb up a steep, specially constructed path of paved rock slabs and steps; at the top you can take a well earned breather on the shoulder of Brown Howe. The path steepens again,

and climbs to follow the left side (the true right bank) of Browney Gill. All this path is affected by seepage from the hillside above, and in the grip of winter frosts, tracts of ice form across it. If these conditions prevail, unless you are suitably equipped with ice axe and crampons, you should give it a miss because it has been the cause of innumerable accidents.

The going slackens, and by a crossroads of paths Red Tarn comes into view. The general red discoloration – iron staining – of the ground hereabouts undoubtedly gave the little tarn its name. An old iron pipe sticking out of the ground was once a vent pipe for the mines, but otherwise it is now difficult to recognise any sign of what was once an important and highly productive iron ore site. The ore from here was carted first to Wrynose Pass, then down into Little Langdale to be processed at the Hackett Force Forge; the latter was once of such importance that in the fifteenth century the iron produced was considered to be 'not much inferior to that of Dantzick' (in Germany?). The heavy, dark blue lumps of rock scattered hither and thither are haematite – that is, iron ore.

Turn right and make your ascent to the higher grassy plateau, with Great Knott to the right. Although it is off the main path, a visit is worthwhile, and provides an informative view over the rim across Crinkle Gill to Whorneyside Force waterfall and Hell Gill – the bowels of Oxendale. The grassy shoulder gives way to the long, rocky knoll of the First Crinkle. The deepest dip separates this from the next objective: the Second Crinkle, more properly called Long Top.

Steep scree leads up into a little gully which is barred by a chockstone (no way through, I'm afraid). However, about 10m below the chockstone a short series of steps leads up and out onto the right rib: this is the infamous Bad Step. In dry conditions it is really very straightforward, though you will have to use your hands as well as your feet (it is Scrambling Grade 1). The going above requires the negotiation of rather loose, stony ground on sloping ledges for a short way; this then eases, and the route continues to the highest cairned rock rib, the summit of Long Top – the Second Crinkle. However, the difficulties of the Bad Step can be bypassed altogether should this be

Early morning reflections in Red Tarn. Great Knott to the left followed by Crinkle Crags with Bowfell in the distance. Now a scene of great tranquillity, this was once the site of a bustling red haematite (iron) mine

desirable. A short way above the base of the dip, a well defined path traverses out left beneath the rocks to make a straightforward ascent of a grassy gully which leads in turn to the edge of the summit plateau.

There are three crinkles still to go: all require a slight detour from the main path, nevertheless all are worthy and should be included. Descend along the path and cross the head of a broad scree gully sweeping down to the depths of Crinkle Gill: this is Mickle Door. Ascend the knoll 50m east of the main trod to reach the independent top of the Third Crinkle; this stands a little forward of the others and is the most prominent of the Crinkles when viewed from the valley. It also provides a revealing perspective north to the two remaining crinkles and Shelter Crags beyond. Return to the path by the same route.

The Fourth Crinkle stands 10m east of the path and offers an excellent view over Great Langdale. The Fifth Crinkle, Gunson Knott, lies 20m east of the path, with a summit depression formed from boulders. The path continues to skirt the east flank of the rocky knoll of Shelter Crags, and a short, scrambly ascent to the left is required should you be intent on reaching its top. Whilst it may be possible to trace a rough undulating line along the rim, hereafter the path actually skirts to the left, taking the line of least resistance. Pass a tarn in the depression below, and continue along a well

defined route, also passing an independent rock knoll which stands over to the right. Drop to the large flat col occupied by the Three Tarns: this crossroads of routes offers a wonderful aspect to the mighty Scafells, seen to the west, over their own image mirrored in the water surface.

Should you have the time and energy to spare, you may wish to go on from here, following the steeply rising path towards the summit of Bowfell. If you do, allow an hour to make the round trip back to this point, plus at least another hour to make your return to the Old Dungeon Hotel. Those content and dedicated to the ethical purity of the Oxendale Horsehoe will bear right and follow the path which traverses down towards the long shoulder of the band.

The going is rough, with a few boggy bits and a few rocky bits, mostly connected by loose scree – though who could complain, because the descent of the band is absolutely glorious: it is a rugged mountain scene *par excellence*, with high fell bracken, juniper and red rhyolites framing the greener pastures of Langdale below. It is equally magical by moonlight, with Pike O'Blisco and Pike O'Stickle set black against the stars, and the only sound that of a dog fox howling deep within the depths of Oxendale. Nearing the bottom the path veers right to avoid the tumble over a crag. The path is well worn, and route-finding is straightforward.

The Crinkle Crags and Bowfell seen from Pike O' Blisco

THE SCAFELLS from ESKDALE

Lingcove Beck Bridge, Esk Buttress, Lakeland's two highest mountains, Broad Stand,
Spout Force, Silverybield

Fact Sheet

Location: Eskdale, Scafells, Western Fells, Lake District National Park, north west England

Length: 13.5km (8.25 miles)

Ascent: 900m (2950ft)

Time: 8 hours

Difficulty: A remote and demanding walk over the rooftops of England. It is a long way even to reach the ridges detailed, and once reached they are physically and technically demanding with a high degree of exposure in places. The going is stony along the heights, and there are sections of bog lower down. There is a river crossing which may be impossible in spate conditions. The key stages of technical difficulty are: (1) The ascent of Pen above Esk Buttress on the ascent to Scafell Pike; this requires a moderate scramble in ascent and descent (Scrambling Grade 1). (2) The infamous Broad Stand leading from Mickledore to Scafell (Scrambling Grade 3). (3) The descent of Cam Spout ridge, which is rough and arduous rather than technically difficult. It is a long and difficult expedition under snow and ice (Winter Grade II)

Seasons: Summer conditions may be expected from May to October, and winter conditions from November to April

Map: OS Outdoor Leisure 6, The English Lake District – South West

Start & Finish: By the telephone box at Brotherilkeld, at the foot of Wrynose Pass, Eskdale (NY 212 012). There is some parking here, or in the larger layby car park a little further down the road

Access: Some 18km (11 miles) west of Ambleside along the A593 towards Coniston, then follow the minor road up through Little Langdale and over the mountain passes of Wrynose and Hardknott – a lot of single track, and best avoided at busy times – to Eskdale. From Whitehaven in the west go some 32km (20 miles) south and east along the A595(T) to Gosforth, and then along minor roads into Eskdale

Tourist Information: Egremont (Tel: 01946 820693)

Accommodation: There are all types of accommodation within Eskdale, including campsites and a Youth Hostel

Geology: Rough, reliable rhyolite. Note that Broad Stand is very polished and becomes greasy when wet

The Tops

Pen	762m (2500ft)	(pen = head)
Scafell Pike	978m (3210ft)	(scaw-fal pike = pointed top of a bare rocky fell)
Scafell	964m (3162ft)	(scaw-fal = bare rocky fell)

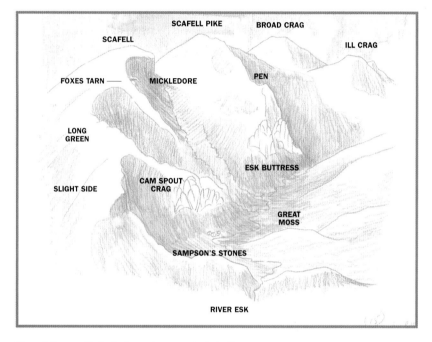

Flora & Fauna: Birds that may be seen include the raven and the peregrine. Rowan trees, stonecrop and butterwort grow here. Wild salmon still spawn in the River Esk, and the more observant might see the mountain ringlet butterfly

Comment: This is a very demanding outing, much more than just a stiff hill walk. It covers some of the wildest and grandest mountain scenery in Britain, including England's two highest mountains. *Bon voyage!*

■ The Scafells form the highest mountain massif in England, and as with Snowdon in Wales and Ben Nevis in Scotland, they know their own importance. An élite, high mountain atmosphere, a certain indefatigable spirit, pervades these sublime, distant heights: crest these tops, scale these steeps, and the

Cam Spout Crag and the mighty Scafell seen above Upper Eskdale's Great Moss. Mickledore, the connecting ridge between Scafell and Scafell Pike, can be seen top right with the formidable crag of Scafell's East Buttress immediately to its left. The roof ridge tile shape of Cam Spout Crag provides an entertaining ridge descent from the summit plateau

huge array of mountains spread out beneath your feet leaves you in no doubt that you are on the roof of the world.

An early start should be made: the track starts at the telephone box and leads to Brotherilkeld Farm. Turn left before the farm, however, and follow the path along the right (the true left) bank of the River Esk. Upper Eskdale sits amongst a wild and rugged landscape, Heron Crag rising to the left, while the steep mountainsides tower high above, protecting the spectacularly placed Roman fort to the right. Continue along the path, to pass over the stone arch of Lingcove Beck packhorse bridge. Ascending, the path follows the right edge of the ravine, passing first below Throstlehow and then beneath the craggy face of Scar Lathing, finally entering the remote and wonderful world of Great Moss.

To the west, two impressive crags dominate the scene: the first, massive and liberally coated with greenery, is shaped like a roof ridge-tile – hence the name 'Cam Spout', or more correctly Cam Crag ('cam' is Old Norse, meaning 'of ridge section'); Cam Spout is actually the name of the waterfall to its right. Our line of descent takes the ridge which

leads down from the broad shoulder of Scafell and then along the rim of this crag. The other crag is that of Esk Buttress (named Dow Crag and Central Pillar on the OS map) and it is one of the finest rock-climbing crags within the Lake District. We take a line above this to climb directly to the Eskdale Cairn of Scafell Pike.

Pick a suitable place to cross the Esk, somewhere above its confluence with the beck flowing from Cam Spout (the waterfall). In normal conditions it is usually possible to keep your feet dry by traversing beneath Esk Buttress and so gaining the entrance of Little Narrowcove up to the left beyond. In a short way it is possible to move out left and climb the shoulder above Esk Buttress to reach the little top of Pen. A corner on its left side offers a sporting scramble with only one awkward step (Scrambling Grade 1). An easier route exists round to the side. Return to the ridge beyond and traverse across to the foot of a little rock wall. An easy scramble will be found to the left, and thereafter the rocky crest of the ridge can be followed, rough and stony but without technical difficulty, to gain the Eskdale Cairn of Scafell Pike.

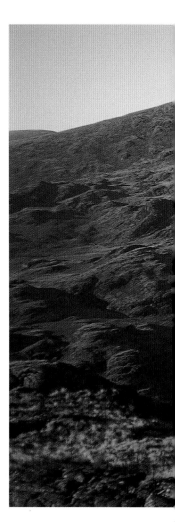

A short walk across the plateau leads to the large circular summit shelter of England's highest mountain.

A path leads down to the curious little crest of Mickledore, which gamely connects Scafell Pike to Scafell. At its far end, down below its crest to the left, there is a large block boulder with a deep cleft on its right side. This is the entrance to Broad Stand, and above lies a series of rocky steps leading to easier ground. There are alternatives, though they necessitate making long detours: the easiest route is to the south, running underneath the overhanging mass of the East Buttress and then by Foxes Tarn; another is to the north, traversing beneath Scafell Face and Scafell Pinnacle and so to the steep rift of Lord's Rake.

Rather out of control, and reputedly – though personally I don't believe this – under the influence of 'Kendal Black' (a particularly strong laudanum mixture of opium and alcohol), Samuel Taylor Coleridge descended this way on 8 August 1802. He managed to negotiate a safe passage down the middle rocky step (1.5m high) by dint of hanging from his hands and letting himself drop – a method still employed by some today. Our way lies in ascent, a feat never accomplished by the late great A.W. Wainwright. Although the technical difficulties are not high, and very many manage it without the slightest problem, exposure is considerable and you cannot afford to make a single slip: the consequences of doing so would be disastrous.

Squeeze your way through the rift to the right of the block, then make a polished traverse out to the left and straighten yourself cautiously into a standing position on the slab: even though you have only just commenced climbing, exposure here is already considerable, as the ground falls away rapidly to the left. Move up the slab to gain the horizontal rock ledge below the next corner. The next section is the crux: either climb directly up the vertical corner – it is only a few feet to get your hands over the top – or move out to the left and then up (very exposed) to gain the rock ledge above. An easier, slabby corner (still exposed) now leads to the scree-strewn rock slab above.

The path leads up and to the left, zigzagging across the slabs – take care not to dislodge any stones as there may be other climbers below – and eventually gaining a notch in the rib to the left. Beyond the notch lies the stone-filled, easy upper section of Mickledore Chimney, a broad rock gully. Move into the gully, being extremely careful not to dislodge any stones as the gully lies directly above the climbers' path which passes beneath the East Buttress, and follow it to easier ground, a straightforward section. Continue taking a south-westerly course along the plateau, passing the twin tops of Scafell Pinnacle and rounding the rim of Deep Gill to the right, and keep going until you reach the summit, some 400m distant.

This grand scene surveys the 'seven kingdoms', as proclaimed by 'Auld Will Ritson': a rich local

Above: The magnificent spectacle of England's highest mountain massif, The Scafells, seen arrayed above Upper Eskdale

Left: A narrow rift formed by a large boulder marks the start of the exposed and demanding scramble of Broad Stand rising from Mickledore through Scafell's formidable rock defences

Top left: A narrow ridge runs across the gap of Mickledore to connect Scafell Pike with Scafell

character known as 'the King O' Wasdal', he was the landlord of what is now the Wasdale Head Inn. In 1856 he added to his farming interests by establishing in his farmhouse what was then the Huntsman's Inn; he also served as a part-time mountain guide. Scafell's 'seven kingdoms' originates from the occasion that he took a clergyman to the summit and proclaimed the surrounding mountain ranges to be the Isle of Man to the west with Ireland beyond, Wales to the south, Scotland to the north, and England to the east – 'and you should know this vicar, there's heaven above and hell below!'

Make your way down the shoulder to the little top of Long Green – easy going – to meet the Cam Spout ridge which falls eastwards. This provides an excellent descent, leading down to, and then curving round the rim of Spout Crag; the going is rough and rocky but there are no technical difficulties. Following the shoulder above the crag it is best to

keep to the left, as a couple of deep gullies run up onto the ridge from the crag below. Bear left again near its base, and cross the stream to find the well eroded path on its north-east side; this leads down the rib alongside Cam Spout waterfall, then bears to the right, crossing the beck at its base and so down to the great boulders known as Sampson's Stones.

Follow above the right bank of the Esk for a way, then when the path divides, take the right fork which leads to the high level route passing by Silverybield Crag. The path travels down a natural corridor between the crags, then crosses a boggy section, and finally zizags down to the left to emerge onto the track near Scale Gill Waterfall. Go right along the track and over the bridge beneath the waterfall, then branch to the left, taking the track down through the fields to Taw House Farm. From the farmyard a stile leads across the field to a footbridge which crosses the River Esk opposite Brotherilkeld Farm.

THE MOSEDALE HORSESHOE – by BLACK SAIL to PILLAR MOUNTAIN continuing over RED PIKE to YEWBARROW

Wasdale Head Inn, lonely Mosedale, Black Sail Pass, Wast Water

Fact Sheet

Location: Wasdale, Pillar group, Western Fells, Lake District National Park, north west England

Length: 16km (10 miles)

Ascent: 1170m (3850ft)

Time: 7.5 hours

Difficulty: There are no great technical difficulties, though this route does have a sting in its tail: the ascent of Yewbarrow's north prow via Stirrup Crag presents a mild scramble (Scrambling Grade 0.5), and the descent of its southern prow is rather rough with unstable scree, and requires careful route-finding

Seasons: Summer conditions generally prevail from April to November, and winter conditions from December to March

Map: OS Outdoor Leisure 6, The English Lake District – South West; and OS Outdoor Leisure 4, The English Lake District – North West. Alternatively Harvey's Superwalker Map, Western Lakeland, covers the whole outing

Start & Finish: The Wasdale Head Inn (NY 187 088). There is limited parking here, or 300m (330yd) back down the road

Access: From Whitehaven in the west, head some 32km (20 miles) south and east along the A595(T) to Gosforth, and then along minor roads into Wasdale

Tourist Information: Egremont (Tel: 01946 820693)

Accommodation: Within Wasdale there are all types of accommodation, including campsites and a Youth Hostel. The Wasdale Head Inn also has a campsite, a bunkhouse, self-catering accommodation and an outdoors shop

Geology: Rhyolite, with some scree and boulder fields

Flora & Fauna: Birds include the raven and the sparrow hawk. Plants that commonly occur include juniper, rowan and gorse, and amongst mammals, the red fox and the polecat may be seen

Comment: This is a high skyline of powerful mountains around one of Lakeland's most desolate valleys.

The Tops

Looking Stead	627m (2057ft)	(looking sted = site of building with commanding view)
Pillar	892m (2927ft)	(pillar = pillar)
Black Crag	828m (2717ft)	(black crag = black crag)
Scoat Fell	841m (2760ft)	(scoat fal = sticking out – into Ennerdale – fell)
Red Pike	826m (2709ft)	(red pike = red rocky pointed hill)
Yewbarrow	628m (2058ft)	(yew barrow = yew tree long hill)

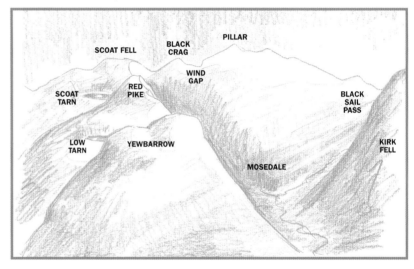

■ The little mountain basin of Mosedale is the remote northerly offshoot of Wasdale Head, a valley ringed by mountains. From its floor they shoot upwards some 750m, to occupy vertical space seven times that of the valley width. The major peak at the head of the valley is Pillar Mountain: much revered, Pillar is named after the great precipice of rock which stands on its northern (Ennerdale) flanks.

Black Sail Pass provides convenient access onto the ridge, and an anticlockwise route will take in all the high tops which are wrapped around Mosedale. In addition to Pillar these include Black Crag, Scoat Fell, Red Pike and finally the great upturned hull of Yewbarrow which protrudes beyond Mosedale to look down upon Wast Water. This is an energetic but immensely rewarding excursion.

Over the head of Mosedale with Wind Gap separating Black Crag (l) from Pillar Mountain (r)
Below: The approach to Pillar Mountain

Behind the inn a track leads to the right to pass an ancient, stone-arch packhorse bridge; continue by the beck until the way forks. Go left and follow the track rising into Mosedale. The path contours the right side of the valley before crossing Gatherstone Beck and rising via Black Sail Pass to the col between Pillar Mountain and Kirkfell.

Go left along the ridge, making a minor detour right to the little knoll of Looking Stead: this offers a good lookout point from which to view the Ennerdale valley and the High Stile range beyond. Beyond this point the ridge steepens, and the rocky spine of Pillar Mountain becomes the next objective. The main path takes the easiest route, lying mainly to the left of the crest. However, should the visibility be clear and you have a long summer's day ahead of you, it is more enjoyable to make your way along the crest itself; this is easy scrambling.

You will cross a subsidiary top which looks down into Pillar Cove, before the summit and trig point of Pillar Mountain are reached. A detour to the northern edge will reveal a limited profile of

the tremendous Pillar Rock far below to the north, though I'm afraid a closer appraisal is beyond the scope of this outing, for there is still a long way to go.

Straightforward descent leads to the appropriately named Wind Gap – indeed, there are quite a few of these amongst the Lakeland fells. A short section of ascent brings bouldery Black Crag to heel: not named on the OS map, nevertheless here it is, offering an open aspect to the summit of Pillar and along the ridge to Scoat Fell. Continue along to the col above Mirk Cove; from here it is best to take the path which veers left to contour above Black Comb. This gains the col beneath the rise to Red Pike, though it misses out the ill-defined top of Scoat Fell – those intent on finding the latter's illusive summit should ascend by the stone wall; the summit lies at the highest indefinite point of the wall.

Ascent from the col leads to a cairn midway along the high shoulder of Red Pike; the latter's summit will be found further on, a little cairn perched on the edge of the rim overlooking

The evocative head of Pillar Rock viewed from the flanks of Pillar Mountain. Far below, the track running up Ennerdale leads to Black Sail youth hostel. Pillar Rock plunges vertically for some 150m and has long been a demanding challenge for rock climbers. It was first climbed by a local shepherd, J. Atkinson, in 1826

Mosedale. Red Pike is a superb mountain and provides an excellent view both back along the horseshoe, and also onwards to the mighty Scafell range on the opposite side of Wasdale.

The path then descends through rock outcrop and boulder without difficulty to the dramatic col of Dore Head. En route it passes a minor subsidiary top: possibly another contender for the name Black Crag, it is actually unnamed on the OS map. This top was once the subject of an enquiry by a television researcher, who asked fell-running legend and local shepherd Joss Naylor if it had a name. Joss replied, 'Aye, I call it Boot Fell'. This was duly written up, but when pressed further for the possible origins of the name, Joss replied with a smile that he had named it so, 'Because I yance found a pair boots on t'spot!'

Should time be running short, one possible descent is from Dore Head directly to the valley floor of Mosedale – indeed, it is a much used route. However, should you do this, have a care because it is very steep and Dorehead screes are now extremely eroded (having been largely washed away). Keep to the left of the scree initially, before traversing right across the gill and descending to the Mosedale valley floor.

Looming directly above the northern end of

Yewbarrow is Stirrup Crag: it always looks daunting, but to continue we must tackle it. In fact the first section of the climb is a series of short walls and grooves with many ledges between, and it is actually quite straightforward, comprising only a moderate scramble. Yewbarrow's north and lesser summit is reached first, an airy, grassy stroll with tremendous views across Wast Water to the Scafells, the route running easily along the crest of the keel to the higher south summit. Try to save film in your camera for these views because they are quite magnificent.

In descent there is much rather unpleasant loose scree, though the path is reasonbly well defined, leading first to Great Door and then towards Dropping Crag; bypass the crag (taking care not to go over it!) by a bouldery rocky gully to its left. The awkward gully soon relents, and a swooping plunge down the sharp, grassy ridge leads to the road, and the gloriously golden yellow gorse by Wast Water. To return by the road may be rather hard on the feet at the end of this long mountain route – but I am sure you will agree that in this valley, after such a day, it is a very small price to pay. Go left, leaving the road, at 'Down in the Dale Bridge', and follow along by the beck till the packhorse bridge leads back to the Wasdale Head Inn.

THE HIGH STILE RIDGE

Buttermere, Sourmilk Gill, Bleaberry Tarn, Birkness Combe, Gamlin End

Fact Sheet

Location: Buttermere, High Stile group, Western Fells, Lake District National Park, north west England

Length: 11km (6.8 miles)

Ascent: 830m (2725ft)

Time: 4.5 hours

Difficulty: Strenuous beginnings, albeit broken by the Bleaberry Tarn basin, lead to a relatively gentle stroll along the crest of the ridge. There are no technical difficulties

Seasons: Summer conditions can generally be expected from April to November, and winter conditions from December to March

Map: OS Outdoor Leisure 4, The English Lake District – North West

Start & Finish: Buttermere; there is parking in the centre of the village opposite the Fish Inn (NY 173 169)

Access: Some 14km (8.7 miles) south-west of Keswick over the Newlands Pass; also from Cockermouth some 15km (9.3 miles) along the B5292 and B5289

Tourist Information: Keswick (Tel: 017687 72645); Cockermouth (Tel: 01900 822634)

Accommodation: Most types are available in Buttermere, including a Youth Hostel and two nearby campsites

Geology: Rhyolite and red granite, with some steep sections of scree in both ascent and descent

Flora & Fauna: Birds include the raven, the peregrine and the goosander. Oak, Scots pine, ling and bell heather and also bilberry can be seen growing throughout this area; and amongst mammals, the stoat and the red fox are relatively common

Comment: Rising from the intimate depths of the Buttermere valley, these powerful mountains offer an inspiring, high-level traverse along their spine. This is a classic Lakeland outing.

■ Located between Ennerdale and Buttermere, the High Stile spine stretches from Red Pike over High Stile itself and on to High Crag. This walk tackles these peaks from the Buttermere side, from whence they present their most appealing aspect. Often in dark shadow, this deepened even further by the hanging basins of Bleaberry Comb and Birkness Combe (named Burtness Comb on the OS map), their considerable heights rise mysteriously to sunlit

The Tops

Red Pike	755m (2478ft)	(red pike = red rocky pointed hill)
High Stile	806m (2644ft)	(high stile = high ridge path)
High Crag	744m (2442ft)	(high crag = high crag)

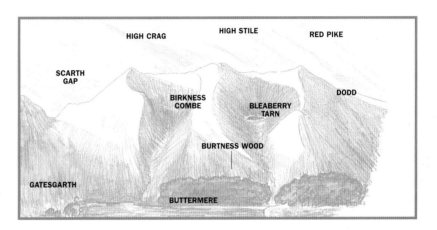

distant edges. Seen like this they have an alpine fascination, one which quite overwhelms the minutiae beauty of pastoral Buttermere. If you love mountains, then you have to climb these.

In days of yore the much celebrated beauty Mary Robinson, daughter of the landlord of the Fish Inn, attracted a whole host of admirers to Buttermere, including all the Lakes' poets. The conman John Hatfield, alias 'the Honourable Alexander Augustus Hope', duped her into marriage with the promise of great riches. Unfortunately for all concerned he wasn't all he claimed to be, because he already had a wife and he didn't have any money. They obviously couldn't take a joke, however, for they hanged him in Carlisle in 1803.

Enticing you away from the present-day attractions of little Buttermere village, the long waterfall of Sourmilk Gill tumbles steeply down the fellside and through the trees to the base of Buttermere lake. It is particularly striking when frozen white with ice, or heavy in spate, and it appears to offer a compulsive line of ascent; in fact today it is bypassed by a good path to the left, though it does serve as a positive waymark, pointing towards Red Pike.

Climbing Gamlin End – our line of descent takes the well-defined path to the side of these rocks

Right (left to right): High Crag, High Stile and Red Pike. With its rim traversed by the High Stile Ridge, the dramatic basin of Birkness Combe hangs high above Buttermere

Leave the car park to follow the little stony lane to the base of Buttermere lake. Cross the footbridge over the wonderfully clear waters of Buttermere Dubs, the beck which makes the short connection between Buttermere and Crummock Water. Bear left along the track through the woods, and in a short distance you will find a path which rises to the right (signed). Follow this: it leaves Burtness Wood (OS name) to zigzag first left and then back right, climbing steeply up the flanks of Old Burtness (OS name) fellside via a series of steps and sections of paving; eventually it gains the left bank (the true right) of Sourmilk Gill where it levels out just below its issue from Bleaberry Tarn.

Cross the gill by the base of the tarn, then follow the well blazoned path up the steep scree to gain The Saddle between Dodd and Red Pike above. A steepening ascent leads to the bouldery summit of Red Pike, the effective starting point of a remarkable high-level ridge. As befits its name, the volcanic rocks of this Red Pike (the other lies above Mosedale) are dramatically coloured.

High above Birkness Combe, a gap in the ridge approaching High Crag reveals a lovely aspect over Gatescarth Farm and the head of Buttermere to Robinson, Hindscarth and Dale Head of the North-Western Fells

This is probably the best point of all from which to view the little known and seldom trod Loweswater Fells to be found on the far side of the Floutern Pass. The pass – once important, now forgotten – is a packhorse route which runs from Crummock to Ennerdale Water: here lie the stately twin tops of Mellbreak and the grassy domes of Gavel Fell and Blake Fell, and further north still, over the Solway Firth, the distant hills of Galloway are topped by Criffel.

A gentle stroll out along the shoulder leads to the ascent of High Stile and its summit rocks and cairn. Look seaward to the Isle of Man, south to Steeple and Pillar, and onward to the giant skull of Great Gable. If you have a little time it is worth walking out to the top of Grey Crag, for this offers the best unbroken aspect over Buttermere to the north-western fells of Grasmoor and Robinson, and eastwards across the darkness of Birkness Combe (named Burtness Comb on the OS map). At the back of the comb stands the

head and profile of the largest climbing crag in Buttermere, the mighty Eagle Crag.

It was on Eagle Crag, on 23 June 1940, that my late friend Bill Peascod, pioneer rock climber, artist and miner, with local schoolteacher Burt Beck, climbed Eagle Front, the most famous rock climb in Buttermere and a very bold effort for those times.

Our way follows the bilberry-crested ridge along the rim of Birkness Combe to High Crag. Pause for an inspection of Ennerdale before descending the infamous grind of Gamlin End – a whole lot easier in descent, however. Scree leads to bucket steps worn into the sharp grassy ridge. Some way before reaching the col and its little tarn, at the base of the ridge, a well worn scree path drops off to the left to follow an old stone wall down to the main track of Scarth Gap Pass. Bear left and follow this to descend to the valley floor. Go left and follow the lakeside path through the woods back to Buttermere.

THE LITTLE DALE HORSESHOE by SCOPE END to HINDSCARTH and the LITTLEDALE EDGE to ROBINSON descending via HIGH SNAB BANK

Goldscope Mine, Hackney Holes, Low High Snab

Fact Sheet

Location: Newlands Valley, Dale Head group, North Western Fells, Lake District National Park, north west England

Length: 10.5km (6.5 miles)

Ascent: 760m (2500ft)

Time: 4.5 hours

Difficulty: Although this round is steep in ascent and descent, with a little rocky section down to High Snab Bank, on the whole it offers straightforward and pleasant ridge-walking

Seasons: Summer conditions can generally be expected from April to November; winter conditions from December to March

Map: OS Outdoor Leisure 4, The English Lake District – North West

Start & Finish: The small car park by Chapel Bridge, near Little Town in the Newlands Valley (NY 232 194)

Access: It is situated some 8km (5 miles) south west of Keswick: take the A66(T) to Portinscale, then minor roads through Swinside and Stair to Little Town. It is 7km (4.3 miles) north-east from Buttermere over Newlands Pass

Tourist Information: Moot Hall at Keswick (Tel: 017687 72645); also the National Park Information Centre at Keswick (Tel: 017687 72803)

Accommodation: There are many facilities in this area: the Swinside Inn, 'B&B' and self-catering within the Newlands Valley, and all facilities at Keswick; the nearest campsite is at Braithwaite, and the nearest Youth Hostel at Buttermere

Geology: Skiddaw slate veined with quartz provides good going, though it is slippery when wet

Flora & Fauna: Raven, peregrine and buzzard can be seen, and amongst trees, rowan, sycamore and crab apple. Red squirrel, badger and fox inhabit this area, but are secretive

Comment: This is a superbly defined, high ridge walk around the secretive Little Dale and above lovely Newlands.

The Tops

Scope End	412m (1352ft)	(scope end = the mined end of the ridge)
Red Knott	452m (1483ft)	(red knot = red rocky knoll)
High Crags	529m (1736ft)	(high crags = high crags)
Hindscarth	727m (2385ft)	(hind-scarth = female deer hill above the gap)
Robinson	737m (2418ft)	(robinson = robinson)

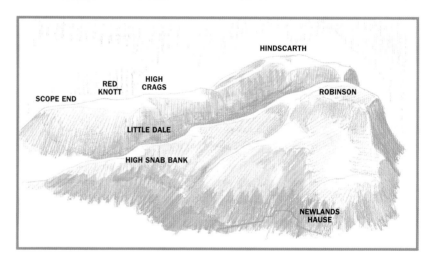

■ Served only by the Newlands Pass rising over from Buttermere to the south, and open only at its distant northern end, the Newlands Valley is a lovely quiet backwater, a narrow dale of woods and small, sloping fields, overlooked by high fells. One tributary feeding its tree-lined river is that of Scope Beck falling from Little Dale, a secretive basin nestling high between the shoulders of Hindscarth and Robinson. At its head is the Littledale Edge, with Buttermere beyond, and running either side are the sharp aesthetic ridges of Scope End, rising to Hindscarth, and the continuation of High Snab Bank rising to Robinson.

The horseshoe around Little Dale is described here in a clockwise direction, though it is equally enjoyable walked either way. Indeed it must be amongst the most delightful ridge walks in the Lake District, one that is challenging without being too

Seen over the head of the Newlands Valley (from Maiden Moor), Scope End rises to snow-capped Hindscarth (l). To its right, separated by Little Dale, stands Robinson

Right: Evening shadows begin to fall over the ridge of High Snab Bank leading from Robinson

Left: Hot work ascending to the large cairn situated high on the nose of Hindscarth (reached before the summit)

technically demanding, airy on the ridges, open on the tops with extensive and revealing views, and with plenty of interest on the ground.

Apart from a few more trees, little has altered the appearance of Chapel Bridge since Beatrix Potter painted the scene overlooking Little Town in 1905 (in *The Tale of Mrs Tiggy-Winkle*). Climb the road

back towards Little Town to branch out right over the stile, climbing to gain the track which runs up the head of Newlands. The view up Scope End and down the ridge falling from Robinson to High Snab Bank is impressive. You will come to a stone wall; follow it, passing a stone building (now a climbing hut), until at the wall's end a path bears off right to cross Newlands Beck via a little footbridge.

Ahead, the spoil-heaps of Goldscope Mine rise up the hillside, the legacy of a mineral-rich vein within the Skiddaw slate. Containing lead and copper, the latter with a high percentage of silver and a quantity of gold, the mine is known to be of ancient origin: the German miners prospected its worth in 1607, and written records go back to Henry III. It is hard now, looking at the remnants, to understand its economic importance, although history tells us that Thomas Percie, Earl of Northumberland, fell out with Queen Elizabeth regarding the 'Queen's prerogative' – this stated that if a mine produced a greater worth of gold and silver than of the copper or lead, it became the property of the monarch. In fact he lost his head as a result of it.

The path now rises to the right, passing Low Snab Farm to the right, and then following the contour to gain the nose of the ridge. A steep, straightforward ascent leads directly to the minor top of Scope End. Whilst the main path now follows a line to the left, the more atmospheric route follows the crest, with excellent perspective to High Snab Bank and the ridge falling from Robinson. Rather undulating and heathery, it takes in the small rocky knolls of Red Pike and then High Crags before a steeper ascent leads to the large cairn on the edge of the Hindscarth summit plateau. This is a good place for a rest and a bite to eat, even though the actual top lies just a little further on.

Pass the summit cairn and continue along the gentle shoulder to reach the top of the Littledale Edge and a view over Buttermere to Fleetwith Pike. Bear right and descend to the grassy col, then climb upwards again with a wire fence to your left. The curious may like to know that after an initial period of ascent, Hackney Holes may be located, over the fence to the left: bearing in mind the other evidence on the ground, including nearby cists and burial mounds, it is likely that these elongated shallow rifts running up the hillside are the remnants of a Bronze Age copper mine. Ascending to the corner of the fence line, a path bears off to the right across the shoulder to gain a corridor through the quartz-streaked rock summit of Robinson.

Cross the summit plateau and, with the shadows of Littledale growing ever longer, make your way down the ridge – this is a fine, open descent. Before the route joins High Snab Bank it steps through a little outcrop of rock and turns left; a delightfully easy grassy crest follows. A green path cuts down to the right through the bracken to make a straightforward, though steep descent diagonally down the hillside; when it meets the track at the bottom, go left (signed 'Public footpath') to pass the delightful buildings of the quite logically named Low High Snab.

The way becomes surfaced, and falls charmingly through the trees, passing the combined school and chapel, returning to Chapel Bridge.

Crossing the head of Little Dale, the Littledale Edge connects Hindscarth to Robinson. The Hackney Holes, ancient copper workings, lie left of the path ascending to Robinson

THE HIGH RIDGES around COLEDALE

The Matterhorn of Lakeland, seven tops over 610m (2000ft),
Force Crag Force, Causey Pike, Stoneycroft mines

Fact Sheet

Location: Braithwaite, Grasmoor and Grisedale Pike groups, North Western Fells, Lake District National Park, north west England

Length: 14km (8.7miles)

Ascent: 1140m (3740ft)

Time: 7 hours

Difficulty: This round is long and sustained, with a number of strenuous ascents and descents. The technical difficulties are low, however, though the ascent from Coledale Hause involves steep, scrambly scree, and for the initial descent from Causey Pike you may need to use hands (or bottom!) as well as feet (Scrambling Grade 0.4)

Seasons: Summer conditions generally prevail from April to November, and winter conditions from December to March

Map: OS Outdoor Leisure 4, The English Lake District – North West

Start & Finish: Braithwaite. There is limited parking on the hill above the village in the old quarry by the side of the Whinlatter Pass Road (NY 227 237). The track emanating from the quarry – barred to all vehicles – leads up Coledale to the now-disused Force Crag Mine

Access: Some 5km (3 miles) west of Keswick

Tourist Information: Moot Hall at Keswick (Tel: 017687 72645); also the National Park Information Centre at Keswick (Tel: 017687 72803)

Accommodation: There are most types of accommodation in Braithwaite, including two inns and a campsite. The nearest Youth Hostel is at Keswick

Geology: Skiddaw slate, heavily mineralised in places, provides reasonable going, though it is slippery when wet and there is a fair amount of loose scree

Flora & Fauna: Peregrine and buzzard may be seen. The sessile oak grows here. Amongst animals the red squirrel is an inhabitant

Comment: The North Western Fells are noted for their elegant ridges and graceful architecture. This long, high horseshoe around Coledale, which includes the pyramidal Grisedale Pike (the Lakeland 'Matterhorn') and the cone of Causey Pike, is one of the finest outings to be had.

The Tops

Kinn	374m (1227ft)	(kinn = cheek or fountain)
Grisedale Pike	792m (2593ft)	(grise-dale pike = swine dale rocky pointed hill)
Hobcarton Crag	739m (2425ft)	(hob-carton crag = the crag of Carton's hill rising from boggy ground)
Eel Crag	807m (2649ft)	(eel crag = eel crag)
Crag Hill	839m (2751ft)	(crag hill = hill of crags)
Sail	773m (2536ft)	(sail = heel)
Scar Crags	672m (2205ft)	(scar crags = scar crags)
Causey Pike	637m (2090ft)	(causey pike = rocky pointed mound)
Rowling End	433m (1421ft)	(row-ling end = end of heather ridge)

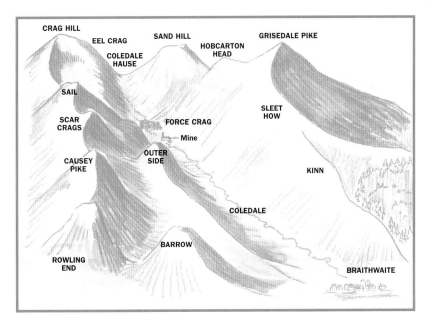

■ The high deserted valley of Coledale cuts deep into the heart of the North Western Fells. At its foot lies the village of Braithwaite with the flat plains of the River Derwent beyond, and all around is a breathtaking panorama of high hills comprising fells from both the Grasmoor and Grisedale Pike groups. Buttermere lies some way beyond to the west, whilst the passes of Newlands and Whinlatter define them to the south and north respectively.

The Skiddaw slate predominant here is

Looking up Coledale to Force Crag with the waterfall frozen solid by winter cold. Beyond, to the left, rise (from r to l) Eel Crag, Crag Hill and Sail

Left: The ridge of Skiddaw slates falling from Scar Crags to Causey Pike (which lies behind this winter walker)

Lakeland's most ancient rock, and it has weathered dramatically. Long exposed ridges, soaring peaks and wonderful vistas make this one of the premier ridge walks – if not the premier walk – in the North Western Fells; when white with snow the scene is positively alpine. On the northern leg the pyramidal angularity of Grisedale Pike fully justifies its comparison to its more famous namesake in Switzerland as Lakeland's Matterhorn; it is completed on the southern leg by the piercing sharpness of Causey Pike, a veritable Aiguille du Géant. At the head of the horseshoe, aloof and seemingly inaccessible, is the highest and mightiest of them all, Crag Fell.

The greater horseshoe (for lesser circuits can be made) is described here in an anticlockwise direction, starting with the ascent of little Kinn en route to climbing the east ridge of Grisedale Pike, then dipping across the head of Hobcarton and down to Coledale Hause. A rough, scrambly ascent then takes you up to Eel Crag and Crag Fell. The long southern leg from Sail over Scar Crags and Causey Pike to Rowling End is quite magnificent,

looking down on the tops of the lesser horseshoe, namely Outerside, Stile End and Barrow. Despite numerous craggy faces and dizzy exposure, safe escape into Coledale can be made at a few key points, notably from Coledale Hause (though beware of the great drop over Force Crag, barring access to the valley below), and from the notch-like col between Sail and Scar Crags.

From the quarry, or more directly from the village, follow the signed paths to access the long aesthetic east ridge which falls from Grisedale Pike. Once Little Kinn is crossed, the going steepens. To the right, the heavy conifer green of Hospital Plantation fills the slopes around Whinlatter Pass: it was named after the isolation hospital situated by the side of the pass and initially thought to be suitably remote; it is now a guesthouse and well frequented. The going steepens to pass Lanty Well and up the fine crest of Sleet How. The top of Grisedale Pike befits its perfectly pyramidal appearance: it is a barren, rocky place, the wind always seems to buffet, and little can be found in the form of shelter.

Make your descent south west to the col, with

the little top of Hobcarton Head just beyond; the going here is straightforward. The main path is well defined, and drops diagonally to the left to the col of Coledale Hause. The most arduous section of the round now lies ahead. To the right of the nose above, a scrambly path leads steeply up the broken scree; the first cairned top that you come to is that of Eel Crag, a satellite of Crag Hill. Bear right and climb to the main cairn and trig point of Crag Hill, a broad, rather featureless summit plateau with an expansive view, but not a place to lose one's way in poor visibility because of the menacing drops below. If in doubt, follow a compass bearing to access the ridge known as The Scar, which connects with Sail.

As you dip down The Scar, Scott Crag to the north and Scat Crag to the south present moderately high exposure; here there are a few rocky steps to negotiate, though nothing too severe before you reach the bottom of the dip – plain going now leads to Sail. A straightforward descent leads to the col below Scar Crags; above, the rocks steepen with the ascent and caution should be exercised when making your way up to the rocky knoll top.

Below, to the south, a wood of dwarf sessile oaks, the indigenous trees of the area, clings to the slopes. To the north, in the rocks immediately below and ranging beyond Outerside to Force Crag, the Skiddaw slate has yielded a crop of metal-rich minerals, namely cobalt from Scar Crags, copper from Barrow, and zinc with barytes from Force Crag; indeed, the Force Crag concern was the last working metaliferous mineral mine within the Lake District.

The ridge now falls lazily, with loose slate scree tinkling underfoot, until it is necessary once again to tighten the muscle for the short pull up the distinctive rock cone of Causey Pike; this offers a very fine position looking to Skiddaw and the Northern Fells, over Derwent Water, and up into the Newlands Valley. Take care now, because the ridge continues here with a steep, rocky descent. The going soon eases, however, and a path worn through the heather and bilberry leads out along Sleet Hause to Rowling End. Finally the way falls steeply due north down the hillside, meeting the road by the stone-arched bridge at Stoneycroft. Cross the bridge and follow along the road for about a kilometre. Before the wood and the cattle grid, bear left across the flanks of the hillside, taking the path above the wood which leads to Braithwaite Lodge. Descend the track back to the village.

Seen over the foot of the Newlands Valley the unmistakable cone of Causey Pike (left) rises elegantly above Stoneycroft

SKIDDAW by ULLOCK PIKE
and descent via BIRKETT'S EDGE

A Lakeland three-thousander, the highest of the Northern Fells with superb views, Whitewater Dash

Fact Sheet

Location: Bassenthwaite, Skiddaw massif, Northern Fells, Lake District National Park, north west England

Length: 13.5km (8.4 miles)

Ascent: 1015m (3330ft)

Time: 6 hours

Difficulty: In ascent there is a little scrambly walking over rocks, though nothing technically difficult

Seasons: Summer conditions can generally be expected from May to October, and winter conditions at other times

Map: OS Outdoor Leisure 4, The English Lake District – North West; and OS Pathfinder 576 – Caldbeck: both are required. Alternatively, Harvey's Superwalker Northern Lakeland covers the whole walk

Start & Finish: There is limited parking in a small lay-by at the side of Orthwaite Road, a little above the junction with the A591 above Bassenthwaite village (NY 237 311)

Access: It is 5km (3 miles) north of Keswick, taking the A591 and then the minor road to Orthwaite. From Cockermouth it is 15km (9 miles) east along the A66, B5291, A591 and then the Orthwaite Road

Tourist Information: Moot Hall at Keswick (Tel: 017687 72645); also the National Park Information Centre at Keswick (Tel: 017687 72803)

Accommodation: Accommodation around Bassenthwaite village is limited; this includes the Sun Inn and a campsite. The nearest Youth Hostel is at Keswick. Notably there is a cosy farmhouse in Uldale which offers accommodation and is famed for its excellent meals

Geology: Skiddaw slate, with igneous intrusions; slippery when wet with a fair amount of loose scree

Flora & Fauna: Merlin, peregrine and raven may be seen in this area; amongst flowers, cranesbill and moss campion are particularly notable; and the red fox and the mountain hare are furtive mammal inhabitants

Comment: The curving ridge of Ullock Pike and Longside is a stimulating walk and provides a tremendous way to climb to the great summit of Skiddaw. By contrast, the descent down the northern ridge of Birkett's Edge explores a quiet and different Lake District.

The Tops

Watches	333m (1093ft)	(watches = look-out place)
Ullock Pike	692m (2270ft)	(ullock pike = rocky pointed hill where wolves play)
Long Side	734m (2408ft)	(long side = long edge)
Skiddaw	931m (3053ft)	(skider = the divided – into many tops – mountain)
Broad End	831m (2726ft)	(broad end = broad terminus)
Bakestall	673m (2208ft)	(bak-stall = back table of the mountain)

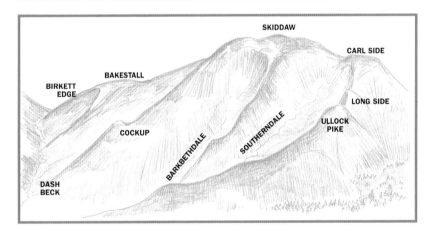

■ Skiddaw is a large mountain of many tops and satellites, standing impressively at the south-western corner of Lakeland's isolated Northern Fells. There are two distinct sides to her character: her well known and much loved southern aspect, characterised by sensuous curves, floating serene above Keswick and Derwent Water; and her dark northern face overlooking Skiddaw Forest – a misnomer, since there is barely a tree in sight – expansive, untamed and private. This exciting ridge, quite the most interesting way to scale the mountain, experiences both.

Above Derwent Water, Ullock Pike and Longside Edge merge with the whole to form the west shoulder of the massif, an elegant ridge curving around Southerndale, only joining with the bulk of Skiddaw at Carl Side; they are best viewed from the shores of Bassenthwaite Lake or

Skiddaw High Man summit trig point

Skiddaw (left) and Ullock Pike (right) seen above the Bassenthwaite road

from the village. Here the route is described in an anticlockwise direction, first tackling the sharply defined ridge and climbing the flank of Skiddaw, then descending by Broad End, Bakestall and Birkett Edge to Dash Beck above and Whitewater Dash falls.

From the stile with its 'Public Bridleway' sign, cross a stream and take the lesser path which breaks away and climbs upwards to the right. A grassed-over track with a line of thorns leads up the field, then bears left to a stile. Follow the track rising up the field until it bears right to a gate/stile leading over the fell wall. Go right alongside the wall until you come to a path which climbs directly up the crest of the shoulder to gain the rocky knoll summit of Watches. A curious area of blocky pinnacles follows (witches?); then continue upwards over a series of undulating knolls on the ridge.

The going steepens, and you will have to climb a substantial subsidiary knoll before finally reaching the true twin-topped summit cone of Ullock Pike. The narrow edge leads on up the lovely crest of Longside Edge to top Long Side. Here there is a fine sense of exposure, though this diminishes rapidly as you make the easy traverse across the flank of Carl Side, at the head of Southerndale, to Carlside Tarn. Next is a rather arduous ascent up the path which rises diagonally to the left across the great scree slope falling from Skiddaw's summit plateau. It emerges by the cairn/shelter of Skiddaw's Middle Man.

After a stop to admire the view and regain your breath, continue easily along the stony shoulder to gain the highest top and trig point: this is Skiddaw High Man, where a veritable desert of grey-blue slates extends across the entire summit shoulder. Just to the west stands a 'Silver Jubilee' plaque which helps to identify some of the range of mountains to be seen from here. It is a tremendous

Looking north to Skiddaw High Man

Below (left to right): Whitewater Dash waterfall, Birkett Edge and Bakestall lead to Skiddaw's Broad End

panorama of a hugely contrasting nature: south, towards the heart of Lakeland, is the intense, vibrant young beauty of tree, lake and jagged crag of the Borrowdale volcanics; to the north is the desolation and emptiness of a vast expanse of peat bog and heather, the mature roundness of the ancient Skiddaw slate. Between these two extremes is a whole world of contrast.

Descend north to find the little North Top; then a col and a rise lead to the aptly named Broad End. Bear right, and follow down the line of the wire fence to the summit of Bakestall; bear right again to make your way down the heather of Birkett Edge, with dark Dead Crags to the left. You will intercept the track leading to Skiddaw House, now a Youth Hostel. Our way lies to the left, through the gate, with Whitewater Dash waterfall below.

Follow the track all the way to the surfaced road, where you keep left to gain the Orthwaite Road just along from Peter House Farm.

Bear left; in about 400m you will find a gate to the left, at a right-angled bend in the road. Go left and then right, to follow the public footpath along the track to Mill Beck. Bear right, and follow the path across the fields, crossing a footbridge over Barkbeth Gill, then climbing upwards to pass Hole House, and left to Barkbeth Farm. Follow the pleasant 'Permissive Path' around the farm (don't follow the one signed 'Public Bridleway' which unnecessarily goes right through the farmyard in a confusion of sheds and tractors); this leads to a well signed path above the farm, which on rounding the flanks of the hillside, will be found to be the 'Public Bridleway' taken at the start.

BLENCATHRA by SHARP EDGE and descent via HALLSFELL RIDGE

Lakeland's two most difficult ridges, with high exposure and a superb mountain position

Fact Sheet

Location: Threlkeld, Blencathra Group, Northern Fells, Lake District National Park, north west England
Length: 7.5km (4.7 miles)
Ascent: 690m (2270ft)
Time: 4 hours
Difficulty: Sharp Edge involves negotiating an exposed, narrow rock crest with steep ground on both sides. Technically it isn't actually too difficult, although there is an awkward section balancing around a rocky knoll where the rock slab underfoot is highly polished – when wet or icy it is very slippery. Beyond the crest the rocks steepen and the route follows an exposed groove (Scrambling Grade 1). It is possible to miss out most of the difficulty along the crest by following a well worn path down to the right; even so, this steepens at the end of the ridge and it is still necessary to climb the groove above the ridge. Hallsfell Ridge looks deceptively easy from the top, but in fact if you keep to the crest, the difficulties match those of Sharp Edge and they are remarkably sustained (Scrambling Grade 1). This should be considered a climbing expedition under winter conditions of either snow or ice (Winter Grade I)
Seasons: Summer conditions may be expected from April to November; winter conditions from December to March
Map: OS Outdoor Leisure 5, The English Lake District – North East
Start & Finish: At the lay-by which lies on the A66 above Threlkeld (NY 339 267)
Access: Some 9km (5.6 miles) east of Keswick along the A66(T), and about 19km (11.8 miles) west of Penrith, also along the A66
Tourist Information: Moot Hall at Keswick (Tel: 017687 72645); also the National Park Information Centre at Keswick (Tel: 017687 72803)
Accommodation: Threlkeld has most forms of accommodation, and campsites can be found nearby on the south side of the A66. The nearest Youth Hostels are at Keswick and Legburthwaite
Geology: Skiddaw slate, which is slippery when wet; however, it is reasonably sound to pull on, though caution should be exercised
Flora & Fauna: Raven and buzzard may be seen; amongst

The Tops

Atkinson Pike	845m (2772ft)	(atkinson pike = Atkinson's rocky pointed hill)
Blencathra/Saddleback/ Hallsfell Top	868m (2847ft)	(blen-cath-ra/saddleback/halls-fell top = the mountain of steeply falling ridges/ Hall's fell top)

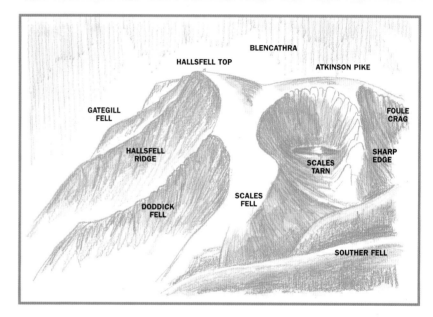

the plants, wavy hair moss and alpine club moss grow here; and the red fox, the mountain hare and the stoat are notable amongst the mammal inhabitants
Comment: The two most challenging ridges in Lakeland also offer a very fine mountain expedition.

■ Separated from the Skiddaw massif by the deep rift valley of Glenderaterra, 'Saddleback' is the modern local name for the splendid mountain located on the south-eastern periphery of the Northern Fells. Especially when clad white in snow, the Threlkeld face of Blencathra presents a breathtaking sight from all regions south. A high, apparently knife-edged spine cutting along the skyline, defining the huge mountain face below. A face buttressed by three great ridges. Hallsfell Ridge

Top right: Hallsfell Ridge falling steeply directly from the summit of Blencathra

Right: The spectacular view down the length of Sharp Edge with Scales Tarn below

Pages 84–5: A fine aspect of Sharp Edge's knife-edged ridge with the awkward rock tower, passed by a polished slab, prominent

falling directly from the summit of the mountain is the centralmost of these and the most challenging of the three. This we take in descent. However, the most spectacular ridge of all is Sharp Edge, lying round the corner on the more secretive east face. The logical way to combine these two ridges is first to ascend Sharp Edge to top Atkinson Pike (sometimes referred to as Foule Crag), then to proceed to the summit both of the mountain and of Hallsfell Ridge, finally using the latter to make your descent. This is a veritable tour de force, one of the most exciting mountain walks in the Lake District.

The busy A66 makes for a rather incongruous start to an otherwise delectable mountain walk. (A quieter alternative may be found on the little road which passes the White Horse Inn; there is limited parking over the bridge below Mousthwaite Comb, which can be taken in ascent.) Pass the cottage and bear left, following the path to gain the open hillside; traverse right, high above the stone wall, following the rising path across the brackened flanks. This leads to the rocky edge of Mousthwaite Comb.

Follow the path up the edge. It is quite exposed, and you should proceed with care because of the little crag lying below. As the going eases and improves, our path bears right to flank the River Glenderamackin below to the right; follow it to the point where Scales Beck can be seen tumbling down the hillside a little distance in front. Here a path bears off up to the left to intercept the beck; cross it and follow its right side (the true left bank) making

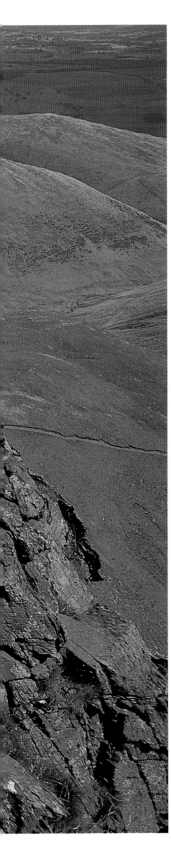

a steep and rough ascent to the little col above the aquamarine blue of Scales Tarn.

The ascent here is steep; follow the path over loose, slaty scree to gain the rocky outcrops which effectively mark the start of Sharp Edge. The exposure is already noticeable. To begin with you scramble pleasantly up through the rocks, picking your own route; then suddenly you emerge onto the horizontal, and the crest of Sharp Edge lies stretched out in front of you. This is a reasonable place to pause and gather your strength.

Most interest will be found by keeping to the crest, and this involves fairly continuous scrambling over a distinct rock pinnacle and on to a leaning tower which effectively bars the way; this is passed on its right side. It is just a simple step round the corner and up onto the ridge beyond, and in good conditions most people will not think twice about its implications. Unfortunately, however, handholds are lacking, and the rock slab which provides the footholds is extremely polished; if it is wet it can be precarious.

Beyond this the edge fuses with the mountainside, and steep rocks must be climbed. A little gully/groove on the right provides the least exposed route, though the rocks straight above provide excellent, positive handholds and footholds and are easier than first appearances suggest. Around 30m of climbing leads to a good ledge at the top of the groove, and instant respite. Admire the view – it's a long way down to Scales Tarn from here!

There are a number of easier routes down to the right of the crest. With the exception of the leaning tower, you can miss out all the hardest bits by taking a route just below and to the right of the crest. The easiest way, however, and well blazoned, is to traverse right from the end ledge, keeping on a low, horizontal path; this ends at the continuation of the gully/groove, below the point where the crest of the ridge joins the mountain. It should be noted that there is still a rather awkward section of scrambling ascent to reach the main route.

From the ledge above the main difficulties a path ascends to the left, or direct ascent can be made up the easy rocks above. At the point where the rocks disappear and grass takes over, a path traverses out to the left to cross the head of the combe above Scales Tarn. This leads directly to Hallsfell Top.

However, for very little extra effort I would recommend that you climb up the grass to take in the worthy summit of Atkinson Pike. Before you reach the cairned, rock-scar summit you will observe a cross, apparently ancient, formed from gathered stones. The summit is a lovely satellite of the main mountain, with extensive views incorporating the grassy northern flanks as well as the distant Scottish hills.

The dip of relatively flat grassy ground between here and Hallsfell Top is known as The Saddle of Saddleback; it holds a little tarn, and provides a simple means to pass from one to the other. Interestingly, just beyond the cairns of Atkinson Pike, you will pass another stone cross of blue-grey Skiddaw slates, nestling in the grass; and in another 25m, yet another well documented and much larger modern cross formed from white quartz rocks. Above the tarn a stony rise leads to the summit.

Hallsfell Ridge plunges away directly below: it looks so easy you may feel that you will reach the grassy shoulder beyond the initial steeps without any effort – however, that would be a false impression. After an initial section of descent the rocks begin to steepen, and there are numerous exposed sections which provide plenty of interest; although difficulties can be mitigated to either side in most cases, this is not always so. Exposure is high, too, though perhaps not quite so extreme as on Sharp Edge. Furthermore the difficulties continue for some surprising length before the relatively comforting grass and heather of the lower shoulder is finally reached.

The path cuts a swathe through the heather and bilberry – wonderfully purple in August – making a straightforward descent down the shoulder; as the slope begins to steepen again, it cuts over to the right and then zigzags down the edge of Gate Gill. Many remnants of the old lead-mining industry are in evidence within the confines of the ravine. At the foot of the ridge, traverse left to follow the distinct path above the fell wall.

Continue to cross the deep-cut gills of Doddick and Scale Beck; there is great beauty at the foot of Blencathra, too, the jagged heights above providing shelter for lovely rowan, silver birch and yellow gorse, these giving way to stands of old bent larch and sycamore. Finally the opening to the right leads back to the road and our starting point.

HELVELLYN by STRIDING EDGE and descent via SWIRRAL EDGE

(Starting up The Nab and finishing down Catstycam North-West Ridge)

3000ft massif by Lakeland's two most classic knife-edge ridges

Fact Sheet

Location: Lake District National Park, north west England

Length: 12km (7.5 miles)

Ascent: 915m (3000ft)

Time: 5 hours

Difficulty: In summer Birkhouse Moor's North East Ridge (The Nab), Striding Edge, Swirral Edge and Catstycam's North East Ridge lie somewhere between an easy scramble and a walk (Scrambling Grade 0.5). Exposure is considerable, particularly along Striding Edge and down Swirral Edge. In winter conditions the expedition becomes much more difficult (Winter Grade I)

Seasons: Summer conditions can generally be expected to be found between April and November; winter from December to March

Map: OS Outdoor Leisure 5, The English Lake District – North East

Start & Finish: Glenridding's Beckside Car Park (NY 386 169)

Access: From Ambleside proceed north up The Struggle to Kirkstone Pass then down via the A592. South along the A592 from Penrith

Tourist Information: National Park Information Centre at Glenridding, Beckside Car Park (Tel 01764 82414)

Accommodation: Greenside Youth Hostel at head of Glenridding. Camping and all other types of accommodation in Glenridding and Ullswater area

Geology: Of volcanic origin the rock mass is rhyolite and although polished in places, by many feet, it is generally rough and dependable

Flora & Fauna: A number of rare alpines grow on the east face of the Helvellyn massif, including a variety of saxifrage. Ravens are commonly sighted on the heights. On the summit you are more than likely to encounter Herdwick sheep – guard your lunch!

Comment: Striding Edge and Swirral Edge are amongst the most popular mountain outings in the whole of the Lake District. A word of caution. In anything less than perfect conditions both become serious propositions and

The Tops

Birkhouse Moor	718m/2356ft	(birk-hoos moor = birch moor on the summit)
Helvellyn	950m/3118ft	(hel-vel-lin = hill of the high lake)
Catstycam	890m/2919ft	(cats-ti-cam = wild cat ridge path)

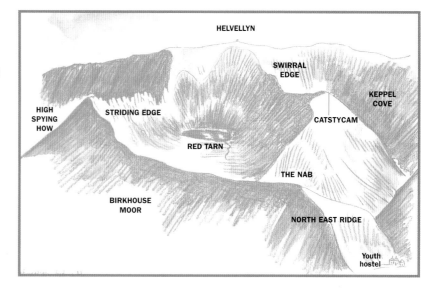

the route described here includes ascent of The Nab (Birkhouse Moor's North East Ridge) and descent of Catstycam's North West Ridge, making for a long and sustained horseshoe. The eastern face of Helvellyn, sheltered by the mountain's bulk and distance from the wet westerlies, and bearing the full brunt of the colder drier easterlies, can retain a snow covering longer than any other Lakeland mountain.

■ Located centrally within the Lakeland fells, the whaleback of the Helvellyn range runs due south to north with fine views to all other areas. This the second highest massif in Lakeland, a powerful and desolate mountain with similarities to Scotland's Cairngorm. It turns a long curving back west to Thirlmere and bares its craggy teeth east to Ullswater. This easterly aspect presents a long

Down the steeps of Swirral Edge, rising again to the pyramidal summit of Catstycam. Catstycam's North West Ridge can be seen sweeping grandly (left of summit) into Keppel Cove. Ullswater lies beyond

fringe of rocky crags and soaring pikes, which run across the heads of the Grisedale and Glenridding valleys to culminate with the summit of Helvellyn.

At the rugged heart of it all, beneath an east face which plunges directly from the summit plateau, lies the remote cove of Red Tarn (the high lake), held fast between the long fangs of Striding and Swirral Edges. Starting from Glenridding, at the head of Ullswater, and taking in the very tips of these fangs, up The Nab and down the shapely pyramidal peak of Catstycam, this route takes a magnificent natural horseshoe around the tarn. The long aesthetic knife blade of Striding Edge and the steep plunging descent of Swirral Edge combine perfectly to provide an absorbing and memorable outing.

Leave the car park and bear left to ascend Glenridding's main (and only) street. A little way above the village, at the S bend in the road, go left

to cross Glenridding Beck via Rattlebeck Bridge. Pass the caravan site and rise along the track to gain the open fellside above Miresbeck. Do not follow the path rising directly by the side of Mire Beck – although this is the main route to Striding Edge, we are going a different way. Above the fell wall an old water leat, a rough-bottomed though mainly dry ditch, rises directly above the gate. This may be obscured by bracken growth in summer. Follow this to a levelling and then, passing a tree, continue to follow the steepening leat until the angle slackens and it bears off horzontally rightwards. Traverse along the leat until it is desirable first to ascend and then move rightwards to gain the bottom crest of Birkhouse Moor's North East Ridge. With a sense of position and increasingly rewarding views, make rough scrambly ascent avoiding the small crags as necessary to gain The Nab and on to the plateau of Birkhouse Moor.

Continue to gain and follow a stone wall which crests the actual top of Birkhouse Moor and leads to the main trod along the open shoulder. Low Spying How is traversed on the Red Tarn side of the crest before ascent is made to the rocky cone of High Spying How. In front, unveiled below your feet, the magnifcent prospect of Striding Edge.

With the edge cutting a fine line, the ground plunges steeply away to Nethermost Cove to the south, and Red Tarn to the north. Keeping to the absolute crest is the most difficult route, though in summer it is possible to find an easier alternative below. In winter, when thick with snow or ice, this is not always obvious or possible. Three lesser pikes are crested before a final rocky tower terminates the edge proper. Descent from this, down a steep little chimney gully towards the south side, presents the most difficult section. Once down, cross the gap in the ridge to gain a little rocky buttress. This submits with mild scrambling and leads to the

Moving along the exposed crest of Striding Edge under full winter conditions

easier scree-strewn east flanks of Helevellyn. Steep ascent levels, and the path leads rightwards to pass the Gough Memorial and on to the crossed stone walls of the summit shelter. Just beyond, the actual top of Helvellyn is marked by a cairn and offers views to Red Tarn far below.

Should the weather be fair and visibility good, a panorama of high fells extends in all directions. Conditions on the high exposed summit plateau are not always so. I have experienced widely differing conditions. Once, when the plateau was plastered in ice, the ferocity of the wind was so extreme that the only way to make progress, indeed to maintain the status quo, was to crawl, prone, along using my two ice axes (used for technical climbing) and crampons. The three memorials to be found hereabouts may bear testimony to these differing conditions. The Dixon Memorial 1858, situated on the Nethermost Cove flank of Striding Edge, marks the spot a local huntsman fell to his death. The Gough Memorial 1805, commemorates a fatal fall down the east face. Just south of the summit shelter a plaque reads 'The first aeroplane to land on a mountain in Great Britain did so on this spot on Dec 22nd 1926. John Leeming and Bert Hinkler in an Avro 585 Gosport landed here and after a short stay flew back to Woodford'. No high-tech back-up there, I imagine, just an indefatigable spirit of adventure and a little old-fashioned bravery.

From this point the summit rim strikes an aesthetically symmetrical 'C' shaped curvature with the trig point found centrally and the cairned top of Swirral Edge at its far end. If snow should lie here keep well back from the edge as large cornices, prone to collapse, build up in the lee of the wind. The first few feet of descent down Swirral Edge can feel most exposed and intimidating. However, the angle slackens after 25m and rocky outcrops serve to provide some security. Routes can be found either to the right (south) or left. As the edge slackens near the base the path follows the right flank and so avoids a final craggy drop to the col. Beyond the col keep straight on up the crest (ignoring the main path veering down rightwards) to gain the top of Catstycam, a fine peak which would feel even more distinguished if located other than in the shadow of the mighty Helvellyn.

The North West Ridge falls steeply down from the summit. Keep to the crest, with a little zigzagging in places to avoid unneccesary hardships, and all will prove well. The going is very steep but not unduly technically difficult.

Over Red Tarn to the summit of Helvellyn, Swirral Edge profiled to the right and Striding Edge to the left

At the base of the ridge follow on down the hillside to Kepple Cove Dam. In October 1927 a cloudburst saw the reservoir behind it burst the banks and the resulting tidal wave caused devastation down below at the Greenside lead mines and in Glenridding itself.

It is usual to cross the beck here and follow the main trod on the other side. However, a more interesting way is to follow the old water leat, found a little way below the dam, which leads rightwards to traverse the flanks of Catstycam along the 525m contour. Though boggy in places the leat is easy to follow and disappears at one point only – where it rounds a craggy outcrop and was once supported on now rotted timber supports. At the point where the grassy leat intercepts the unmistakeable main trod falling from Red Tarn descend the latter. After levelling it crosses a wooden footbridge over Red Tarn Beck and continues to descend, traversing the hillside above Glenridding Beck.

Keep along this track bearing right to follow along above the wall opposite Greenside. The old lead mine buildings are now converted for various uses including those of the Youth Hostel. In a further kilometre and a half, long shadows may well have begun to fall as you pass beneath the foot of Birkhouse Moor's North East Ridge and rejoin the original route above Miresbeck. This sustained mountain adventure of quality draws to a close.

Symmetrical curvature along Helvellyn's summit rim. Beware of unstable snow cornices – keep back from the edge in wintry conditions

A DEEPDALE CIRCUIT – FAIRFIELD via HARTSOP above HOW RIDGE and descent via COFA PIKE and ST SUNDAY CRAG

Fairfield's most demanding horseshoe; a view to Dove Crag's Priest Hole Cave

Fact Sheet

Location: Patterdale, Fairfield group, Central Fells, Lake District National Park, north west England

Length: 14.5km (9 miles)

Ascent: 910m (2985ft)

Time: 6 hours

Difficulty: The length and comparative remoteness of this walk are important considerations. Technically the most difficult sections fall just short of bonafide scrambles: these are the short initial ascent of Hart Crag (Scrambling Grade 0.5), and the descent from Cofa Pike, which is very steep and stony, and demanding in winter (Winter Grade 0.5)

Seasons: Summer conditions can generally be expected from April to October, and winter conditions from November to March

Map: OS Outdoor Leisure 5, The English Lake District – North East

Start & Finish: The lay-by situated on the A592 by the telephone box at Deepdale Bridge (NY 399 144)

Access: Some 20km (12 miles) south west of Penrith along the A592; alternatively 11km (7 miles) or so north of Ambleside over the Kirkstone Pass

Tourist Information: Ambleside (Tel: 015394 32582); also the National Park Information Centre at Glenridding, Beckside car park (Tel: 017684 82414)

Accommodation: All types are available in Patterdale, including a campsite and a Youth Hostel

Geology: Rhyolite, rough and dependable, is predominant in this area

Flora & Fauna: Amongst birds, the raven, peregrine, buzzard and the barn owl frequent these parts. Mountain sorrel and alpine saw-wort grow happily here; and you may be lucky enough to see the red fox and the badger

Comment: The high ridges around Deepdale provide a long, remote circuit, and undoubtedly Fairfield's most challenging horseshoe.

The Tops

Gale Crag	512m (1680ft)	(gale crag = crag above the ravine)
Gill Crag	582m (1909ft)	(gill crag = crag above the stream runnel)
Hart Crag	822m (2698ft)	(hart crag = female deer crag)
Fairfield	873m (2863ft)	(fair-field = sheep fell)
Cofa Pike	823m (2700ft)	(cofa pike = rocky pointed top of the adjoining fell)
St Sunday Crag	841m (2758ft)	(St Sunday Crag)
Birks	622m (2040ft)	(birks = fell of the birch trees)

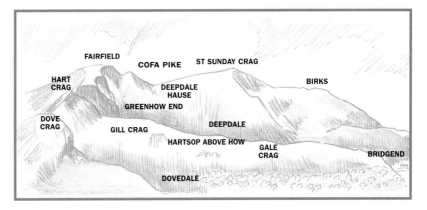

■ This is a walk on the wild side of Fairfield, that follows airy ridges and cuts through impressive steeps to make a powerful circuit around Deepdale. Overlooking substantial portions of the Helvellyn massif and the Eastern, Southern and Western Fells, and high above the heads of both Windermere and Ullswater, it offers a frequently changing kaleidoscope of mountain scenery. Walking in a clockwise direction – as the circuit is described here – keeps to a minimum the sections of strenuous ascent; it also provides an inspirational view down over the head of Ullswater from the steep nose of Birks.

Just beyond the telephone box a signed track leads through the fields to an old stone barn on the edge of the woods. Make your way up through the mixed deciduous trees to gain the open crest, by the stone wall, of the Hartsop-above-How ridge.

Follow the route over the little rocky knolls of Gale and Gill Crags to the steep toe of Hart Crag; the going is straightforward. To the north is the long expanse of Deepdale, its boulder-littered moraine overshadowed by the dark and foreboding cliffs of Greenhow End. To the south is Dovedale, with the formidable Dove Crag and its mysterious Priest Hole cave towering above.

The way up through the rocks is steep; you will come to a long rock slab which you must climb, then move first to the right edge of the crest, overlooking Link Cove, then left to follow a central line. The angle soon relents and the way leads directly up to the long, rocky crest summit of Hart Crag. Bear right and follow the well defined, though stony path down to cross over Link Hause: take care in winter, because large cornices can build here along the north-eastern rim. The path now rises to curve left, passing the top of Scrubby Crag to the right, and then follows

A winter's study of the head of the horseshoe, looking over the secluded valley of Grisedale. Our ridge can be seen falling from the domed summit of Fairfield (right) down over Cofa Pike before rising again to St Sunday Crag (left)

Top right: Deepdale, headed by the heights of Fairfield

Right: Cofa Pike rising from the ridge below Fairfield with St Sunday Crag beyond

due west along the broad shoulder and across Flinty Grave to the summit cairns of Fairfield. It is a magnificent outlook; however, the top of Fairfield lacks any definite feature and is notoriously difficult to navigate successfully in poor visibility. If such conditions prevail, be sure to use a compass – there are four ridges falling from Fairfield's broad shoulder and it is easy to take the wrong one.

Bear right (due north), and drop over the rounded edge of the plateau: you will quickly gather momentum down to the saddle col at the foot of the distinct little rocky knoll of Cofa Pike. Beyond this, the going is very steep indeed, right down to Deepdale Hause. From here it is a gradual ascent along the shoulder ridge to the broad, cairned top of lovely St Sunday Crag; from this summit there is a tremendous aspect over the Grisedale valley to the mighty east face of the Helvellyn massif. A continuous line of crags and pikes runs from

Grisedale Tarn over Ruthwaite and Nevermost Cove to Striding Edge and Helvellyn summit.

Only if battered by a cold north-easterly will you want to quit this favourite Lakeland Fell. The descent is easy, and leads to the grassy col beneath Birks. A word of caution, however: although in summer the going is straightforward, be very careful in winter because considerable accumulations of snow can build on these slopes, and they have been known to avalanche, with fatal consequences.

Next, a gentle pull leads to the top of Birks. From here, head north down the nose: a moderate incline at first, it steepens considerably down the crest of Thornhow End, offering a matchless view over the head of Ullswater. A few trees begin to change the bold, open nature of the ridge, and soon a horizontal track is intercepted. Follow this to the right until it enters an area of scrubby trees behind the Patterdale Hotel. Bear right to gain the road in the hamlet of Patterdale, and go right again.

Whilst ascending the ridge to Hart Crag a break in the snowfall reveals a view over Link Cove to Scrubby Crag

Opposite: By the cairn marking the top of Mardale Ill Bell with Haweswater Reservoir visible beyond (right)

THE MARDALE HORSESHOE – HIGH STREET via RIGGINDALE RIDGE descending HARTER FELL via GATESCARTH PASS

Drowned Mardale, golden eagle country, High Street Roman Road

Location: Mardale Head above Haweswater, High Street group, Eastern Fells, Lake District National Park, north west England

Length: 11km (6.8 miles)

Ascent: 750m (2465ft)

Time: 4.5 hours

Difficulty: A rugged, high-level walk with no technical difficulty. Escape may be made down Nan Bield Pass

Seasons: Summer conditions may be expected from April to October, and winter conditions from November to March

Map: OS Outdoor Leisure 5, The English Lake District – North East

Start & Finish: The car park at Mardale Head above Haweswater (NY 469 107)

Access: Some 23km (14 miles) south west of Penrith along minor roads through Askham, Helston and Bampton; alternatively 40km (25 miles) or so north of Kendal along the A6 to Shap, then on minor roads

Tourist Information: Penrith (Tel: 01768 867466); also the National Park Information Centre at Pooley Bridge (Tel: 017684 86530)

Accommodation: There are most types available within the area; nearby Bampton has a campsite, and the St Patrick's Inn. The nearest Youth Hostels are at Kendal and Patterdale

Geology: The rock is mainly rhyolite, so the going is rough and stony in places

Flora & Fauna: You may be lucky enough to see the golden eagle; also the raven may be glimpsed amongst these wild crags. Liverwort and sheep's fescue grow in this region; and red fox, red deer and the Lakeland Fell pony are indigenous to these parts

Comment: On the eastern fringe of the National Park, this ridge walk extends around the rugged head of one of Lakeland's most remote valleys. Note that the RSPB may make it 'out of bounds' if the golden eagles are nesting, between April and July inclusive, and it is important for the survival of the eagle in Lakeland that any such restriction is strictly observed.

The Tops

Rough Crag	628m (2060ft)	(rough crag = rough crag)
High Street	828m (2718ft)	(high street = high road)
Mardale Ill Bell	761m (2496ft)	(mar-dale ill bell = Mardale's bad bell-shaped fell)
Harter Fell	778m (2552ft)	(hart-er fell = fell of the female deer)

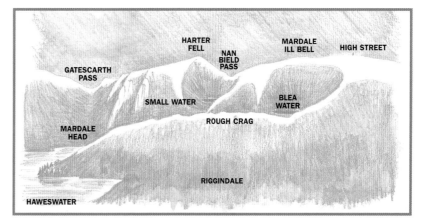

■ In 1940 Haweswater valley was flooded to create a reservoir, and a whole community disappeared beneath its waters – the church, the Dun Bull Inn and the school are now on the reservoir bed, leaving the head of Mardale quieter and more secluded than ever. Nevertheless, the daunting black cliffs and the hanging combes holding Blea Water and Small Water still present a stunning skyline – and into this wild environment the golden eagle has returned.

Go through the gate that marks the start of Gatescarth Pass, then bear right to pass above the reservoir. Cross Mardale Beck by the footbridge. Take the bouldery path to the right, traversing above the wall, then climbing up to reach the bracken-covered end of the shoulder of Riggindale ridge. Below lie the conifers now afforesting The Rigg. The well defined path follows the crest of the ridge, its outlook becoming increasingly impressive: initially it ascends to the left of the stone wall, then makes its way over the open rocky knolls until it reaches the summit section of the aptly named Rough Crag. The col beyond holds a tiny tarn and is known as Caspel Gate; it provides a possible way off the ridge.

Beyond this point the ridge is known as Long Stile: it steepens in descent until it ends abruptly by a cairn on the substantially flat summit plateau of High Street. Bear left to find the summit cairn and trig point. It takes this name from the High Street which identifies the highest point of the Roman Road between Troutbeck and Penrith. Our summit is also called Racecourse Hill, for which the possibilities are reasonably obvious. Native Lakeland Fell ponies still graze wild over these grassy slopes.

Mardale Ill Bell – not to be confused with the nearby Ill Bell of Kentmere – lies at the southern end of the rim of the Blea Water basin. The route off the great shoulder of High Street is an easy, grassy descent which leads down left to this slightly raised cairned knoll; it is an advantageous viewpoint from which to peruse the details of the Riggindale ridge – and perhaps, if you are lucky, from which to watch the soaring, unmistakable flight of the golden eagle.

Continue heading south down the shoulder until the well worn path bears left to descend steeply through the rocky knolls which guard the head of Nan Bield Pass. A ruined stone building, now without roof, still acts as an effective wind-break. The way left leads to Small Water, and escape back to Mardale Head; descent to the right leads into Kentmere. The next section is probably

Over Haweswater to Riggindale (right) and the head of Mardale (left) with the Riggindale ridge rising to High Street between. A remote corner of Lakeland now famed for its golden eagles

the most strenuous of the whole round.

Climb up from the col and traverse the rocky crest, with Black John's Hole menacing to the left. The ascent is steep and best tackled in zigzags, until eventually you reach the large summit cairn of Harter Fell. From here there is a good prospect over Small Water and to the curved back of High Street, though the best viewpoint from this fell will be found a little way on. Go left from the cairn along the easy, grassy shoulder, and in about 500m you will find another substantial cairn; this one marks the northernmost extent of the summit plateau, from which there are handsome views over the head of Haweswater Reservoir. Turn sharp right and descend with the line of the fence, passing the craggy knoll of Little Harter Fell to the left, and continue until a path sweeps off down to the left.

This falls, rather wet and peat-boggy near its end, to join the old packhorse route of Gatescarth Pass.

This track once served as an important route to link Mardale with Mosedale, which drops to Swindale, and Longsleddale (pronounced 'long-sled-dale', and originating from the fact that the quarrymen had a long way to sled out their spoils). The latter valley leads south towards the important wool market town of 'olde grey' Kendal. We drop down to the left, the walk back to the deserted head of Mardale requiring steady effort in the gathering dusk.

Right: The stone wall which runs centrally over the broad plateau of High Street parallel to the route taken by the Roman road

Below: Two summer walkers below Harter Fell, with Small Water down to the right. The ridge snakes over Nan Bield Pass from here and up to Mardale Ill Bell

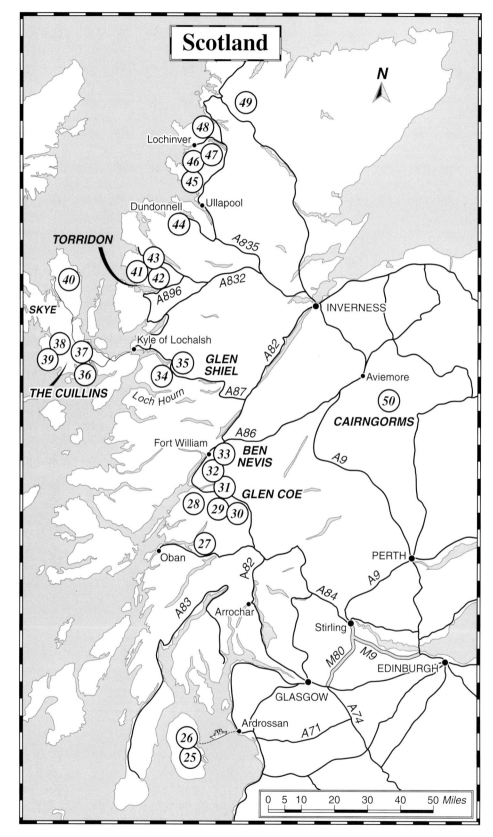

Scotland

Twenty-six ridge walks are described, of varying degrees of length and difficulty, throughout the magnificent Highlands and Islands of Scotland. The diversity of the landscape and mountain form, of the climate and of the geology, and of the flora and fauna, is absolutely breathtaking. Some of these ridge walks rise from the road, some from the sea, others are set in regions of vast wilderness. All are wild, untamed, majestic.

The area represented by the walks in this book covers something like a staggering 90,000 sq km (34,750 sq miles). Longitudinally it stretches some 350km from Cape Wrath, the far north-western tip, southwards to the Island of Arran floating in the Firth of Clyde. Although the coastline is so irregular as to make a definition of width fairly irrelevant, for the sake of the exercise, if we look at the midway point it extends for some 275km from the westerly Island of Skye, eastwards to Aberdeen.

Although, at the time of writing, there are no designated National Parks in Scotland, there are a great number of key mountain groups. For the purposes of this book I have taken a representation from six major mountain areas: the Islands (the Isle of Arran and the Isle of Skye, the Southern Highlands (stretching up the west coast from Oban to Ballachulish), the Central Highlands (from Glencoe to Ben Nevis), the Western Highlands (Glen Shiel), the Northern Highlands (from Wester Ross to Sutherland, Torridon to Cape Wrath) and the Cairngorms (to the east). With such a huge area of choice I have selected the ridge walks principally for their quality of walking and scrambling over a wide range of difficulty; however, I have also portrayed something of the huge diversity of the area. The order of the book weaves northwards from the Isle of Arran, up the west coast almost to Cape Wrath, then returns to the Cairngorms in the east.

The wild and rugged grandeur of Glencoe epitomises the magnificent Highlands of Scotland. Two of the Three Sisters are portrayed here; seen centrally the rocky bastion of Gearr Aonach and to her right the mighty head of Aonach Dubh

Over BEINN NUIS and BEINN TARSUINN – THE CIRQUE of COIRE a' BHRADHAIN

Wreck sites, Old Man of Beinn Tarsuinn, granite archway of Fhir-bhogha

Fact Sheet

Location: Above Glen Rosa, Isle of Arran, south-west Scotland

Length: 15km (9 miles)

Ascent: 985m (3,230ft)

Time: 7 hours

Difficulty: Despite this walk's benign appearance, the distances are not to be underestimated: it is fairly remote, with a long, boggy approach and return. In execution the technical difficulties are low, with only the descent of Beinn Tarsuinn presenting short sections of easy, rocky scrambling (Scrambling Grade 0.25)

Seasons: Summer conditions may be expected from April to October; winter conditions from November to March

Map: OS Outdoor Leisure 37, Isle of Arran

Start & Finish: From the small car park above the campsite at the end of the surfaced road leading to Glen Rosa (NS 001 376)

Access: There are good Caledonian MacBrayne ferry connections to the island, which provide regular sailings. The main link is the Ardrossan to Brodick ferry, south of Glasgow; it has co-ordinated rail linkage directly to Glasgow. The Lochranza (Arran) to Claonaig ferry sails from the northern tip of the island to the Kintyre peninsula allowing travel to and from the north. For information for both ferries, tel. Ardrossan 01294 4634570; for bookings, tel. 0990 650000. To reduce the cost of sailing it is perfectly feasible to leave vehicles on the mainland and hire a bicycle on Arran. Cheap bicycle hire is plentiful in Brodick, and distances to the hills are short and flat. Glen Rosa lies some 3km (2 miles) outside Brodick: follow the A841, then the B880 Blackwaterfoot Pass road for 250m before bearing right down a minor road leading to the campsite

Tourist Information: On the pier at Brodick (tel. 01770 30214); also Brodick Country Park Ranger Service (tel. 01770 302462)

Accommodation: Brodick has most types of accommodation; the nearest Youth Hostels are at Whiting

The Tops

Beinn Nuis	792m (2,597ft)	(by-an an-oosh = mountain of the fawn)
Beinn Tarsuinn	826m (2,710ft)	(by-an tarsh-yn = transverse mountain)
Beinn a' Chliabhain		
	675m (2,215ft)	(by-an a khlee-av-yn = creel mountain)
Cnoc Breac	401m (1,316ft)	(nock bree-akh = little knoll)

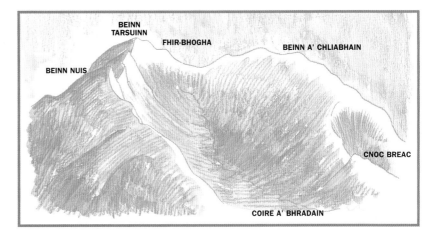

Bay and Lochranza, and the nearest campsite is at the foot of Glen Rosa (basic facilities). The Co-op supermarket is open '8 till 8' including Sundays

Geology: Typically the rock is coarse-grained, light golden/silvery/pink/red-coloured biotite granite. It is very rough and dependable to walk on (though beware of the coarse grit which can be unstable, as if you were walking on ball bearings)

Flora & Fauna: Golden eagle, raven, basking shark and red deer may be seen. Arran whitebeam and Arran service-tree grow in this area

Comment: Situated above Brodick Bay in the north-east quarter of the island, and belying their gentle surroundings, the jagged hills of Arran are amongst the most spectacular in the whole of Britain. This circuit serves as perhaps the gentlest introduction to their magnificent granite ridges (note that inclusion of the A'Chir Ridge makes this walk into a mountaineering expedition).

Sheltering from the weather under the granite arch beneath Fhir-bhogha

In terms of general character the island of Arran, that great sleeping warrior of the Clyde, lies somewhere between the sublime dales of the Lake District and the wild glens of the Scottish Highlands. Yet above a sylvan coast, above the enchantments of Glen Rosa and Glen Sannox, rise a series of granite peaks and fine knife-edge ridges, the like of which are hardly rivalled outside the Chamonix Aiguille. This dramatic mountainscape results from the effects of the last glacial epoch.

Whilst ice smothered the lower hills and valleys, planing them smooth, the high tops of the granite batholith were left protruding, and it was the intense frost-shattering of these that produced the splintered edges and jagged pyramidal shapes we see today. These granite hills and connecting ridges, which occupy the north-eastern quarter of the island, form a giant letter 'H'. The horizontal bar of the H is known as 'The Saddle', and it divides the long valleys of Glen Rosa to the south and Glen Sannox to the north. The eastern leg of the H includes the highest top, that of Goatfell overlooking Brodick Bay. This route occupies the peaks and ridges of the southern end of the western leg of the H. This limb terminates with Beinn Nuis and is crossed by Beinn Tarsuinn (transverse mountain); the latter continues over Beinn a' Chliabhain to form Coire a' Bhradain. It is the skyline of this hanging valley, falling into

Glen Rosa, that provides the fine mountain walk described here.

With the golden brown of Glenrosa Water to your right, follow the track which leads up Glen Rosa. The distant mountain of Beinn Nuis, the first objective, can be seen up to the left, just before you pass a rusting pipe bridge. The pyramidal magnificence of Cir Mhor comes into view at the head of Glen Rosa; soon after, you come to a wooden bridge that crosses the Garbh Allt burn which falls from Coire a' Bhradain. On crossing the bridge, bear left and start climbing immediately; the route rises above the right side of the burn (the true left bank) and comes to a kissing gate which leads through a deer fence into the 'Garbh Allt Enclosure' – an attempt by the National Trust for Scotland to keep out sheep and deer and so promote the regeneration of natural woodland.

The path is straightforward, though very boggy and heathery, and climbs steeply to exit the enclosure by another kissing gate; as the angle slackens, the peat bogs seem to get worse. Keep to the right of the burn. Shortly after it begins to sink into a ravine, a kissing gate gives access to yet another wired-off enclosure. Continue above the ravine until, after about 250m, a faint path veers left and makes a short, easy descent into the gorge; it crosses the Garbh Allt and then climbs the other

The Coire a' Bhradain horseshoe. Beinn Nuis stands to the left, Beinn Tarsuinn centrally, with the knoll of Fhir-bhogha below and to the right the lesser peak of Beinn a' Chliabhain

side. The view across the lonely coire reveals a distant though imposing rock buttress, the Meadow Face, on the front of Beinn Tarsuinn. (Two parallel crack lines may be visible to the discerning. A long time ago – on 17 September 1972, to be precise – I climbed the left-hand one, named Brachistochrone, then rated as one of the most difficult rock climbs on Arran. It is an experience still vivid in my memory.) Above the basin all the ridge of this high cirque can be seen in fine array.

The path up the shoulder is well defined and provides a pleasant climb. It levels out along the shoulder and passes through a natural trough between granite outcrops, then moves right towards the imposing cliff face of Beinn Nuis. Whilst there is no difficulty, this is a compelling place: airy and enjoyable in sunshine, it is formidable and daunting when the clouds roll across the sky. Down below to the left, near the head of Coire Nuis, note the visible remains of a wrecked aircraft: this was Lodestar which crashed on 1 October 1943 carrying top secret dispatches. Not so obvious is another crash site to the right, on the rock face, now only really to be seen using binoculars. A Flying Fortress went down here on 10 December 1944, and although most of the wreckage has been removed, some can be seen still jammed in the vertical cracks which run up the face of Beinn Nuis; the rocks above bear the scars of the huge explosion that surely followed its crash. Due to extreme winter conditions this site was not located, nor the ten bodies removed, until 3 March the following year.

The path veers left, above Coire Nuis, then back right to traverse directly above the cliff face, and finally ascends to the summit of Beinn Nuis. A short, easy descent leads to the ridge which runs along to Beinn Tarsuinn; it offers great interest though little difficulty. The way along the broad ridge is easiest just left of, and below, the crest of tilted granite blocks; the path then continues, passing beneath an impressive overhanging boulder. The initial ascent to Beinn Tarsuinn passes layer upon layer of granite blocks, then you reach a ridge adorned with remarkable natural rock sculptures of rounded granite: one, looking down a deep gully to the Meadow Face far below, is unmistakably the Old Man of Beinn Tarsuinn. The rock platform summit is surrounded by blocky overhangs of granite. The view is particularly

dramatic across the head of Glen Rosa to Goatfell and North Goatfell above The Saddle.

The route descends in a north-easterly direction and is reasonably well defined though a little scrambly in places, and the large granite boulders require thoughtful negotiation; one such cluster forms an enclosure, and you must pass in and out of this in the shadow of granite overhangs. A short section of steep slabs also requires care (they constitute an easy scramble) before the col, Bealach an Fhir-bhogha, is reached beneath a rocky granite tower of An Fhir-bhogha. The path bears down to the right, then to the left and traverses beneath the rocky tor, actually passing through a rock arch, to reach the easy shoulder which leads to Beinn a' Chliabhain. The archway is nicely formed from granite shaped like a door handle when looking from the south, and more like a rounded arch looking back from the north. It is actually a section of the granite slab/bluff above, which has slipped a few feet across the path, leaving this natural passageway.

The path is well defined and leads down to the col; good views left reveal the tremendous ridge of A'Chir. (This could have been reached by traversing left and making your way around the west side of An Fhir-bhogha. It leads on to Cir Mhor and is one of the finest ridges in Scotland: however, it is a mountaineering challenge with some considerable difficulty and exposure, and usually involves ropework even for experienced climbers. From the col the main path flanks the ridge of Beinn a' Chliabhain. However, it is much better to leave this and climb up left to the crest of the mountain; there is no particular difficulty, and the views over Glen Rosa are tremendous.

The blocky granite outcrop which tops Beinn a' Chliabhain is a worthy prize. Descent is straightforward, picking the simplest way down the nose. Continue across the shoulder to little Cnoc Breac, then make your way downwards in a slightly circuitous descent back to the bogs and the kissing gate which leads to the first enclosure of Garbh Allt. The enclosure wasn't there in 1972 when I returned, drunk on moonlight, from Brachistochrone, on a curve of descent occupying the shortest possible time.

In retrospect I'm rather pleased it didn't intrude into what felt like a perfect mountain wilderness.

With the fearsome East Face to the right, the path winds its way past beautifully sculpted granite to the summit of Beinn Nuis

Along the crest of Beinn a' Chliablain, bristling with blocks of granite

THE GREAT GLEN SANNOX HORSESHOE

Witch's Step, pitchstone, Cir Mhor, The Saddle, The Devil's Punchbowl

Fact Sheet

Location: Around Glen Sannox, Isle of Arran, south-west Scotland

Length: 14km (8¾ miles)

Ascent: 1,630m (5,350ft)

Time: 9 hours

Difficulty: A long and arduous mountain walk involving numerous sections of strenuous ascent, sections of scrambling and considerable exposure. Unavoidable scrambling sections include the Witch's Step (Scrambling Grade 1, or if directly over the first pinnacle and down into the gap, Scrambling Grade 3); and the ascent to, and descent from Cir Mhor (Scrambling Grade 1). This is a mountaineering expedition under winter conditions (Winter Grade II). The difficulties, though not the distance, can be halved by descending Glen Sannox (an awful peat bath at the time of writing, though footpath works have begun) from The Saddle

Seasons: Summer conditions may be expected from April to October; winter conditions from November to March. There is unrestricted access to the hills, though culling of the red deer takes place between mid-August and mid-October (tel. 01770 302363)

Map: OS Outdoor Leisure 37, Isle of Arran

Start & Finish: Sannox car park beside the road (NS 016 454)

Access: There are good Caledonian MacBrayne ferry connections to the island, providing regular sailings; the main link is the Ardrossan to Brodick ferry south of Glasgow, with co-ordinated rail links directly to Glasgow. The Lochranza (Arran) to Claonaig ferry sails from the northern tip of the island to the Kintyre peninsula, allowing travel to and from the north. For information for both ferries, tel. Ardrossan 01294 4634570; for bookings, tel. 0990 650000. To reduce the cost of sailing it is perfectly feasible to leave vehicles on the mainland and hire a bicycle on Arran. Cheap bicycle hire is plentiful in Brodick, and distances to the hills short and flat. The easiest and quickest way to approach Ardrossan from the south is to follow the M74 to Junction 2, then take the A71 to Kilmarnock, thence following signs to Irvine or Ardrossan. Glen Rosa lies some 2 miles (3km) outside Brodick: follow the A841,

The Tops

Suidhe Fhearghas	651m (2,136ft)	(soo-ya era-ghaysh = Fergus' Seat)
Ceum na Caillich		(kame na kyle-yikh = Witch's Step)
Caisteal Abhail	847m (2,779ft)	(cash-ty-al av-al = castle of the fork)
Cir Mhor	799m (2,621ft)	(keer voar = big cockscomb)
North Goatfell	818m (2,684ft)	(north geitar fjall = north hill of the wind)
Mullach Buidhe	829m (2,720ft)	(mull-akh boo-ya = golden rounded hill)
Cioch na h-Oighe	661m (2,168ft)	(kee-okh na haw-ya = the virgin's breast)

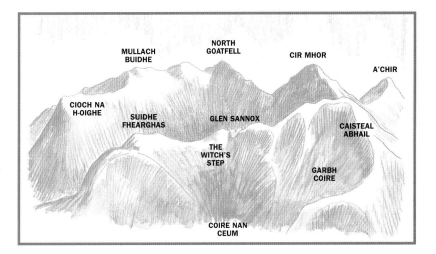

then take the B880 Blackwaterfoot Pass road for 250m before bearing right down a minor road leading to the campsite

Tourist Information: On the pier at Brodick (tel. 01770 30214); also Brodick Country Park Ranger Service (tel. 01770 302462)

Accommodation: Brodick has most types of accommodation. The nearest Youth Hostels are at Whiting Bay and Lochranza, and the nearest campsite is at the foot of Glen Rosa (basic facilities). The Co-op supermarket is open '8 till 8' including Sundays

Geology: The rock is typically coarse-grained, light golden/silvery/pink/red-coloured biotite granite. It is very rough and dependable to walk on (though beware of the coarse grit which can behave like ball bearings beneath the feet). The friction under the boot is tremendous, though positive handholds may sometimes be lacking.

Approaching the summit of North Goatfell

The great cleft of the Witch's Step is formed by more rapid erosion of a vertical dyke of quartz-dolerite which has intruded through the granite

Flora & Fauna: Golden eagle, raven, basking shark and red deer may be seen; amongst flowers, bog asphodel and thyme-leaved speedwell grow in this area

Comment: This complete round must be rated as one of the finest and most demanding in Britain. There are only two feasible escape routes which lead safely down into Glen Sannox: from the shoulder before the ascent of Cir Mhor, and from The Saddle (the half-way point) after Cir

Mhor. Note that you must descend from The Saddle into Glen Sannox by the cairn which marks where the path from Glen Rosa arrives; any other way and there are steep cliffs. The path first moves left (west) then right, and follows a natural rake through the cliffs; there is a short section of scrambling near its end (Scrambling Grade 1).

■ The fact that you start from sea level – the views across Sannox Bay and the Firth of Clyde are tremendous – is significant for two reasons. First and most obvious is that to reach the first top,

The first leg of the Great Sannox Horseshoe with the pinnacles of the Witch's Step seen from Suidhe Fhearghas followed by the heights of Caisteal Abhail. To the left the striking angularity of Cir Mhor

Suidhe Fhearghas, of this anticlockwise round of Glen Sannox you really have to climb its full height: 650m of ascent. The second is that you may well see basking shark, as well as golden eagle and red stag, particularly in late August.

Though supremely rewarding, this is a physically and technically demanding outing negotiating the whole of the northern half of the 'H' formation of Arran's granite mountains. The great nose of Cioch na h-Oighe, the Witch's Step and the distant pyramid of Cir Mhor are all prominent from the near environs of the road, giving an instant visual taste of just some of the delights to be encountered. 'Escape' from The Saddle at the present time involves some two hours of struggle through peat bog and heather.

Opposite the car park, a tarmac lane by the cottage leads past the graveyard; it then becomes unsurfaced. Pass the tall white mast (one of three, matched by another set one mile north: when aligned, these start the nautical mile for measured speed trials); you will soon enter Glen Sannox beneath the spell of Cioch na h-Oighe. Follow the track until just before a row of beech trees: here a path leads down to the right, to cross the burn via a wooden footbridge. Go left, passing the spoil heaps and hollows of the old barytes mines. Bear right, and pick up and follow the old railway incline leading directly up the hillside.

The skyline around Glen Sannox paints a formidable picture; most noticeable are the spiky rock turrets of the Witch's Step. Continue to the top of the smooth incline; from here a narrow path leads to the left (to the side of the spoil heaps), then steeply up through the bracken – though no more than a sheep track, it is well defined. Trending left, it rises to the foot of the eastern shoulder of Suidhe Fhearghas. Go round this to the right until you see a path that rises steeply left through the heather and granite; a little scrambly, it emerges onto a modest level shoulder, with a fine view to the imposing nose of Cioch na h-Oighe opposite. From here the way is straightforward, occasionally over golden gravel, to the granite summit seat of Suidhe Fhearghas.

Ahead, the pinnacles of the Witch's Step look formidable. Take heart, for the regular route around the first pinnacle is much less difficult than first appearances would suggest. Descend initially,

then follow the broad, pleasant ridge over a gentle mixture of grass, rock outcrop and boulders. Now climbing, you will pass a large rock, 3m high, standing with its flat face toward the path. As the ridge begins to narrow, continue along the cleats of granite; the way steepens, climbing towards the first rock tower which guards the Witch's Step. Just before it becomes really steep, a good path breaks off right: the normal route follows this, avoiding the most difficult section, first descending and then skirting around the tower; there is one awkward exposed step which leads to a final little scramble into the bed of the gully. Climb the gully to the saddle neck of the Witch's Step. Alternatively, the direct route (Scrambling Grade 3) climbs the tower, then descends steeply, directly to the gap – the final slabby corner of the last 10m provides the main difficulty.

Climb from the gap, taking the well worn route up the slabby wall; there are many possible variations (Scrambling Grade 1). There are three further minor pinnacles along the crest of the ridge; most interest can be had by scrambling over them (Scrambling Grade 1), though the most popular route lies down to the left. A little col marks the end of the pinnacles and the beginning of the ascent of Caisteal Abhail. The path is reasonably well defined, and leads through granite bluffs to the first flat block top of Caisteal Abhail. Over a col beyond, a second granite bluff provides another distinctly separate top. The OS indicates that the first top is the higher, though with the naked eye it is impossible to be sure. Descent from the first top may be made directly (Scrambling Grade 2), or by returning via the line of ascent; then swing north around the head of the col to gain the second (most southerly) top.

The south-westerly ridge gives a straight-forward, curving descent to the col beneath the north-western shoulder of Cir Mhor. This stunning pyramidal peak of granite seems to concentrate the whole of Arran's mountain energy; from it, three ridges spiral outwards – ours from the north-west, the A'Chir ridge from the south-west, and The Saddle ridge which rises to North Goatfell from the east. Before reaching the col you may come across a spring, and scattered around it the sharp black/green shards of vitrified pitchstone, a glass-like form of lava resembling obsidean; elsewhere this rock has

been fashioned into tools by mesolithic man.

Though steep, the ascent of the shoulder of Cir Mhor is straightforward until the last crown of granite, where a little scrambling is required (Scrambling Grade 1): immensely exposed, this final rocky perch is simply one of the very best places to be. Make your way down in the direction of the east ridge; there is no great exposure, and there are few variations until a short gully which steepens to about Scrambling Grade 1; this drops down to a path which bears out left to an easier shoulder of grass and heather. An easy descent over another little shoulder leads to The Saddle, the ridge which divides Glen Rosa from Glen Sannox. A cairn marks the junction of paths; you should descend from here, should that option be taken.

Around 400m of grinding, scrambly ascent leads to the summit of North Goatfell and, hopefully, a new lease of life. The path along the crest, over the rocky knolls via Mulloch Buidhe and then bearing left to Cioch na h-Oighe, is interesting though straightforward. Descend to the narrow ridge, and follow it to its final granite

protuberance: the summit of Cioch na h-Oighe.

The summit is narrow, and awesome steeps plunge directly to Coire na h-Oighe (The Devil's Punchbowl) to the right, and the depths of Glen Sannos far below to the left. One could be forgiven for feeling a little apprehensive, although in execution it isn't in fact so bad: though narrow, the ridge is by no means knife-edged, and similarly beyond the summit, frequent ledges break up the steepness of the descent – there is surprisingly little difficulty until around the last 450m contour. Here the slabs do become continuous and caution should be exercised in order to negotiate safely this section of scrambling (Scrambling Grade 1).

A ledge at 400m signals the end of the difficulties; the path here runs horizontally across to the right to the base of the Punch Bowl and on to the Allt a' Chapuill, so avoiding the final section of the nose which continues to fall directly into Glen Sannox. Follow the path, which descends by the left bank of the burn until finally it crosses it at the 125m contour; continue down the right bank of the burn to intercept the main track which runs up Glen Sannox. Turn right and head for the sea.

Arran's Glen Sannox; at the head stands the pyramidal rock perfection of Cir Mhor. To the right can be seen Suidhe Fhearghas, followed by the pinnacles of the Witch's Step. Opposite, guarding the entrance, the conical steeps of Cioch na h-Oighe plunge to the valley floor

BEN CRUACHAN

Cruachan dam, five tops over 3,000ft, fine aesthetic ridges, spacious views over the sea

Fact Sheet

Location: The eastern end of the Pass of Brander (A85), above Loch Awe, southern Highlands of Scotland

Length: 14km (8¾ miles)

Ascent: 1,265m (4,150ft)

Time: 8 hours

Difficulty: Although rough and scrambly in places, in general reasonable paths prevail. All technical difficulties can be avoided

Seasons & Restrictions: Summer conditions may be expected from April to October; winter conditions from November to March. Stalking may be in progress from late August: contact Castles estate (tel. 01838 200638)

Map: OS Landranger 50, Glen Orchy

Start & Finish: From the wide verge on the north side of the A85, just east of the power station by the Falls of Cruachan (NN 080 268)

Access: Some 30km (19 miles) east of Oban, and 35km (22 miles) west of Crianlarich along the A85

Tourist Information: At Oban (tel. 01631 561322) and Tyndrum (tel. 01838 400246)

Accommodation: There is an assortment within the area; the nearest Youth Hostels are at Oban and Crianlarich, and the nearest campsites at Ledaig, North Connel and at Tyndrum

Geology: Fine-grained grey and red granites predominate. Several sections of rough bouldery scree will be encountered, not least that falling from Ben Cruachan to the col below Meall Cuanail – fortunately taken in descent

Flora & Fauna: Raven and wheatear may be seen, also red deer, Highland cattle and the chequered skipper butterfly. Blaeberry and heather grow in these regions

Comment: With its tops invisible from the A85 beside Loch Awe to the south, the sheer size and scale of Ben Cruachan is difficult to assess. In fact it is a considerable undertaking, with most of its length, save the section rising by Cruachan Falls, spent negotiating the very fine ridges which connect the five tops described, all of which are situated above the 3,000ft level. This is a logical horseshoe around Coire Cruachan, and worthy of its classic status.

The Tops

Stob Garbh	980m (3,215ft)	(stob gar-av = the rough top)
Stob Diamh	998m (3,272ft)	(stob dyv = peak of the stag)
Drochaid Ghlas	1,009m (3,312ft)	(droch-ahd ghlas = the grey bridge)
Ben Cruachan	1,126m (3,695ft)	(byn kroo-ackh-an = conical hill on the mountain)
Meall Cuanail	918m (3,004ft)	(me-owl koo-aneel = hill of the flocks)

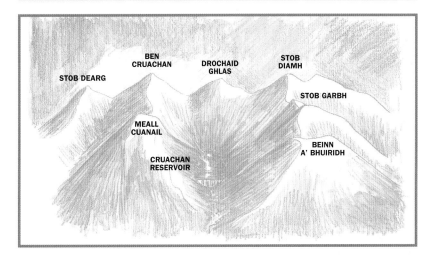

■ With seven tops rising to over the 3,000ft mark, with Loch Awe to the south, Glen Noe and Glen Mhoille to the north, and Loch Etive running past the north-western toe, Ben Cruachan is a major and much favoured mountain. Even when sunshine and clear skies prevail around its periphery, it has an almost legendary capacity for hiding its tops in cloud. Perhaps this is one of the reasons why William Wallace moved his troops over and around the mountain's flanks to such good effect, in 1298 winning a bloody battle in the Pass of Brander. On a clear day the horseshoe of Coire Cruachan, taking in five of the tops, is a magnificent ridge walk. Even in swirling mists – and I speak from some experience – it has considerable intrinsic merit.

Start by the steps leading to a passage under the railway line. On the other side our path leads up and left, to nudge alongside the Falls of Cruachan, then climbs right out from the trees

Brocken Spectre seen when looking over Coire Cruachan from Meall Cuanail

Snow-capped Ben Cruachan rising above Loch Awe

onto open hillside. Contour back left, however, and take the rickety ladder stile over the deer fence; the path continues through a boggy morass, but this can be avoided by climbing the hillside to the right and continuing until you reach the private road; here you bear right and climb to the surfaced road feeding the dam. Turn right along this lower road, then left at the junction: progress is easy, right to the eastern end of the dam.

Pass the end of the dam and go through the gates, over a concrete sluiceway channelling the water from a rather mysterious tunnel portal, and continue along the path, boggy in places, that traverses the flanks of the hillside above the reservoir. Cross the foot of a deep gorge, then climb the rib to its left, following a well defined path. Once you reach the survey marker – a little stone tower with a metal post – the angle slackens, though the path continues to rise until it gains the broad crest of the shoulder which runs up towards Stob Garbh (the col beneath Beinn a' Bhuiridh lies

below to the right). As the shoulder levels it passes two small, bouldery knolls to the left, before climbing to the summit of Stob Garbh.

Descend easy rocks; a path of granite and grass leads to the fine-grained, grey rock cairn marking the summit of Stob Diamh. The ridges from here to Ben Cruachan are superb. Descend to the west; as it leaves the summit the route is surprisingly rather broad and featureless, particularly in reduced visibility. However, the well defined, narrowing crest of the ridge below promises greater interest. Follow the ridge, a comfortable walk until the steep ascent of red scree and blocks that leads to a cairn in a little notch col. The next top, that of Drochaid Ghlas, is offset north from the ridge (aptly named 'the grey bridge'); it is an easy two minutes away and should be visited, as in good visibility it provides an excellent aspect west along the next section of ridge to the summit of Ben Cruachan.

Return to the col and bear right; either descend the narrow slabby granite crest, or take the easier path to the left, until approaching the low point of the ridge before the climb starts to Ben Cruachan. A large area of granite slab is best avoided by taking a path that runs down to the left; it leads to a shallow gully. Take this for a short way until you come to a short, exposed, balancey traverse (perhaps Scrambling Grade 0.3); this leads across the granite to a nick in the col. A steep ascent follows, initially to gain a small shoulder, with a thimble-like needle of rock standing above, and then up the larger red-grey boulders. The most popular route lies to the left of the nose and is straightforward, leading to the summit bower of Ben Cruachan; those seeking a little more adventure will find it by scrambling the blocky granite nose direct (Scrambling Grade 1). Not included in this round, the most westerly peak of Stob Dearg (Taynuilt Peak) lies below and beyond.

Descend to the south, to the col of Coire Dearg below the next objective of Meall Cuanail; this involves negotiating rough boulder scree. The first third of the descent is the most awkward – keeping the edge of Coire Cruachan just over to your left, the path repeatedly disappears and reappears within the boulder field. There is no easy way: dogged determination will ultimately bring you to a better defined shoulder and path lower down, then a pleasanter descent leads to the col and little lochan. It is possible to descend left from this point, though the next objective provides excellent views over Loch Awe and really should not be missed.

Ascend directly to the summit of Meall Cuanail, following the ruined fenceline – fortunately this is easier than it looks. Descending, the main path again follows the old fenceline, though the best aspect back across Coire Cruachan is to be had by moving left along the edge, following a slight ridge for a little way before breaking down to the right. As the going levels at the shoulder, a path continues straight on. However, many people bear left, to descend a wide, grassy gully; this leads down to the road flanking the west side of the reservoir, a few hundred metres above the dam – go carefully, because steep little cliffs lie either side of the gully. Beyond the dam, whilst it is possible to follow down the right side of the falls of Cruachan (so providing a different finish) I recommend crossing the dam and returning via the line of ascent.

Cruachan Dam with Meall Cuanail beyond

Descending Meall Cuanail, with Beinn a' Bhuiridh over Coire Cruachan to the left and the waters of bonny Loch Awe spread below

BEINN a' BHEITHIR via the north ridge of SGORR BHAN and descending the north ridge of SGORR DHEARG

Forgotten paths, soaring ridges, exceptional view along Loch Leven

Fact Sheet

Location: Above Ballachulish (A82), the Central Highlands of Scotland

Length: 8km (5 miles)

Ascent: 1,060m (3,480ft)

Time: 4 hours

Difficulty: Rough paths prevail, a strenuous ascent followed by a gentler descent

Seasons & Restrictions: Summer conditions may be expected from April to October; winter conditions from November to March. There are no restrictions

Map: OS Landranger 41, Ben Nevis

Start & Finish: The lay-by car park by St John's Church on the south side of the A82 just west of Ballachulish (NN 068 584); leave room for those using the church, particularly on a Sunday. Alternatively 200m west (past the railway signal) there is a wide junction and verge

Access: Some 22km (14 miles) south of Fort William along the A82

Tourist Information: Ballachulish (tel. 01855 811296) and Fort William (tel. 01397 705922)

Accommodation: There are all types within Ballachulish and Glencoe; the nearest campsite is at Invercoe, and the nearest Youth Hostel in Glencoe

Geology: Chiefly quartzites, providing an excellent crunchy base to walk on, with a smattering of gneiss, a few scatterings of slate, and brown/pink granite

Flora & Fauna: Raven, ptarmigan, ring ouzel and crossbill may be seen; also the Scotch argus butterfly. Purple saxifrage is just one of the plants that grows in this region

Comment: The north ridges which fall from Sgorr Bhan and Sgorr Dhearg form the forked tongue of the great serpent of Beinn a' Bheithir. Linked by a sharply defined crest of classical curvature, they provide a superb route to top Beinn a' Bheithir.

■ Situated above the bridge spanning the narrows at the end of Loch Leven as it ebbs and floods into the larger straits of Loch Linnhe, the massif of Beinn a' Bheithir holds a commanding position. Whilst it

The Tops

Beinn a' Bheithir		(by-an a vay-heer = great snake mountain)
Sgorr Bhan	947m (3,104ft)	(sgor vaan = white peak)
Sgorr Dhearg	1,024m (3,361ft)	(skor jer-ak = pink/red mountain)

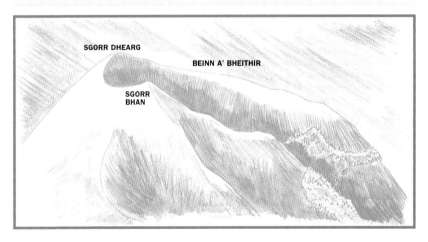

has little of the rugged rocky malevolence and grandeur of nearby Glencoe, it has nevertheless a powerful elegance; this is most associated with its fine ridges and the aesthetic curvature of the crest between the tops of Sgorr Bhan and Sgorr Dhearg. Its Gaelic name of 'great serpent' or 'sea monster' is typically descriptively accurate, the north ridges falling from Sgorr Bhan and Sgorr Dhearg forming the forked tongue, and Creag Ghorm its thick, wriggling body curving down from Sgorr Dhonuill to the tip of the tail.

The lower reaches have now been cleared of obtrusive firs revealing an ancient and secretive path, and I know of no more satisfying or enjoyable way to climb Beinn a' Bheithir than by this route. It is both logical and exhilarating, of reasonable length and immediately interesting. Described here in a clockwise direction, it would prove equally satisfying if you were to follow it the other way.

Go over the stile by the gate and join the track

Moss campion seen on the descent of Sgorr Dearg

behind the church; by the first bend, within 10m, climb the peaty bank on the left into the rhododendron bushes. A little path leads off to the right; it runs parallel to the track, then leads into the larches and zigzags to the left, becoming much better defined. At the time of writing, the recent careful felling of firs by the Forestry Commission has kept the path free of brushwood. The way is marked by little bamboo sticks complete with ribbon. The path zigzags upwards to the right of the stream/gully, then swings left below the little crags, to cross the stream below a rocky cascade. Next it bears left, almost to the edge of the cleared area, and zigzags upwards, finally to traverse right, near the top of the clearing, to cross the stream and gain the edge of the firs.

Continue along the path that runs between the fir and the silver birch above the little crags to the right, like a corridor running into the darkest depths of the plantation. Follow the path through the conifers for some distance until a stand of Scots pine and silver birch allows some light to penetrate the canopy; cross to the right edge of this, and follow the steep, zigzagging path upwards, within the firs, by its side. Finally the path moves first left across the stand, and then out

right again. Continue to the right through the firs until another opening of silver birch. Follow the path zigzagging in ascent, then to the right through the thinning trees, until above the open heather to the left a little ladder stile crosses the wire fence.

Follow the vague path to the right until a well worn sheep track traverses out to the left. Follow this, across the flanks of the hillside and out, onto the open front face. From the first high point a vague path climbs diagonally up to the left; alternatively keep traversing around the front face until on the eastern edge of the nose a well defined path climbs up to the right. Follow this white quartzite trail, marked by cairns, to gain a level shoulder above. Cross the shoulder until the going steepens and the ridge proper begins. It is a steep climb: zigzag up the middle of the rocks of grey gneiss; where the path bears to the right, ascend steeply to the left, to gain and follow the crest of the ridge. This offers a commanding position overlooking the north face of Sgorr Bhan. Cross a band of slate/shaley rock to regain the quartzite, now of a grey disposition. The daunting, horizontally bedded steeps of the north face over to the left, although black in colour, also appear to be composed of quartzite.

Looking down the north-east ridge of Sgorr Bhan to Ballachulish and over Loch Leven and the burial island of Eilean Munde

Looking north to Sgorr Bhan with steep ground plunging away either side

Summit cairn perched on the narrow ridge top of Sgorr Bhan

Above the steep north face the angle slackens, and the shoulder displays a pyramidal tip; initially the crest curves to the left and is joined by the north-east ridge. The route passes some crater-like basins in the quartzite boulder field to the right, and finally climbs steeply upwards to the sharp-edged, blocky summit of Sgorr Bhan. It is a precise and narrow top, the scree falling away steeply on each side, giving a tremendous feeling of openness and exposure. Beyond this top can be seen the slender curving crest that drops to the col and then rises to Sgorr Dhearg: this is sheer perfection of mathematical symmetry, beautiful to behold and a joy to walk. Under snow it forms a razor-sharp edge requiring mountaineering ability.

The summit of Sgorr Dhearg, with its ruined trig point, is equally well defined, its western slopes forming a sharp edge above the steeply sweeping concave slopes of its north-east face. The highest top of Beinn a' Bheithir, it offers no protection against the prevailing westerlies, but the views along Loch Leven, over the burial isle of Eilean Munde and the Pap of Glencoe, must surely have made the Norseman, used to the spectacular sea fjord scenery of Norway's west coast, feel perfectly at home. It really is breathtaking.

An easy path runs down the long and elegant north ridge. About two-thirds of the way down, a stile crosses a wire fence. Continue slightly to the left

of the crest until it levels out and a rocky knoll rises in front of you, crossed by a little cairned shoulder to its right. Descend to the final grassy shoulder, from where the path drops to the right through the bracken and then diagonally left through a stand of silver birch. Keep to the left, down the blunt nose to the left of the broad gully; this is a rough descent through the brushwood (hopefully this will not be replanted with conifers). Pass through the rhododendrons and down onto the track. Descend the track, initially going left until at a junction you bear right to ford the burn between the concrete abutments of a missing bridge. Finally make your way either behind St John's Church, or go left to the parking place by the solitary railway signal.

BIDEAN by the LOST VALLEY HORSESHOE

The Lost Valley, Gear Aonach Zig-Zags, Argyll's highest peak, the Bad Step

Fact Sheet

Location: South side of Glencoe (A82), Argyll, the Central Highlands of Scotland

Length: 12km (7½ miles)

Ascent: 1,380m (4,528ft)

Time: 9 hours

Difficulty: Long, sustained, remote, exposed and potentially serious, with three key sections of difficulty: the Gearr Aonach Zig-Zags (Scrambling Grade 1), the Bad Step to reach the col beneath Stob Coire Sgreamhach (Scrambling Grade 1), and the descent from the end of Beinn Fhada to the floor of the Lost Valley (requiring careful route finding, though not technically difficult). A very demanding expedition in winter (Winter Grade I). Escape west can be made from the southern end of the Gearr Aonach ridge down into Coire nan Lochan (there is a good path to the valley) and from Bealach Dearg north-eastwards down into the Lost Valley (Coire Gabhail)

Seasons & Restrictions: Summer conditions may be expected from June to September; winter conditions from October to May. There are no restrictions

Map: OS Outdoor Leisure 38, Ben Nevis and Glen Coe

Start & Finish: Glencoe, the upper lay-by car park south of the pass (NN 171 569)

Access: Some 35km (22 miles) south of Fort William along the A82

Tourist Information: Ballachulish (tel. 01855 811296) and Fort William (tel. 01397 703781)

Accommodation: There are all types within Ballachulish and Glencoe: campsites in Glencoe and at Invercoe; the nearest Youth Hostel is in Glencoe

Geology: Typically the rock is rhyolite and andesite, reasonably rough and dependable though it can be slippery when wet/damp, and there are sections of loose scree (take care not to dislodge stones onto parties below)

Flora & Fauna: Golden eagle, raven and ptarmigan may be seen; also red deer. Drooping saxifrage, blaeberry, moss-campion and stag's horn moss grow in this region

Comment: In a sea of rugged mountains and great steeps, this is one of the most powerfully impressive outings in the British mountains. Despite its formidable appearance, the nose of Gearr Aonach, up the the Lost Valley face, is breached by an interlinking series of natural

The Tops

Gearr Aonach	692m (2,270ft)	(gear-oe-nokh = short ridge mountain)
Stob Coire nan Lochan	1,115m (3,657ft)	(stob kora nan loch-yn = peak of the corrie of the lochans)
Bidean nam Bian/Beann	1,150m (3,773ft)	(beed-yan nam by-own = head of the mountain peaks)
Stob Coire Sgreamhach	1,072m (3,517ft)	(stob kora screv-akh = peak of the menacing rock corrie)
Beinn Fhada South Top	952m (3,123ft)	(by-an at-a = long ridge mountain)
Beinn Fhada Central Top	931m (3,054ft)	
Beinn Fhada North Top	823m (2,700ft)	

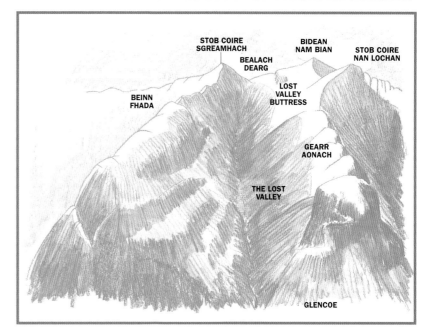

diagonal ledges, known as the Gearr Aonach Zig-Zags. These provide the key to its ascent, unlocking a masterly traverse of the high ridges encircling the Lost Valley.

■ Three rocky bastions dominate the south side of the Glencoe mountain pass. From the east they comprise Beinn Fhada, Gearr Aonach and Aonach Dubh, commonly known as the Three Sisters. Impressive as they are, in point of fact they are merely the gable end, so to speak, of three great

ridges which run to the highest mountain of the region, the mighty Bidean nan Bian. Gearr Aonach and Aonach Dubh join at the peak of Stob Coire nan Lochan before proceeding onwards and upwards. Beinn Fhada, below Stob Coire Sgreamhach, and Gear Aonach joined with Stob Coire nan Lochan leading directly to Bidean nam Bian, form the enclosing ridges, respectively east and west, of the Lost Valley (more properly called Coire Gabhail). This walk makes an anticlockwise circuit of the valley.

Set in the spiritual heartland of the magnificent Highlands of Scotland, this must surely be one of the best mountain ridge walks in the world. It has just the right balance between ease of movement and technical difficulty, between challenge and intimidation, exposure and danger, mountain grandeur and desolation, wildness and wilderness. Even though technical difficulties are reasonably low (two short, easy, Scrambling Grade 1 sections), it will

test your mountain mettle. It comprises a continuous circuit of high ridges where there is no room for error, very few places to make escape, and where a deterioration in conditions should be treated very seriously indeed.

Drop from the car park to the old road; bear left and follow this for only a little way before a constructed footpath leads down to the ravine. Cross the footbridge and follow the path, over the ladder stile, up into the Lost Valley. Keep climbing until you reach a little rocky knoll just above your route, then continue to a boulder where a lesser path scrambles up to the right. Soon it levels out and bears to the left. Keep along this for a short way until you are opposite the imposing nose of Gearr Aonach. Here a faint path rises directly up the hillside to the right. Follow this to the foot of the buttress.

To begin the Gearr Aonach Zig-Zags, climb diagonally to the left up the steep grassy ramp beneath the cliffs. Keep traversing beneath the rock

High above the Valley of Glencoe and marking the sensational start to the Lost Valley Horseshoe, the dominant rocky head of Gearr Aonach stands between the Lost Valley (Coire Gabhail) left and Coire nan Lochan right. The peaks of Stob Coire nan Lochan (right) and Stob Coire Sgreamhach (left) can be seen beyond with the ridge and three tops of Beinn Fhada forming the left-hand skyline

slabs and higher overhangs until you reach a little corner, formed by a blocky pinnacle; here there is a short rocky slab about 8m high, at the top of which is a long, narrow little cave beneath an overhang. On reaching the cave (Scrambling Grade 0.75), a rock shelf is suddenly revealed, traversing diagonally to the right: this unexpected natural phenomenon seems the work of some supernatural hand. It is quite level and of ample width, and provides easy going through the vertical rock steeps.

It gains the front of the nose – the car park is visible far below – where a slab leads up to the left into a little corner. Climb this (Scrambling Grade 1) to gain another broader terrace, of heather and rowan; this leads off diagonally to the left. Climb a short, slabby corner and continue along the terrace; as it begins to shelve, keep going left until you reach a series of rocky steps; up these (Scrambling Grade 0.5) and you will emerge onto a fan of scree. You may feel a sense of victory, but hold on – you aren't up yet! You will see that, a little lower to the right, the path continues to traverse diagonally right: follow it to regain the front nose of the buttress, at which point it is best to climb a little rock chimney leading up to the left (Scrambling Grade 0.75; the path that continues to the right is best avoided as it becomes very exposed). An easier, well defined path now leads to the summit knoll of Gearr Aonach. The mountain scenery is stunning, with great steeps on all sides.

Before beginning the traverse of the broad ridge beyond it is advisable to cast the eye over the end flanks of Beinn Fhada to the east and carefully pick out the line of descent – binoculars are useful here, if not essential (see the end of this walk for a detailed description). Descend to the col, then climb again to the next flat-topped rise. Continue along the broad spine, passing the little lochan to the left, and over another rise to gain the steeply curving ridge ascending Stob Coire nan Lochan. A strenuous haul follows. Keeping to the crest is most difficult (up to Scrambling Grade 1); however, the main path, though rough and blocky, bypasses all technical difficulties.

Stob Corie nan Lochan represents the merging of the Aonach Dubh and Gearr Aonach ridges, and is a wonderful vantage point. When you continue, an elegant ridge of grey, then salmon-pink rhyolite rocks descends southwards to the col. From here it

The view over Glencoe from halfway up the Gearr Aonach Zig-Zags

is an awkward, blocky ascent, but it finally eases; you will cross a flat shelf before the final pull to the slender cone summit of Bidean nam Bian. Quite justifiably known as the head of the peaks, this is the highest point in Argyll; from the depths of Glencoe the summit of this great mountain cannot be seen, nor its grandeur be truly envisaged. It offers a panoramic outlook over rank upon rank of mountains: the magnificent, unparalleled, Highlands and Islands of Scotland.

Tempting as it may be to linger, there is still a considerable distance to travel. The well defined path leads along the ridge and down to the domed head of the Lost Valley Buttress, then falls to the col of Bealach Dearg. Pleasant stony slopes above lead to the slender, elongated top of Stob Coire Sgreamhach; the summit cairn is found on its northern spur and it offers an uninterrupted view of the whole Lost Valley horseshoe. It is a good place to identify the three distinct tops of Beinn Fhada. (If anyone should find a pair of binoculars hereabouts, I would greatly appreciate their return; they are not very expensive, but they are of great sentimental value.)

Descend the narrow rocky crest, which is exposed though not difficult; nearing the col, the flying tower summit which is the south top of Beinn Fhada is now ahead and above. At a point some 25m above the col the rocks begin to steepen: this is the 'Bad Step' section. Climb down for some 12m (just about Scrambling Grade 1); it is then best to veer horizontally right (eastwards – do not continue straight down). Descend again (Scrambling Grade 0.5) to easy ground and traverse back left to the col.

Continue along the delightful, undulating, airy traverse of Beinn Fhada, over the tower of the South Top, to the next substantial tower-like knoll; this is the Central Top. Continue to descend to a cairned, flat, saddle-like col below, south of the cloven-hoof North Top. From this point it is possible, though steep, to descend (westwards) directly to the floor of the Lost Valley, keeping to the ground on the left (south) side of the gully; the most interesting way, however, is to complete the ridge of Beinn Fhada.

If the latter course is taken, the following points should be carefully noted: first, whilst there are no technical difficulties, precise route-finding is essential (see below) because bands of steep cliffs lie above and below the route described; second, at the time of writing there is no well blazoned trail, but only a

track fashioned by red deer and sheep; and third, there is scree and bouldery ground lying above steep cliffs and the exposed head of sheer gullies, and this must be traversed.

To complete the ridge walk, therefore, continue over the cleft of the North Top; you will reach a second, lesser cleft summit and a small lochan. There is a further knoll and tiny lochan en route to the cairned end of the ridge, which lies opposite the Zig-Zags of Gearr Aonach. The purpose of descending from here is to gain a natural shelf that slopes back towards the Lost Valley. It cannot be gained directly because cliffs lie below, therefore keep descending grassy slopes to the north; the tiny cottages of the Alt na reigh will now be in view by the side of the main road. You will come to a short, rock corridor gully around 25m in length, on your left (its location should be pin-pointed from Gearr Aonach whilst making the ascent). Do not attempt to descend this gully, but follow the nose for a further 30m until it is possible to swing left and traverse beneath its foot. Continue to descend diagonally to the left, over scree, towards the Lost Valley.

Keep left beneath the minor crags here, crossing a bouldery gully and streamlet, and keep going until it is possible to make a more direct descent down to a little grassy shoulder – take care, as there are cliffs immediately below. Traverse diagonally left, crossing the head of a gully, and continue to make your way down across grass and scree, crossing little streamlets below some slabby crags; keep going, diagonally and to the left across easy grass – eventually you will come to a broad, easy open gully, distinguished by a dark corner above. Follow the actual course of this down, keeping to its right for a little way, until you will see it is best to move back left and cross it.

Keep down the steep, easy grass to its left (south); as you approach the valley floor, you come to a water-polished rock slide – descend the left side of this to gain the main tourist path down the Lost Valley. Keep on the east side of the burn until rocky steps lead awkwardly down and it is possible to cross the boulders amidst the rowan trees. The high path on the left provides the most straightforward descent.

Looking east from Bidean nam Bian down over the Lost Valley Buttress to Stob Coire Sgreamhach and on over the Buachaille Etives Beag and Mor beyond

BUACHAILLE ETIVE MOR by CURVED RIDGE

The Curved Ridge beneath the Rannoch Wall, with views down the glen to Loch Etive

Fact Sheet

Location: Above Rannoch Moor (and the King's House Hotel) at the entrance to Glen Etive and Glencoe (A82), Argyll, the Central Highlands of Scotland

Length: 13km (8 miles)

Ascent: 1,100m (3,620ft)

Time: 7 hours

Difficulty: A strenuous and technical ascent of Buachaille Etive's north-east face by the Curved Ridge leads to a high mountain traverse. The Curved Ridge follows an impressive line beneath the great pink face of the Rannoch Wall, providing reasonably easy scrambling initially, then steepening at the top. A few rocky steps have to be climbed; individually these are perhaps no greater than 10m (30ft) high and with good ledges beneath, but there is no easier alternative; however, the climbing is of only moderate difficulty, and is short-lived (Scrambling Grade 3). Even so, this is a demanding mountain expedition in winter, and the Curved Ridge can be tough (Winter Grade II)

Seasons & Restrictions: Summer conditions may be expected from June to September; winter conditions from October to May. There are no restrictions

Map: OS Outdoor Leisure 38, Ben Nevis and Glen Coe

Start & Finish: Parking is by the buildings of Altnafeadh, by the side of the A82 (NN 221 563)

Access: Some 41km (25 miles) south of Fort William, and 21km (13 miles) north of the Bridge of Orchy along the A82

Tourist Information: Ballachulish (tel. 01855 811296) and Fort William (tel. 01397 703781)

Accommodation: The nearby Kingshouse Inn provides a variety of accommodation including full hotel, self-catering, bunkhouse and camping; it also does bar meals, restaurant. There are all types of accommodation within Ballachulish and Glencoe, also campsites in Glencoe and at Invercoe; the nearest Youth Hostel is in Glencoe

Geology: The predominant rock is rhyolite, which is reasonably rough and dependable although it can be slippery when wet/damp, and there are sections of loose scree (take care not to dislodge stones onto parties below)

Flora & Fauna: Golden eagle, raven and ptarmigan may

The Tops

Buachaille Etive Mor/Buachaille Eite Mor

(boo-kel etiv moar/boo-uc-heel-ya ay-tya moar = great shepherd of etive)

Stob Dearg	1,022m (3,353ft)	(stob jerrak = red peak)
Stob na Doire	1,011m (3,316ft)	(stop na dur-ra = peak of the copse)
Stob Coire Altruim	941m (3,087ft)	(stop kora al-trim = peak of nursing)
Stob na Broige	956m (3,136ft)	(stop na braw-ika = peak of the shoe)

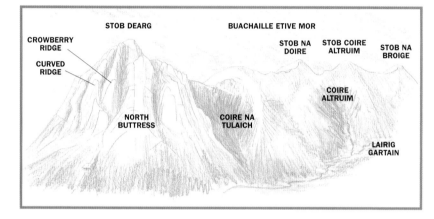

be seen; also red deer. Purple saxifrage, crowberry, blaeberry and heather grow in this region

Comment: The north-east face of Buachaille Etive Mor, going by the Curved Ridge and the long (4½km/3 mile) traverse of the summit ridge, offers an oustanding ridge walk; its attraction is immediately obvious to anyone driving north along the A82. It should be carefully noted, however, that the route described requires basic rock-climbing ability, and is for the technically competent only. In winter conditions it becomes a fully fledged mountaineering expedition.

Climbing Curved Ridge

■ Guarding the entrances to Glen Etive and Glencoe, a great pyramid of red/pink rhyolite rises for some 2,500ft from the purple heathers and vast empty expanse of Rannoch Moor. The 'Great Shepherd' – or more properly, 'Herdsman' – of Etive, Buachaille Etive Mor, is one of Britain's most evocative mountains: to climb it by the Curved Ridge, then continuing along its sinuous summit

Facing the expanse of Rannoch Moor, guarding the valleys of Glen Etive and Glencoe, the Buachaille Etive Mor – the great shepherd of Etive – is one of the most evocative mountains in the whole of the Scottish Highlands

ridge high betwixt lovely Glen Etive and the lonely mountain pass of the Lairig Gartain, is surely the stuff that dreams are made of!

The track leads to a footbridge crossing the River Coupall. Pass the buildings of Lagangarbh and continue upwards towards Coire na Tulaich – though don't go too high: the path divides, and you should follow the left fork. The route is well defined, and leads to a leftward (eastern) traverse beneath the flanks of the mountain. Keep rounding the mountain until you pass beneath the great Water Slide Slab; the path then begins to rise steeply until it reaches an easy rock barrier. Pick your way up this – it is easiest to the right – then, with Great Gully soaring above (it is named thus on the OS map, though climbers know it as Crowberry Gully) traverse left; this will bring you to the ridge to the left of another diagonal rock gully. You are now about to start the ascent of the Curved Ridge; the gully to its right separates it

from a sheer red wall, the Rannoch Wall so well loved by rock climbers (the right end of this wall forms a very steep ridge known as Crowberry Ridge, which is also named on the OS map).

It is just moderate scrambling up the ridge, with impressive views all round; near the top, however, where it curves left beyond the gaze of Rannoch Wall, it steepens, and a number of little rock wall/steps necessitate some basic rock climbing. Even so, the way is well scratched by crampon marks, there are good ledges, and the rock is wonderfully clean and sound; moreover you soon reach easy ground. Make your way up a broad, bouldery scree gully, passing Crowberry Tower and the top of Crowberry Gully, then climb up and left to the top of Stob Dearg.

The most demanding section of this round is now complete, but the topmost spine of Buachaille Etive Mor is a wonderful ridge walk of some length. First the route drops down to the col of

Coire na Tulaich, where escape can be made directly down to Lagangarbh, then it climbs the slight rise to an unnamed top (height 902m – is this the Tulaich, meaning knoll?). A steep, zigzag path to the south-west descends to the col by Feadan Ban (white chanter), then climbs in a long curve around Coire Cloiche Finne to Stob na Doire. Descending in a south-westerly direction again, it reaches the col above Coire Altruim – but you must return in order to make your descent. Cross over to a level shoulder above Coire na Doire, then cross back in a north-westerly direction to the top of Stob Coire Altruim. Gradual descent leads out along the summit ridge until finally you begin to ascend again to reach the most south-westerly top, of Stob na Broige. The reward is an exceptional view down Glen Etive.

Return to the col above Coire Altruim and descend (north) by the burn of Allt Coire Altruim to cross the River Coupall; here you will join the Lairig Gartain path. Bear right along this, and follow it back to the A82 by the quarry car park (where mobile teas are sometimes available).

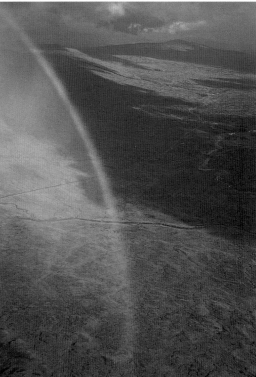

Commencing the climb up Curved Ridge; airy open scrambling heightens to a fine crescendo near the top

Rainbow seen from Curved Ridge with the vast openness of Rannoch Moor stretching beyond

THE AONACH EAGACH RIDGE

Exhilarating scrambling with tremendous exposure, the classic ridge of Glencoe

Fact Sheet

Location: The north side of Glencoe (A82), Argyll, the Central Highlands of Scotland

Length: 7km (4⅓ miles)

Ascent: 1,125m (3,690ft)

Time: 6 hours

Difficulty: The jagged north skyline of Glencoe provides a fine challenge. Horizontally from Am Bodach to Sgorr nam Fiannaidh the distance traversed is some 3km (2 miles), and it must be stressed that there is NO SAFE DESCENT FROM THE RIDGE between these points. The traverse is best tackled from east to west, and the difficulties begin with the descent of Am Bodach (Scrambling Grade 1). Thereafter it is The Pinnacles section, between Meall Dearg and Stob Coire Leith, which provides the main area of interest. Here, problems come thick and fast, and there are numerous short scrambling sections with not inconsiderable exposure in places; the hardest is the very last pinnacle, at Scrambling Grade 2. In winter conditions this walk becomes a mountaineering expedition, of Winter Grade I/II severity. The descent west of Clachaig Gully is steep and demanding, with exposed sections of scrambling which, although technically easy, should still be tackled with considerable care

Seasons & Restrictions: Summer conditions may be expected from June to September, and winter conditions from October to May. There are no restrictions

Map: OS Outdoor Leisure 38, Ben Nevis and Glen Coe

Start: From the small lay-by car park on the north side of the A82, below the cottages of the Alt na reigh (NN 173 567)

Finish: At Clachaig Inn (NN 128 567)

Access: Some 35km (22 miles) south of Fort William, and 21km (13 miles) north of the Bridge of Orchy along the A82

Tourist Information: Ballachulish (tel. 01855 811296) and Fort William (tel. 01397 703781)

Accommodation: There are all types within Ballachulish and Glencoe, including campsites in Glencoe and at Invercoe; the nearest Youth Hostel is in Glencoe. The Clachaig Inn has a variety of accommodation, from hotel to self-catering chalet, and it does bar meals

The Tops

Aonach Eagach		(oe-nokh ee-gokh = the notched ridge)
Am Bodach	943m (3,085ft)	(am bo-tokh = the old man)
Meall Dearg	953m (3,127ft)	(me-owl jerrak = the red hill)
Stob Coire Leith	940m (3,088ft)	(stob kora lay = peak of the grey corrie)
Sgorr nam Fiannaidh		
	967m (3,173ft)	(skor nam fee-a-nee = the peak of the fair-haired warriors)

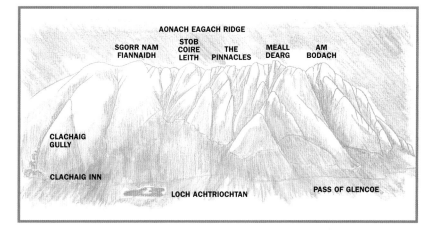

Geology: The rock is rhyolite, except for the shoulder below the last peak of Sgorr nam Fiannaidh which is quartzite; it is reasonably rough and dependable, though it can be slippery when it is wet/damp. There are sections of loose scree, particularly by the side of the Clachaig Gully (so take care not to dislodge any stones onto parties below)

Flora & Fauna: Raven and stonechat may be seen. Yellow saxifrage, crowberry, rowan and autumnal hawkbit grow in this area; the red fox and the mountain hare are shy inhabitants

Comment: A compelling, classic outing that fully lives up to its reputation for excellence. It is best tackled as a linear trip, from east to west. If an additional car or a lift cannot be organised at the Clachaig Inn, it is usually easy to hitch a ride back up the glen. Extra time should be allowed in case you come up against other parties on The Pinnacles – there isn't much room for overtaking, and this may slow you up.

Viewed from the shadows of Glencoe, a winter sun illuminates the Aonach Eagach Ridge

■ Glencoe was created when the great ice cap flowed inexorably down from Rannoch Moor, carving an uncompromising line through ancient volcano and on to the sea. It is truly a most magnificent valley: incomparably intense, intimidating yet intriguing, of savage grandeur and spectacular rock architecture, it is one of the most hallowed of mountain sanctuaries. The south flank, sometimes seeming perpetually dark, is comprised of the Three Sisters – Beinn Fhada, Gearr Aonach and Aonach Dubh; to the north, kissed by the sun, is a towering, jagged rock edge held aloft by unassailable steeps – the Aonach Eagach Ridge.

For many hillwalkers, Glencoe *means* the Aonach Eagach: it is the touchstone Scottish ridge walk, the classic outing which sets the standard by which most others are judged. If you have the ability, pick the weather, and take care: the Aonach Eagach should not be missed. (The fact that it ends by the doors of the Clachaig Inn is merely coincidental and adds hardly anything to my enthusiasm …)

From the roadside car park a well blazoned path leads up the hillside, then tracks diagonally to the right to climb the grassy ridge to the left of the Allt Ruigh. On reaching a little buttress, the path splits: the most interesting approach is to bear left, and in steep, zigzagging ascent, pick the easiest line up through the broken rocky buttresses (Scrambling Grade 0.5). Soon the angle relents, and the route leads directly to the first summit: Am Bodach.

The path heads west to a small, horizontal platform, then suddenly seems to drop into space; this is the first difficult bit, involving a rock climb of Scrambling Grade 1. Start by moving right – the descent is steep, though with good holds and plentiful little ledges eventually; towards the bottom the best route is to spiral left and then back right to gain the crest of the ridge below. An old iron fence-post provides a useful final handhold. Interestingly, remnants of this old boundary can be found along most of the length of the ridge. The well defined path along the undulating crest leads with interest, though without difficulty, along and up the summit of Meall Dearg.

The next section, leading eventually to Stob Coire Leith, is known as The Pinnacles and constitutes the crux of the traverse. It is exposed,

in places acutely so, and sustained, in that there are frequent sections of unavoidable scrambling (Scrambling Grade 2). The way is well worn, linear, and on the whole follows the crest – route-finding is straightforward, certainly in summer conditions. Nevertheless I feel it is worthwhile highlighting the key features. Thus, following the initial descent ridge from Meall Dearg, there are three distinct tops: from east to west these are the Long Pinnacle, which includes a long grassy section; the Middle Pinnacle, consisting of two pronounced knolls; and finally the tallest of them all, the Great Pinnacle. Within each of these separate areas there is a multitude of problematical features and pinnacles.

The ascent of the Long Pinnacle begins by way of a deep chimney rift. Beyond this, a little slabby corner steps up and round to the left; it marks the start of the Middle Pinnacle. In climbing the Great Pinnacle you will have to negotiate two small rock towers before you tackle the steep rock ascent of the crest itself (easier ways to the right of the crest can be found); technically this is the hardest section so far. The descent of the Great Pinnacle is tricky; it leads to a fine, broad rock tower lying astride the crest and which is climbed by a chimney crack just left of centre. The route beyond this goes from a deep notch to one further tower: a difficult start, possibly technically the hardest section of all, leads to easier climbing above.

A short traverse leads to the ascent of Stob Coire Leith, steep and strenuous, though technically easy. Once achieved, the way forward

Looking east back to Am Bodach – whose descent provides the first tricky section

Looking west to Stob Coire Leith (right) and the distant Sgorr nam Fiannaidh (left) from the broad rock tower encountered beyond the Great Pinnacle

along the gently curving ridge to the last top, Sgorr nam Fiannaidh, is very pleasant. From the summit, views which have previously been extensive to the north, over the Mammores to mighty Ben Nevis, now range over the sea to Ardgour, Garbh Bheinn and the west.

Head west down the narrowing shoulder of white/grey quartzite boulder scree; bear left before the next cairned top on the crest (don't go too far), on a well defined, rocky path which heads south directly for the top of the Clachaig Gully. Pass over the top of the gully and follow down its right flank. Extreme care should be exercised, for the walls of this deep rock gully are precipitous and the path is very exposed, actually touching the edge of the gully in places. The descent is steep and strenuous, made awkward by sections of bouldery scree and outcrops of slabby rock which necessitate easy scrambling. Directly below, the Clachaig Inn beckons: make sure you reach it!

HIGH RIDGES around THE MAMORES – THE COIRE a' MHAIL HORSESHOE

Himalayan Glen Nevis, the wire rope bridge, the 300ft waterfall of An Steall, the ridge of Sron Coire nan Cnamh leading to east ridge of Sgurr a' Mhaim, the Devil's Ridge

Fact Sheet

Location: The Mamores, head of Glen Nevis, above Fort William, the Central Highlands of Scotland

Length: 14km (8¾ miles)

Ascent: 1,700m (5,570ft)

Time: 8.5 hours

Difficulty: Despite what you may read elsewhere, the crags around the An Steall waterfall which guards the entrance to the Coire a' Mhail, are both precipitous, difficult and dangerous, and there have been serious accidents here. THERE IS NO STRAIGHTFORWARD, EASY WAY TO REACH DIRECTLY THE FLOOR OF COIRE A' MHAIL FROM THE BASE OF AN STEALL WATERFALL. The way described is the most straightforward: it ascends to the right (west) side of the waterfall (Scrambling Grade 1), and allows a link across to the east ridge (Sron Coire nan Cnamh) of Sgurr a' Mhaim (Scrambling Grade 0.5). It is strongly recommended that this route is only attempted in ascent (so that you can see the route ahead) – that is to say, THE HORSESHOE SHOULD ONLY BE TACKLED IN AN ANTICLOCKWISE DIRECTION. The Devil's Ridge provides plenty of exposure, though only very mild scrambling, over a shallow dip and a couple of gaps on either side of a small pinnacle (Scrambling Grade 1). The route along the knife-edged crest between An Garbhanach and An Gearanach involves some pleasant scrambling, with the most difficult section descending north from the former (Scrambling Grade 1). On the whole, however, the route offers straightforward hillwalking with good going, with only a few sections of strenuous ascent. Nevertheless it is a mountaineering expedition in winter (Winter Grade I)

Seasons & Restrictions: Summer conditions may be expected from June to September, and winter conditions from October to May. Stalking may be in progress between September and October: contact West Highlands Estates (tel. 01397 702433)

Map: OS Outdoor Leisure 38, Ben Nevis and Glen Coe or Harveys Superwalker Ben Nevis

Start & Finish: From the small car park at the head of Glen Nevis (NN 167 691)

Access: Some 35km (22 miles) south of Fort William, and

The Tops

The Mamores/mam mor		(big breast-shaped hills)
Sgurr a' Mhaim	1,099m (3,606ft)	(skoor a vaa-eem = peak of the great breast)
Stob Coire a' Mhail	992m (3,250ft)	(stob kora a vaa-il = peak of the barrier corrie)
Sgor an Iubhair	1,001m (3284ft)	(skor an yoo-ar = peak of the yew tree)
Am Bodach	1,032m (3,386ft)	(am bo-tokh = the old man)
Stob Coire a' Chairn	981m (3,218ft)	(stob kora a chairn = peak of the corrie of cairns)
An Garbhanach	975m (3,199ft)	(an ga-ravan-okh = the rough one)
An Gearanach	982m (3,222ft)	(an gear-oe-nokh = top of the short ridge)

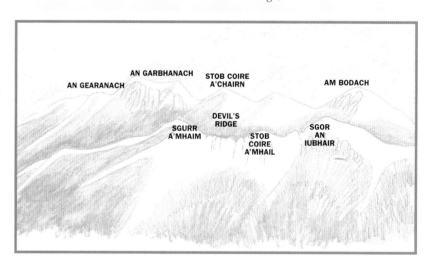

21km (13 miles) north of the Bridge of Orchy along the A82

Tourist Information: Fort William (tel. 01397 703781); also the Countryside Ranger Visitor Centre in Glen Nevis (tel. 01397 705922)

Accommodation: There are all facilities at Fort William; campsites and a Youth Hostel may be found in Glen Nevis

Geology: The rocks which predominate on this walk are mica schist and rugged quartzite, both of which can be particularly slippery when wet

Flora & Fauna: Golden eagle, raven, ptarmigan and dipper

Steall Wire Bridge – an adventure in itself

The scene over the head of the horseshoe from Am Bodach looking to Sgor an Iubhair with Stob Coire a' Mhail to its right

may be seen, also red deer and badger. Blue hyacinth, rowan, silver birch, dwarf oak and Scots pine are typical of this region

Comment: This walk has seven tops of over 900m (3,000ft), including the second-highest summit of the whole group; it has four sections of reasonably easy scrambling, and it has a great position – all things considered, it provides an interesting and adventurous way to explore the special charm and outstanding beauty of The Mamores.

■ At the head of Glen Nevis the flanks of the valley narrow to become a deep ravine, with plunging steeps and roaring waters. The angular crags of the gorge are bedecked whimsically with Scots pine, the dark chocolate rock unexpectedly flashes silver in the sunlight, and the lesser slopes are cloaked with the luxuriant green of rowan, silver birch, dwarf oak, bracken and fern. Even in bright sunshine it portrays an evocative, almost mystical feeling, and this feeling is considerably enhanced once you pass beyond its portals, because suddenly it opens up to reveal a veritable Shangri-la: a wide, flat-bottomed valley of mellow greensward and hanging, vertical sides, complete with a huge waterfall which tumbles from the permanent snow whiteness of The Mamores above.

Such is the overpowering atmosphere of this place, you might think you were approaching the high Himalaya. It isn't, of course, because the silver is mica and the whiteness is quartzite, and the Mamores can be traversed quite easily in a day without the use of either sherpas or oxygen. Overlooked by Ben Nevis, and rising from Kinlochleven with the mountains of Glencoe beyond, Loch Linnhe to the west, and the wilderness of Rannoch Moor to the east, The Mamores are hills of serene character.

This anticlockwise outing takes the high ridge-line around Coire a' Mhail. It starts within earshot of the roar of An Steall waterfall, and includes four challenging sections: gaining and crossing the north-east ridge of Sgurr a' Mhaim; the east ridge of Sgurr a' Mhaim (Sron Coire nan Cnamh); the Devil's Ridge; and the An Garbhanach ridge. Leave the car park and follow the path through the trees, below the cliffs and above the ravine, until the latter opens to a reveal a flat green valley; ahead can be seen the white cascade of the great An Steall waterfall, a drop over steep slabs of some 100m. As you near the waterfall, before the bend in the Water of Nevis, a steel rope bridge can be seen crossing the river: this is an adventure in itself! The path leads to the Steall

*Left: Beyond Devil's Ridge
with Sgurr a' Mhaim
behind*

*Far right: On the
pyramidal summit of Am
Bodach*

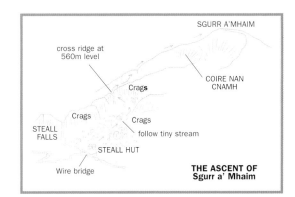

cross ridge at
560m level

SGURR A'MHAIM

COIRE NAN
CNAMH

Crag**s**

Crags

STEALL
FALLS

Crags

follow tiny stream

STEALL HUT

Wire bridge

**THE ASCENT OF
Sgurr a' Mhaim**

Cottage, the corrugated, zinc-roofed Lochaber
Mountaineering Club hut. From the hut, head south-
westwards (right), then west following the line of the
stream, clambering up the hillside to a point where
the stream enters a broad depression. At around the
400m contour, and with the rock knoll of Creag nan
Eun standing above to the right, bear hard left: this is
so you can traverse up and across a little hanging
basin beneath the crest of Sgurr a' Mhaim's north-east
ridge. Pick the easiest line, making your way over
the rocky slabs, until it is possible to move up and
out to the left to gain a flat shoulder on the ridge
(map ref. NN 1763 6798) at an altitude of 560m.

Go round the ridge and down a little way, to the
source of a small stream; continue to cross the base
of Coire nan Cnamh, passing the lochan. The
amazing folds in the quartzite cliffs above are like
bare ribs, and give rise to the corrie's name: the
corrie of bones. Cross to follow the line of Sgurr a'
Mhaim's east ridge, the lower section of which is
called Sron Coire nan Cnamh, meaning 'the nose of
the corrie of bare bones'; this follows a sensuous line,
snaking to the very summit of Sgurr a' Mhaim. It is
technically easy until one minor rib provides an
exposed move (the 'Bad Step'); soon after this it
peaks and flattens at a col, and is crossed by a
wonderfully engineered stalker's path. Continue up
the crest to the crunchy, granular, sugar-white
quartzite summit rocks of Sgurr a' Mhaim, the
second highest Mamore.

Descend to the south; now comes the Devil's
Ridge (unnamed on the OS map), which is crossed
by a little notch called Bealach a Chip. Despite its
fearful name, it proves to be a straightforward
traverse of a narrow rock crest, with the exception of
a recessed pinnacle which can be passed to the side.
The next top is Stob Coire a' Mhail; this is followed

by a further delightful airy ridge, at the end of which
another zig-zag ascent leads to Sgor an Iubhair (both
these tops are unnamed on the 1998 OS map). A
straightforward, westward-curving traverse leads
around the head of Coire a' Mhail and up onto the
pyramidal summit of Am Bodach.

From here the descent is very steep and a little
difficult: first it plunges to the col, then there is an
easy walk over a small, unnamed top, before it falls
and rises again to Stob Coire a' Chairn. Descend to
the Bealach Chadha Riabhaich, then climb the steep
ascent to the slender rocky cockscomb of An
Garbhanach. The next crest is exhilaratingly
exposed, initially steep and rocky and requiring care
in descent, before easier going leads to the final top
of An Gearanach. This is an excellent vantage point
from which to admire the fruits of your labour: the
complete horseshoe of Coire a' Mhail thus described
is a tremendous feather in anyone's cap!

It isn't over yet, however. Descend the nose in a
northerly direction, until the angle slackens for a
short way, and on down, until at the 830m contour
the path bears off hard right (east); DON'T GO
STRAIGHT DOWN BECAUSE STEEP GROUND
LIES BELOW, but follow the path. The descent into
Coire Chadha Chaoruinn is straightforward, and you
can zig-zag down to the floor of Glen Nevis. Bear left
and cross beneath the great waterfall of An Steall.
The wire bridge awaits.

BEN NEVIS by CARN MOR DEARG ARÊTE – the HORSESHOE of the GREAT NORTHERN CORRIE

Exposed arête, summit shelter, a ruined observatory, and the highest mountain in Britain

Fact Sheet

Location: Fort William (A82), the Central Highlands of Scotland

Length: 17km (10½ miles)

Ascent: 1,420m (4,600ft)

Time: 9 hours

Difficulty: Whilst there is no great technical difficulty, the Carn Mor Dearg Arete is exposed and a little scrambly (Scrambling Grade 0.3), and the going is particularly arduous throughout. Peat bog and heather will be found by the side of the Allt a' Mhuilinn, and on the higher ground rough, stony, bouldery ground predominates. Ben Nevis is the highest mountain in Britain, so conditions and weather can be extreme and may change very quickly. In poor visibility precise navigation on the summit plateau is essential, because to the north vertical cliffs plunge 650m directly from the rim, and to the south many hazards await. Never underestimate this mountain: benign and smiling, Ben Nevis can become 'Big Bad Ben' in the wink of an eye

Seasons & Restrictions: Summer conditions may be expected from June to August, and winter conditions from September to May. There are no restrictions

Map: OS Outdoor Leisure 38, Ben Nevis and Glen Coe

Start: From the Allt a' Mhuilin (North Face) car park in the forest above Torlundy (NN 145 764)

Access: Some 5km (3 miles) north-east of Fort William along the A82, turn right (east) at Torlundy and continue through the buildings to cross the bridge over the railway (there are traffic lights). Turn immediately right, and continue down the forestry lane; the car park is on the left

Tourist Information: Fort William (tel. 01397 703781); also the Countryside Ranger Visitor Centre in Glen Nevis (tel. 01397 705922)

Accommodation: All facilities will be found at Fort William, including a campsite; there are further campsites and a Youth Hostel in Glen Nevis

Geology: Red granites and dark andesite are predominant in this area; for walking, friction is good and the rocks sound and dependable

The Tops

Carn Beag Dearg	1,010m (3,314ft)	(kaarn bayk jerrak = smaller red conical hill)
Carn Dearg Meadhonach	1,179m (3,870ft)	(kaarn jerrak mee-a-nakh = middle red conical hill)
Carn Mor Dearg	1,223m (4,012ft)	(kaarn moar jerrak = bigger red conical hill)
Ben Nevis/ Beinn Nibheis	1,344m (4,409ft)	(ben nevis/by-an nee-vash = venomous mountain)

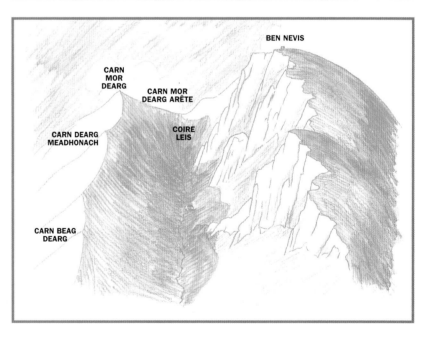

Flora & Fauna: Raven and snow bunting may be seen, also adder, stoat and mountain hare. Many saxifrages will be found in this region – alpine, yellow, starry and purple – also moss campion, starwort mouse-ear and alpine lady's mantle

Comment: The finest view of the great north face of Ben Nevis is from the higher ground of the approach; it is also the most interesting hillwalking route to the summit of the mountain. A new car park has recently been provided, no doubt in an attempt to accommodate the increasing

Camping below the raised summit shelter – in a hard winter this can be buried under the snow

The huge, impressive North Face of Ben Nevis plunges directly from the summit plateau; traversing the Carn Deargs provides an opportunity to inspect its intricacies in safety

volume of hillwalkers and climbers now taking this route to the northern face of Ben Nevis (as opposed to the so-called 'tourist route' from Glen Nevis). However, it has not really helped solve the problem, because the approach path that follows the bank of the Allt a' Mhuilin burn is, at the time of writing, in a terribly boggy and eroded state. A privileged few have the key to the forestry gate and can drive to a parking space above the initial section of path. But considering that this is Britain's principal mountain both for walking and climbing, the situation is less than satisfactory.

■ Unless you actually climb the great northern precipices of the mountain – and that option is for experts only – there is no better route than the one described here from which to view, or begin to understand, something of the sheer size and formidable character of Ben Nevis. Rising by the Allt a' Mhuilin, the impressive ridge climbs in a great horseshoe around the rim of the huge glaciated basin, the great north corrie, scooped between the

forbiddingly black north face of Ben Nevis and the high, broad red shoulder of the Carn Deargs. Gentle at first, the stony back of the Deargs sharpens until it becomes the wonderful, rocky knife-edge of Carn Mor Dearg Arête, that curves in a graceful, aesthetic line around the head of the corrie (Coire Leis) to connect with the southern shoulder of Ben Nevis. Thereafter the climb is a steep, slogging ascent – but your reward is finally to have gained the highest summit in Britain.

Continue along the track from the car park, and cross the bridge over the Allt na Caillich; you will come to a right-angled bend. From here go right, cutting across the corner of the golf course, and pick up the 'Old Puggy Track' – the line of an abandoned mineral railway. Bear right along this to intercept the path rising directly from the golf course along by the wire fence: this is a veritable mud bath. Things improve, however; soon you will pass a track and a level car park (gained by a rough forestry track, accessible only for those with a key). With the

Allt a' Mhuilin to the right, continue on the path rising into the great north corrie; you will just have to pick the best line you can through the peat bogs. As the bouldery slopes of the Deargs begin to beckon on the left, swing up the hillside to Carn Beag Dearg; the going is rough.

Traverse the high shoulder, first to Carn Dearg Meadhonach, and then to Carn Mor Dearg – at over 4,000ft this is Britain's seventh highest mountain – before descending to the delectable knife-edge of the Carn Mor Dearg Arête. It is exposed, and the going is a little bouldery and awkward; however, there are are no real technical difficulties. In winter conditions large cornices can build here (and of course overhang the north face of Ben Nevis) and extreme care is required; in thaw or unstable snow conditions, stay away. Now, you will climb a minor shoulder, then the gradient steepens as finally you approach the summit plateau of Ben Nevis. (The way was once marked out by intermittent poles, but at the time of writing these were the subject of some controversy and have been removed.)

On the summit of Ben Nevis a cluster of old walls and cairns marks the site of the observatory, which was used between 1883 and 1904, and that of a hotel which ceased trading a little later. In addition to the trig point and summit cairn there is also a strange corrugated shelter, somewhat crazily

elevated above the bare rocks; such is the hostility of the climate that sometimes even this gets buried in winter. Best of all, of course, is the view: a sea of mountains in all directions. Sometimes people have a strong compulsion to peer over the northern rim down and across the impressive cliffs of the north face. Have a care, however, because great cornices build here, lingering well into the summer months, and overhanging the steeps below by some considerable distance; under the right conditions, they do collapse.

Heading west along the summit plateau, the path skirts above the heads of a number of deep gullies that cut in from the depths to the right. Take care along all this section, really until you come to the zigzags which follow the declivity around the Red Burn watershed, then lead down the western flank of the mountain. In descent, don't go too far left (south): there have been many accidents in poor visibility, with parties by default attempting to descend the notorious Five Finger Gully. Take the path that leads off to the right, and crosses above the waters of Lochan Meall an t-Suidhe; continue until you round the corner of the mountain, above the Allt a' Mhuilinn, where the shortest route home is to quit the path and descend directly to the burn. Cross it as best as possible – and good luck through the peat bogs!

Carn Dearg Meadhonach and Carn Mor from Ben Nevis; the mountaineer in the foreground is standing at the top of the North East Ridge on the edge of the summit plateau

Ben Nevis summit plateau; overhanging the North Face considerable snow cornices can linger long into the summer months. Here we are looking west, over the head of Tower Gully, from near the summit trig point

THE SADDLE OF GLENSHIEL by the FORCAN RIDGE continuing by THE CIRQUE OF COIRE UAINE

An exposed and challenging steep ridge scramble, the three saddles of The Saddle, and a pristinely elegant skyline above a lonely corrie

Fact Sheet

Location: Above the west side of Glen Shiel (A87), the western Highlands of Scotland

Length: 15km (9⅓ miles)

Ascent: 1,365m (4,480ft)

Time: 9 hours

Difficulty: The Forcan Ridge is a magnificent rocky scramble of considerable exposure and interest; climbed directly it is Scrambling Grade 2; however, by choosing the easiest line it can be done at Scrambling Grade 1. The high ridge that curves round Coire Uaine provides no technical difficulties, although it is undulating and of some length (it can be made shorter and easier by using a stalker's path)

Seasons & Restrictions: Summer conditions may be expected from May to September; winter conditions from October to April. The visitor may expect deer stalking to be in progress between 11 August and 20 October: for information, tel. 01599 511282

Map: OS Landranger 33, Loch Alsh, Glen Shiel

Start: From the lay-by on the north side of the A87 some 1km (⅔ mile) south-east of the old quarrry (NG 968 144)

Finish: At Sheil Bridge; there is parking on the old road by the campsite (NG 938 187)

Access: Some 30km (19 miles) south-east of the Kyle of Lochalsh along the A87, and some 85km (53 miles) north-west of Fort William along the A82 and A87

Tourist Information: The Kyle of Lochalsh (tel. 01599 534276); also Fort William (tel. 01397 703781)

Accommodation: There is a reasonable selection of places to stay, and a campsite at Glen Shiel Bridge; there is also a Youth Hostel at nearby Ratagan

Geology: The lower rocks are of mica schist – they are solid and offer sharp-edged flake holds, though they become slippery when they are wet. Higher and beyond, the rocks are of grey gneiss banded by quartz and pegmatites, and these are rough and solid, a delight to walk or scramble over

The Tops

Meallan Odhar	615m (2,018ft)	(my-owl-an oa-ur = brown hill)
Sgurr nan Forcan	958m (3,143ft)	(skoor nan forr-acan = little fork peak)
The Saddle/Sgor na Diollard (trig point)	1,010m (3,314ft)	(skor na dioll-aih = peak of the saddles)
Spidean Dhomhnuill Bhric	940m (3,084ft)	(speed-yan ghaw-il brie = peak of Spotted Donald's high ground)
Sgurr Leac nan Each	919m (3,015ft)	(skoor ly-ekh na ee-akh = peak of the slab of the horses)
Sgurr a' Gharg Gharaidh	683m (2,241ft)	(skoor a garav gaa-ra = rough roaring peaks)

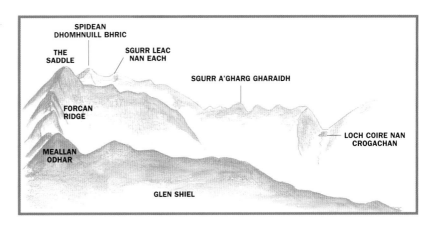

Flora & Fauna: Golden eagle, raven and ptarmigan may be seen, also red deer and weasel. Mountain avens, rowan and alder grow in this region

Comment: In an area which is unsurpassed for the quality of its ridge walks, this is the most challenging and aesthetic of them all. Until the OS information is updated to 1:25,000 scale with modern technology, all the spot heights given here should be taken with a pinch of salt. For the route as described you need to be dropped off at the start and met at the end, or you need two vehicles. Alternatively you can always walk the 6km back up the road – I did, and it took me an hour.

■ Heading west on the 'Road to the Isles', before you reach Loch Duich and the famous island castle of Eilean Donnan, before the Kyle of Lochalsh and the magical Island of Skye, you will come to Glen Shiel. It divides two sublime areas of mountains, both famed for their outstanding ridge walks: to the south Glenshiel, and to the north those of Kintail and its famous Five Sisters. The outing described here lies within the Glenshiel group and is considered by many to be the most challenging and rewarding ridge walk of the region: to climb the steep, slender, rocky nose of the Forcan Ridge, to cross the (apparent) twin peaks of The Saddle, and finally to traverse the peaks skirting the sharp-rimmed basin of Coire Uaine – this is a truly glorious expedition.

Driving west down the A87 the most breathtaking sight of all is undoubtedly the twin peaks and connecting saddle of Sgor na Diollard, The Saddle. However, such is the intricate complexity of this area that it is difficult to match the OS Landranger (1:50,000 scale) map with ground detail; therefore, in order that the reader and potential walker has a clear idea of the features as they actually appear, I think it is worth describing here in detail the summit area of The Saddle.

In actual fact there are three saddles – that is, three concave connecting ridges between peaks. The one seen from the A87 joins the pyramidal independent rocky top of Sgurr nan Forcan (left) and the Saddle East Top (right), with a rocky crest falling to the right to Sgurr na Creige. On the walk you will find that the next pronounced saddle lies between the Saddle East Top and the Saddle West Top (unseen from the road). To complicate things even further, the trig point, a circular column, will be found on a saddle (not so obvious) ridge of high ground connecting the West Top and the Far West Top (which overlooks Coire Uaine) – for convenience we will call the top with the trig point, the Saddle Middle Top! Sadly for those who rely on the order and statistics of Munro tables, the Saddle Middle Top does not appear to be the highest point. Not to worry, The Saddle remains a magnificent mountain.

Following the well worn path along the south

Two figures standing on the Saddle East Top with the fine edged ascent ridge sweeping (rightwards) down to the pointed top of Sgurr nan Forcan. Beyond and far below lies the upper section of Glen Shiel

Approaching The Saddle trig point over the apparently higher Saddle West Top

verge, head east up the road from the lay-by until a path branches right to a gate; beyond this a superb stalker's path zig-zags upwards, then bears to the right to gain the col between Meallan Odhar (left) and Biod an Fhithich (right). The vista before you is truly breathtaking, from the forbidding Sgurr nan Forcan over the shapely East Top of The Saddle, falling to the right towards Sgurr na Creigh (known locally as Sgurr Nid na h-Iolaire, 'the peak of the eagle's nest'). It is now an easy climb left to top the shoulder of Meallan Odhar; then continue to the foot of the ever-steepening Forcan Ridge. A path here continues to the left of the nose; it is lined by boulders and appears to be of ancient origin.

A well defined path ascends the grassy nose, passing a slab of Scrambling Grade 0.5, then reaching a short rock corner. This is awkward when wet (Scrambling Grade 2), but it can be passed more easily up rock to the left. The initial section is quite flat, a convenient shoulder from which to admire the impressive nose of naked rock rising above: the 'meat' of the Forcan Ridge. A knife-edged ridge curves round to the base of the nose; to get onto it you must first tackle some smooth, exposed sections of slab. After this the ridge is broken into convenient little ledges, and as a general rule the easiest way up these is to be found on the right-hand side. However, the crest is most interesting if tackled directly, the hardest sections being the one half way, where the route skirts round a protruding block, and the other near the top where the crest is again quite blocky.

The very top of Sgurr nan Forcan provides an airy perch, and with the connecting ridge to the East Top of The Saddle now in front, most will continue without lingering. First, however, a steep and difficult descent of around 18m must be made to a little col. Taken directly, down well worn, steep, slabby rock (it looks much worse than it is), it is about Scrambling Grade 2 in difficulty. However, there is a gully on each side, and these offer easier options. The one to the south is preferable – a steep, grassy incline to start with, then a traverse right, over a rocky gap, will bring you back to the col. The one to the north is more direct, though the going underfoot is rather soily, loose and slippery to begin with.

Thereafter the path leads along the crest; before reaching the next little top you will come to a slabby rise which is most easily passed to the left. Continue the traverse to make steep ascent to the East Top of

The Saddle; then easily down and across to the West Top (this actually appears to be the highest point) and on to the trig point. The Far West Top marks the start of the wonderful slender ridge that leads around the rim of Coire nan Uaine. Below to the left, in a pristine grassy basin, there is a lovely little kidney-shaped lochan; sheltered from the northerlies by the rocky rim, this area is a good place to rest awhile.

The technical difficulties are now minimal; the position, on the very edge of the rim for much of the traverse, remains breathtaking. Old iron fence-posts grace the edge, and you will come to a great block leaning over the path; then short sections of easy scrambling lead over the quartz-banded, grey gneiss rocks to the pyramidal top of Spidean Dhomhnuill Bhric. From here there are marvellous views west over Beinn Sgritheall and to Glamaig on Skye, and to Applecross and Torridon. Our route descends to the col, then we climb the great dome of Sgurr Leac nan Each. Follow down the shoulder, passing rocks of incredible beauty, from gneiss and massive quartz to salmon-red pegmatites and garnet-bearing silver mica schist. Rather than tackling every bump on the crest, it is easiest to follow the vague path on the right-hand side (otherwise awkward little crags may be encountered); keep going until you come to a slender lochan lying in the col.

Ahead lies a series of steep ascents and descents. However, there is a good stalker's path which crosses down to the right; this eventually joins the path which descends from Loch Coire nan Crogachan. Tiring legs will appreciate this route, as there is still a lot of work to do if the undulations above are followed. If the high route is taken, leading to the terminus knoll of 681m altitude, beware the section immediately following the next knoll: between this knoll and Sgurr a' Gharg Gharaidh, the shoulder is cut through by a (50m) deep rift, and this MUST BE passed down to the right. The final knoll is marked by a cairn on a boulder.

Retrace your steps for a short way, as far as the grassy nose; this gives a reasonably straightforward descent. You will intercept the stalker's path just before Loch Coire nan Crogachan; bear right down this to reach the valley, and on, to cross the Allt Undalain by a wooden bridge. Pause on the little rocky rise beyond the bridge for one final look back – a spellbinding view extending from the Forcan Ridge all the way around the Coire Uaine horseshoe.

THE FIVE SISTERS of KINTAIL

Quintessential high mountain spine, a marvellous position without technical difficulty

Fact Sheet

Location: North of Glen Shiel (A87), the Western Highlands of Scotland

Length: 12km (5½ miles)

Ascent: 1,515m (4,970ft)

Time: 8 hours

Difficulty: There are no technical difficulties and generally the going is good underfoot; however, it is a long way, and there are a few sections of strenuous ascent

Seasons & Restrictions: Summer conditions may be expected from May to September; winter conditions from October to April. This region is the National Trust for Scotland, so there are no restrictions

Map: OS Landranger 33, Loch Alsh, Glen Shiel

Start: From the old road lay-by on the north side of the A87, Glenshiel (NH 009 136). Note there is a restriction on tall camper vans, namely a high bar across the entrance

Finish: At Ault a' chruinn (NG 945 202)

Access: Some 35km (22 miles) south-east of Kyle of Lochalsh along the A87, and some 80km (50 miles) north-west of Fort William along the A82 and the A87

Tourist Information: Kyle of Lochalsh (tel. 01599 534276), Fort William (tel. 01397 703781)

Accommodation: There is a reasonable selection of places to stay, as well as a campsite at Glen Shiel Bridge, and a Youth Hostel at nearby Ratagan

Geology: Red-grey volcanics and gneiss provide sound walking and a little bouldery scree

Flora & Fauna: Dotterel and great black-backed gull may be seen, also red deer and stoat. Sea pinks (thrift) and least willow grow in this area

Comment: This is a high mountain classic, packed with interest, of no technical difficulty and with a wonderful position. It is a linear walk which requires pre-arranged transport. However, Scottish Citylink offer a regular bus service (Fort William to Portree) which will pick you up at Ault a' chruin and drop you off at the starting point, if you ask nicely (tel. 0990 505050 for information and timetables).

The Tops

The Gaelic for the 'Five Sisters' is 'Beinn Mhor', meaning big mountain

Sgurr nan Spainteach	990m (3,248ft)	(skoor nan sphan-tyakh = peak of the Spaniards)
Sgurr na Ciste Duibhe	1,027m (3,370ft)	(skoor na keesht-ya doo-ya = peak of the dark burial chamber)
Sgurr na Carnach	1,002m (3,287ft)	(skoor na carn-akh = rocky place)
Sgurr Fhuaran	1,068m (3,505ft)	(skoor oo-aran = peak of the springs)
Sgurr nan Saighead	929m (3,549ft)	(skoor nan sigh-at)
Sgurr na Moraich	876m (2,874ft)	(skoor na moa-reekh = mighty/ majestic peak)

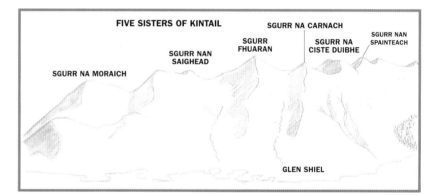

The classic view of all The Five Sisters of Kintail seen over Loch Duich from Mam Ratagan. The profiled peaks from right to left are Sgurr na Ciste Duibhe, Sgurr na Carnach, Sgurr Fhuaran (plus resident cloud), Sgurr nan Saighead (apparent twin tops) and finally Sgurr na Moraich

Left:The south-east end of the route seen at sunset from upper Glen Shiel; to the right is the crest at the point joined by this walk. Sgurr nan Spainteach is seen centrally with Sgurr na Ciste Duibhe to the left

■ Looking back from the Glenelg road over the Shiel Bridge and the head of Loch Duich, it is easy to see why the Five Sisters of Kintail are so named. Rising in a line from an unbroken high mountain shoulder, five fine peaks raise their heads skywards, each connected by a ridge of swooping curve – this is the archetypal mountain range, an artist's dream, a wonderful ridge walk.

Of course, the reality isn't quite that simple, and the peaks and connecting ridges actually weave a slightly snaking route around the elbow in Glen Shiel to the south, and the corries which fall northwards to Gleann Lichd. This only serves to make the route more interesting, however, and allows for a whole array of peaks to be viewed at any one time. Also it will be observed that the Five Sisters form only the western half of a 13km ridge which starts above the Cluanie Inn. So be it: in terms of quality, if not quantity, the expedition as described lacks nothing.

Start by the break in the forestry, and make your way up the grassy hillside straight to the crest of the ridge between Saleag to the east and Sgurr nan Spainteach to the west; this approach has the advantage of both minimising the ascent and maximising the length of the ridge. What is more, you should not miss the chance to walk the section of narrow, rocky, undulating ridge from here over the shapely cone of Sgurr nan Spainteach to the first of the Five Sisters, Sgurr na Ciste Duibhe. Impressively steep, rocky ground lies below to the north, and the view over deserted Coire Dhomdain already extends to the most imposing and the highest of the Five Sisters: Sgurr Fhuaran. In the distant north on a clear day, the grand hills of Torridon grace the skyline, with the central peak of Liathach particularly dominant.

The name 'Sgurr nan Spainteach' is said to refer to the Spaniards who fought for the Jacobites in the Battle of Glenshiel. The drama unfolded directly below, around the area of what is now the old Glenshiel Bridge, on 10 June 1719. Attempting to escape the forces of the Crown, the foreigners crossed over the ridge by the bealach (pass) between this top and Sgurr na Ciste Duibhe – reputedly in such disarray that they didn't even bother with the traverse of the Five Sisters.

It is a steep climb to the rocky crest of Sgurr na Ciste Duibhe, where a well structured cairn marks the summit, and the exciting prospect of Sgurr na Carnach and Sgurr Fhuaran unfolds ahead. The route is straightforward, descending, then ascending to Sgurr na Carnach, with a wonderful view down Glen Shiel and out over Loch Duich. The path leads off slightly left-handed from the stony summit, then swings back right and heads north in a long, steep climb to the summit of Sgurr Fhuaran. This is the highest peak, pyramidal in shape when seen from Glen Shiel, and it is often topped by cloud when the other four sisters bask in sunshine; locally it is known as Sgurr Urain (skoor oo-ran), which could either mean 'peak of the small spring', or 'wolf peak'.

Although a ridge falls to the east, our way lies to the north, and onwards to the craggy peak of Sgurr nan Saighead. The first top reached is the highest point, though there are two more, smaller tops close together at the western end of a ridge formed by steep, sweeping slabs and cliffs of grey gneiss. Bypass the lesser, most north-westerly top by tracking around to its left, then bear right and descend to the col above Coire na Criche. (Note there is an alternative route which swings left instead of right after the last top, and leads over Sgurr an t-Searraich directly down to Shiel Bridge, thus missing out the final sister. This is not recommended, however: this is not the Four Sisters walk.) A gentle climb takes you to the top of Sgurr na Moraich, which, whilst below the 3,000ft mark, is rightly named the mighty or majestic peak: she soars her full height in one unbroken sweep, directly from the salty waters of Loch Duich – what an impact she must have made on the unfortunate Spaniards, landing by boat at Eilean Donnan Castle! The route down to Ault a' chruinn is grassy and straightforward.

Looking south from Fhuaran over the boiling clouds of Choire Dhomdain to Sgurr na Ciste Duibhe (right) and Sgurr nan Spainteach (left)

The BEINN DEARGS and GLAMAIG HORSESHOE – the RED CUILLIN OF SKYE

Easy going, wonderful seascapes and views to the Black Cuillin, volcano mountain

Fact Sheet

Location: The Red Cuillin above Sligachan Hotel (A850), the Isle of Skye, north-west Scotland

Length: 12km (7½ miles)

Ascent: 1,215m (3,990ft)

Time: 7½ hours

Difficulty: There are no technical difficulties, though it is stony underfoot and the slopes of Glamaig are unavoidably steep. Escape is easy from most points

Seasons & Restrictions: Summer conditions may be expected from May to September; winter conditions from October to April. There are no restrictions

Map: OS Outdoor Leisure 8, The Cuillin and Torridon Hills

Start & Finish: From the car park above the Sligachan Hotel, at the junction of the A850 and the A863 (NG 486 298)

Access: Some 15km (9 miles) south of Portree and 36km (22 miles) north-west of Kyle of Lochalsh along the A850. The Isle of Skye is now connected to the mainland at Kyle of Lochalsh by a (toll) road bridge; alternatively there is a small, independent car ferry (summer only) which operates from near Glenelg to Kylerhea; or Caledonian MacBrayne sail from Mallaig to Armadale

Tourist Information: Bayview Road, Portree (tel. 01478 612137)

Accommodation: The Sligachan Inn is a favourite climbing/hillwalking centre, with an excellent bar meals facility and camping for non-residents, in addition to the traditional hotel. The nearest Youth Hostel is in Glen Brittle. Portree is the 'capital' of Skye, with all facilities

Geology: Fine-grained red granite is typical of this area

Flora & Fauna: Hooded crow, kestrel and meadow pippit may be seen. Heather grows in the lower levels of this area, and least cudweed and creeping sibbaldia higher up

Comment: A delightful round of character, with no technical difficulties, taking in the mountains of the Red Cuillin and shapely Glamaig. These hills have a distinctive lightness of character – they are often sunlit when their near neighbours of the Black Cuillin are swathed in cloud.

The Tops

Sron a Bhealach	429m (1,470ft)	(strawn a vee-allakh = nose of the gorge/pass)
Beinn Dearg	649m (2,129ft)	(by-an jerrak = red mountain)
Beinn Dearg Mheadhonach	652m (2,139ft)	(by-an jerrak mee-an-akh = middle-sized mountain)
Beinn Dearg Mhor	732m (2,402ft)	(by-an jerrak moar = big red mountain)
Glamaig/ Sgurr Mhairi	775m (2,543ft)	(glamaig/skoor va-ree = gorge mountain/Mary's peak)

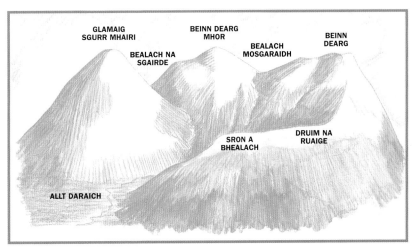

Glamaig – volcano mountain

■ There isn't anywhere in the world to compare with the Island of Skye: its landscape is totally unique. Arriving on a summer's evening from the bridge which arches its way over the narrow sound of Kyle Akin, the prospect that unfolds before you gives an idea of what is in store: inked against a blue-black sky, a fairyland of mountains floats above a sea of silver, the long, rounded shoulders and smooth domes of the Red Cuillin backed by the jagged serrations of the higher Black Cuillin. This is a mountaineer's paradise.

Of course, it isn't always a paradise – the weather can be kind or cruel as it can anywhere, and the Black Cuillin do have a legendary capacity to generate copious amounts of rain. However, this walk on the southern side of Glen Sligachan is effectively in the rainshadow of Sgurr nan Gillean, and so can often be in sunshine when the latter remains invisible beneath a thick, unshifting mantle of cloud. What is more, if the weather should turn bad, then it is a comparatively simple matter to escape and make a quick return to the Sligachan Inn – as did a bare-footed Gurkha before the turn of the century, taking only 18 minutes (after first ascending it in 37 minutes) from the summit of Glamaig to reach the Sligachan Inn (actually I have always wondered, was he demonstrating his mountain agility, or was it that he just couldn't stand the midges?).

Effectively located on a small peninsula formed by Loch Sligachan to the north and Loch Ainort to

the south, with the islands of the Inner Sound scattered like gems beyond, and cut off from the bulk of the Black Cuillin by the great emptiness of Glen Sligachan, this walk has a tremendous position. We start from the Sligachan Hotel – from here Glamaig looks like a volcano, a perfect cone in shape. Cross the old bridge, then bear right and proceed up the Glen Sligachan path. At the point where a small burn comes down from below the end of Druim na Ruiage, bear left and follow it to circumnavigate a peat bog; continue to the foot of the shoulder below the first little summit of Sron a Bhealach, and climb this directly.

Continue along the flat, open ridge, and up the zig-zags which climb the red scree of Beinn Dearg; the rock is hard, fine-grained granite and provides stable, very pleasant walking. The crest of the ridge is effectively the top of Beinn Dearg and it seems to arrive suddenly; the position is quite breathtaking, with some 600m of unbroken scree falling directly towards Loch Ainort. Make your way right-handed, to the top of Beinn Dearg Mheadhonach: carpeted with heather and blaeberry, it is in fact no more than an extension to the ridge, but it offers a tremendous view across to the great dark cliffs of Bla Bheinn (Blaven) which makes it well worthwhile. Laid out below, the islands of Scalpay, Raasay, Pabay and the Crowlins form a mosaic of land and sea between the mainland and Skye.

Head back along the ridge and drop down into Bealach Mosgaraidh, an easy walk. Next comes the

Westwards from the crest of Beinn Dearg nestles the head of Loch Ainort and the island of Scalpay

Red Cuillin; red screes shoot from the spine of Beinn Dearg, with Beinn Dearg Mhor beyond (right) and Glamaig (left)

long climb up to the Beinn Dearg Mhor, highest of the Deargs. The summit is marked by a little cone, then a fine rocky ridge plunges downwards to a scree bank; this broadens out to the dip of Bealach na Sgairde. Above rises the rocky scree of Glamaig, now changed from cheerful red to rather melancholy bluey grey, with some 300m of grinding ascent to the summit, Sgurr Mhairi.

The effort of the climb is more than repaid when you get to the top, however: scree gives way to spongy turf, Storr and the Old Man – that wonderfully different landscape of Trotternish – appear to the north, whilst the prominent volcanic cone of Dun Caan on Raasay catches the eye below. Most magnificent of all – provided, of course, that it is free from cloud – Sgurr nan Gillean stands to the

south-west. Also from here it becomes clear that Glamaig is not just a simple cone, but that it extends for a distance north-eastwards to a second top, that of An Colieach.

You may wish to add An Colieach to your list of summits achieved; most, however, will probably be content just to make their way down, as it is still a long way home. From the summit cairn, keep to the west side of the shoulder and either aim for the road, so avoiding boggy ground below, or head straight for the Sligachan Inn; whilst some portions can be scree-run, there are longer, rougher sections that cannot. Even if you don't beat the 18 minutes, you shouldn't feel guilty about buying a pint; completing this fine Red Cuillin horseshoe is a considerable achievement in itself.

SGURR NAN GILLEAN by the PINNACLE RIDGE – the BLACK CUILLIN of SKYE

Alpine rock ridge adventure, the most evocative mountain in the Black Cuillin

Fact Sheet

Location: The Black Cuillin above Sligachan Hotel (A850), the Isle of Skye, north-west Scotland

Length: 11km (6¾ miles)

Ascent: 1,010m (3,313ft)

Time: 6 hours

Difficulty: Technically this is the most difficult ridge outing described in this book – it should be considered as an easy rock climb rather than a walk. Not only does it entail a good head for heights and steady ability on rock, it also requires the proven ability to handle ropes and make a safe abseil. Descending from the Third Pinnacle requires a 20m abseil (to remove the rope means doubling it and therefore a 40m length of rope is required): consider it to be a severe scramble (Scrambling Grade 3) with one abseil (20m). Descending the so-called 'Tourist Route' also involves a short scramble (Scrambling Grade 1). In winter it is a serious climb (Winter Grade III). Even at 1:25,000 the steeps are so great and the area so complex that the Black Cuillin cannot be truly represented by a map. There is also the fact that within the gabbro rocks are deposits of magnetite which deflect the compass needle away from magnetic north, so a map and compass are of limited use amongst these demanding and serious mountains. Of course, studying a map and knowing the area as well as possible is important, but ultimately the most crucial safety consideration, and one which could make all the difference between success and disaster, is good mountaineering sense and sound judgement

Seasons & Restrictions: Summer conditions may be expected from May to September, and winter conditions from October to April. There are no restrictions

Map: OS Outdoor Leisure 8, The Cuillin and Torridon Hills

Start & Finish: From the car park on the west side of the A863 above the Sligachan Hotel (NG 484 298)

Access: Some 15km (9 miles) south of Portree and 36km (22 miles) north-west of Kyle of Lochalsh along the A850. The Isle of Skye is now connected to the mainland at Kyle of Lochalsh by a (toll) road bridge; alternatively a small, independent car ferry (summer only) operates from near Glenelg to Kylerhea; or Caledonian MacBrayne sail from Mallaig to Armadale

Tourist Information: Bayview Road, Portree (tel. 01478 612137)

Accommodation: The Sligachan Inn is a favourite climbing/hillwalking centre with an excellent bar meals facility and camping for non-residents, in addition to the traditional hotel. The nearest Youth Hostel is in Glen Brittle. Portree is the 'capital' of Skye with all facilities

Geology: Typical of the region is gabbro interspersed with basalt dykes. The course-grained gabbro is renowned for its hard roughness, giving good friction and making it an excellent rock on which to climb. It does vary in quality, however, and there are crumbly and denatured sections. Loose rock and scree will be found on the ledges and paths, so take care not to dislodge any stones for fear of climbers below. Basalt is a darker, more compact rock; it becomes extremely slippery when wet

Flora & Fauna: Golden eagle, meadow pippit and ptarmigan may be seen, also fox, mountain hare and lizard. Moss campion and thrift grow in this region

The Tops

Black Cuillin/Kiolen (black coo-lin/kio-len = high rocks)

Sgurr nan Gillean   964m (3,163ft)   (skoor nan geely-an = peak of the gills)

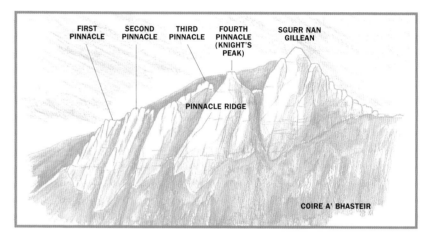

FIRST PINNACLE   SECOND PINNACLE   THIRD PINNACLE   FOURTH PINNACLE (KNIGHT'S PEAK)   SGURR NAN GILLEAN

PINNACLE RIDGE

COIRE A' BHASTEIR

Admiring the breathtaking elegance of Sgurr nan Gillean (high peak on the left) and the northern tip of the great Black Cuillin chain – from the start above the Sligachan Hotel. The independent pinnacle to the right is the Bhasteir Tooth (or executioner's axe) and the peak right again, balancing Sgurr nan Gillean across Coire a' Bhasteir, is Sgurr a' Bhasteir

Left: Steep rocks lead to the top of the Fourth Pinnacle (Knight's Peak)

Comment: This is by far the hardest ridge described in the book – Sgurr nan Gillean is many a mountaineer's favourite, and the Pinnacle Ridge is a classic rock climb. So why include them in a book of hillwalks when their ascent is patently more than a walk? Because primarily I come from a climbing background, and Sgurr nan Gillean via the Pinnacle Ridge I know to be one of Britain's *great* mountain outings – very easy for a climber, perhaps too difficult for even the accomplished hillwalker, Sgurr nan Gillean is a mountain to be respected. Yet why polarise the two worlds? If you are a hillwalker with a will, with the right experience and training, you could bridge that gap.

■ There are many evocative mountains in Scotland, yet the rough, naked blackness of Sgurr nan Gillean – the most romantic peak of the whole Black Cuillin, the most magical mountain on the entire Island of Skye – is so special that there are those who would gladly forsake any mountain range in the world to be by her side. Seen from the Sligachan, end on to the Pinnacle Ridge, Sgurr nan Gillean with Sgurr a' Bhasteir become the twin horns of Am Basteir and the Bhasteir Tooth (the executioner and his axe): it is a fearsomely impressive skyline. Yet only a little further to the

north-west, Sgurr nan Gillean shows her more complex independent nature; four awesome black pinnacles of The Pinnacle Ridge ascend to the finest rock spire of all, the startling pyramidal perfection of Sgurr nan Gillean.

This is not a mountain to be underestimated: it is a proud peak surrounded by great steeps and difficult places, and there is no margin for error. Whilst the rather mischievously named 'Tourist Route' may be the easiest on the mountain, it is far from a simple walk and requires Grade 1 scrambling ability – there are no easy routes to the summit.

Debate has long raged on the origin and correct spelling/pronunciation of what now appears on OS maps as 'Cuillin'. Because the Isle of Skye was a Viking stronghold for centuries, I tend to think that the name comes from the Old Norse (kiolen = 'high rocks'), and that the name of Sgurr nan Gillean is a mixture of Gaelic and Viking (Sgurr nan Gillean = 'peak of the gills', meaning rock gullies which divide the many pinnacles). Alternatively the Gaelic translation of the Cuillin is 'holly trees', and Sgurr nan Gillean 'peak of the young men'.

Climb the bank opposite the car park and aim

for the footbridge over the Allt Dearg Mor burn; you will then cross the great peat moor which extends northwards from the Black Cuillin. The path is well trod – it is non other than the infamous 'Tourist Route'. Where it forks, go left, taking another footbridge over the Allt Dearg Beag and then climbing up onto the shoulder. Above the high point of the shoulder bear right, off the main path, and continue upwards to gain what are in effect the lower slopes of the north ridge which falls from Sgurr nan Gillean. Follow these, with the Allt Dearg Beag burn flowing from the Coire a Bhasteir ravine down to the right.

So far the way is straightforward enough; here the route swings slightly left to gain the base of the Pinnacle Ridge. The First Pinnacle is climbed most easily by first scrambling diagonally left, then moving back right. Thereafter follow the line of least resistance to pass by the left side of the rather inconsequential Second Pinnacle. Steepening ground marks the start of the Third Pinnacle. Sustained scrambling, increasing in difficulty, reaches a very exposed top (Scrambling Grade 3); from here the best way down is to abseil into the gap beyond. A number of slings are usually *in situ* on the top blocks, and you can thread the abseil rope through these – they must be carefully checked, of course, and it may well be necessary to leave your own sling *in situ*. A 20m abseil leads to a rock ledge from where a rocky scramble descends to the base of the gap.

The Fourth Pinnacle (Knight's Peak) is first tackled by following an exposed, though technically easy ramp or rake up to the right; then you zig-zag up the line of least resistance. The descent from the summit of this final pinnacle is straightforward, and leads to the last pyramid. Climb this in an all but direct line to the crest, then contour left to gain the superbly exposed narrow rock table summit of Sgurr nan Gillean: this is just how a mountain top should be. Beyond, in a tremendous curving line south, is the magnificent Black Cuillin Ridge, a mountaineering expedition without parallel in Britain (and beyond the scope of this book). A golden eagle glides effortlessly by – Skye has the densest eagle population in Scotland – confirming this region as one of the grandest of mountain eyries.

Do not underestimate the descent: it is long and

rough, and it begins with a rather tricky section. Move along the crest of the South East Ridge: from the relatively flat slabs of the summit crest it is an awkward and exposed step down a corner to the right, to gain easier ground below. Continue down the rocky spine of the South East Ridge until you come to a cairn: this marks a bouldery descent down to the left, where the going is rough though generally straightforward; the track leads across a rocky basin and meets the traverse above the flanks of Coire Riabhach to reach the shoulder. Join the original path to retrace your steps home.

Parties making descent from the Third Pinnacle of the Pinnacle Ridge. The climber seated centrally is by the rockflake usually used as the anchor from which an abseil is made – the mode of descent recommended here

THE FIONN CHOIRE HORSESHOE – the BLACK CUILLIN of SKYE – BRUACH NA FRITHE by NORTH WEST RIDGE & descent via SGURR A'BHASTEIR

Spectacular mountain scenery – Bhasteir Tooth, Sgurr nan Gillean, The Pinnacle Ridge – and a high mountain summit without technical difficulty

Fact Sheet

Location: The Black Cuillin above Sligachan Hotel (A850), Isle of Skye, north-west Scotland

Length: 14km (8¾ miles)

Ascent: 1,035m (3,392ft)

Time: 7 hours

Difficulty: Amazingly for the Black Cuillin there are no technical difficulties save the sometimes rough going, the length of the walk and its remoteness. Navigation in bad weather is notoriously difficult. It should also be noted that, even at a 1:25,000 scale, the steeps are so great and the area so complex that the Black Cuillin cannot be truly represented by a map. There is also the fact that within the gabbro rocks are deposits of magnetite which deflect the compass needle away from magnetic north, so a map and compass are of limited use amongst these demanding and serious mountains. Of course, studying a map and knowing the area as well as possible is important, but ultimately the most crucial safety consideration, and one which could well make the difference between success and disaster, is good mountaineering sense and sound judgement

Seasons & Restrictions: Summer conditions may be expected from May to September, and winter conditions from October to April. There are no restrictions

Map: OS Outdoor Leisure 8, The Cuillin and Torridon Hills

Start & Finish: The car park on the west side of the A863 above the Sligachan Hotel (NG 484 298)

Access: Some 15km (9 miles) south of Portree and 36km (22 miles) north-west of Kyle of Lochalsh along the A850. The Isle of Skye is now connected to the mainland at Kyle of Lochalsh by a (toll) road bridge; alternatively a small independent car ferry operates from near Glenelg to Kylerhea (summer only)

Tourist Information: Bayview Road, Portree (tel. 01478 612137)

The Tops

Bruach na Frithe	958m (3,143ft)	(broo-akh na free = slope of the wild mountainous land)
Sgurr a' Fionn Choire	935m (3,068ft)	(skoor a fion corri = peak of the fair corrie)
Sgurr a' Bhasteir	898m (2,946ft)	(skoor a basteir = peak of the executioner's corrie)
Meall Odhar	636m (2,087ft)	(my-owl oa-ar = brown hill)

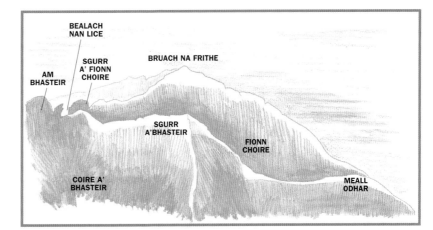

Sgurr a' Bhasteir seen centrally with the Bhasteir Tooth to its left and Bruach na Frithe and Fionn Choire to its right

Accommodation: The Sligachan Inn is a favourite climbing/hillwalking centre with an excellent bar meals facility; there is camping for non-residents, in addition to the traditional hotel. The nearest Youth Hostel is in Glen Brittle. Portree is the 'capital' of Skye, and has all facilities

Geology: Typically the rock is gabbro interspersed with basalt dykes. The course-grained gabbro is famous for its hard roughness, giving good friction and making it an excellent rock on which to climb. It does vary in quality, however, and there are crumbly and denatured sections. Loose rock and scree will be found on the ledges and paths – take care not to dislodge any stones because there may be climbers below. The basalt is a darker, more compact rock; it becomes extremely slippery when wet

Flora & Fauna: Ptarmigan, kestrel and merlin may be seen, also otter and slow-worm. Alpine saussurea and northern rock-cress grow in this region

Comment: This is perhaps the easiest and most accessible of the high Cuillin; nevertheless it is a very rewarding outing amongst breathtaking scenery: Sgurr nan Gillean, The Pinnacle Ridge, The Bhasteir Tooth and the main Cuillin Ridge are all seen to tremendous effect.

Above: A lone figure stands atop Sgurr a' Fionn Choire

Below: On the summit of Bruach na Frithe

This route offers a first-class opportunity to view the formidable Bhasteir Tooth, without having to actually climb it

■ This walk follows the steep ridge which encircles Fionn Choire; there are no real technical difficulties, and the route has a great deal of character and offers superb views, allowing close inspection of the awesome Bhasteir Tooth (the executioner's axe) without actually having to venture onto it. It first goes from Bealach a' Mhaim to Glen Brittle, then quits the path at the head of the pass and climbs the north-west ridge of Bruach na Frithe to make an anticlockwise circuit of the horseshoe around the corrie. This must be one of the best introductions to the Cuillin mountains.

From the road, take the path that heads for the footbridge across the Allt Dearg Mor burn. Don't cross it, however, but bear right to follow the right side of the burn (the true left bank); you will pass Alltdearg House via a dreadful mudbath. Keep following by the burn, then start climbing on a better path; you will pass Tobar nan Uaislean Spring – the source of the Allt Dearg Mor – and will soon reach the head of Bealach a' Mhaim. Bear left and ascend the easy north-west ridge of Bruach na Frithe, with views west over the wilds of Coire na Creiche and down Glen Brittle. For the last kilometre the ridge sharpens, before topping out on the rock summit.

In many respects Bruach na Frithe offers one of the best views of the main Cuillin Ridge. To the east lies Sgurr nan Gillean, the northern terminus, and to the south Gars-bheinn which is the usual starting point in summer. In between stretch eighteen major summits (including Bruach na Frithe), 11km in distance, over 3,000m of ascent, involving difficult route-finding and sections of sensationally exposed rock climbing; it is truly a wonderful expedition (on my last traverse I managed it in 7hr 20mins, summit to summit!).

Our way leads along the rocky crest – a little scrambly, though not difficult – around the head of the corrie to the top of Sgurr a' Fionn Choire above Bealach nan Lice, overlooking the impressive rock fang of the Bhasteir Tooth. A steep crag lies directly below, so back track a little, trending left, then skirt around the north face to gain the bealach. The regular route of ascent up the Tooth is fearfully exposed; used by those traversing the main ridge from south to north, it leads from the right side above Lota Corrie and is known as Naismith's Route. This route was first climbed in 1898.

The Tooth was in fact first climbed by another route earlier in 1898, by Norman Collie. This ascent, whilst impressive enough in itself, was only a small part of Collie's achievements because he was a great character, a climbing pioneer and a scientist of renown. Not only did he explore and pioneer new climbs in the magnificent Cuillin, the Highlands of Scotland and the Lake District, he also did much in the European Alps, was instrumental in opening up the mountains of the Canadian Rockies, attempted the Himalayan giant of Nanga Parbat in 1895, and climbed extensively in Norway and the Lofoten Islands. In the world of science he did much work in isolating the rare gases of helium, argon and neon, and he claimed to have taken the first X-ray photograph. Most of all he loved the Cuillin, and he died at the Sligachan Inn in 1942.

The fine crest leads pleasantly along to the top of Sgurr a' Bhasteir, from where there is a spellbindingly impressive view of Sgurr nan Gillean and The Pinnacle Ridge. Descent down the nose is rough and scrambly, though without undue technical difficulty; the best line is to the right of the crest. Make your way out onto the final lump of Meall Odhar, then continue to descend. Bear left to avoid the small rocky bluffs which lie near the base of the nose; you will reach easy ground and this will take you down to the Allt Dearg Mor – its milky waterfalls and polished rock slides may prove irresistible on a hot summer's afternoon.

THE COIRE NA BANACHDICH ROUND

Eas Mor waterfall, view of the Inaccessible Pinnacle, the Spine of the Main Ridge, an entertaining horseshoe with modest technical difficulty

Fact Sheet

Location: The Black Cuillin above Glen Brittle, Isle of Skye, north-west Scotland

Length: 7¾km (4¾ miles)

Ascent: 1,120m (3,674ft)

Time: 5½ hours

Difficulty: There are a number of short scrambly sections (Scrambling Grade 0.5), the hardest section being the descent of the blade rock which begins the ridge approach of Sgurr nan Gobhar (Scrambling Grade 1). It should also be noted that, even at a 1:25,000 scale, the steeps are so great and the area is so complex that the Black Cuillin cannot be truly represented by a map. There is also the fact that within the gabbro rocks are deposits of magnetite which deflect the compass needle away from magnetic north, so a map and compass are of limited use amongst these demanding and serious mountains. Of course, studying a map and knowing the area as well as possible is important, but ultimately the most significant safety consideration, and one which could well make all the difference between joy and disaster, is good mountaineering sense and sound judgement. Under winter conditions this should be regarded as a climb of severity (Winter Grade I)

Seasons & Restrictions: Summer conditions may be expected from May to September, and winter conditions from October to April. There are no restrictions

Map: OS Outdoor Leisure 8, The Cuillin and Torridon Hills

Start & Finish: There is parking opposite the Glen Brittle Memorial (mountaineering) Hut (NG 412 216)

Access: The end of Glen Brittle is found some 25km (15½ miles) south-west of The Sligachan Hotel; first go along the A863 (the Drynoch road), then along the B8009 (the Carbost road), and finally down the minor road signposted to Glen Brittle that runs down the west side of the Black Cuillin. The Sligachan Inn is located some 15km (9 miles) south of Portree and 36km (22 miles) north-west of Kyle of Lochalsh along the A850. The Isle of Skye is now connected to the mainland at Kyle of Lochalsh by a (toll) road bridge; alternatively a small, independent car ferry operates from near Glenelg to Kylerhea (summer only); or Caledonian MacBrayne sail from Mallaig to Armadale

The Tops

Sgurr Dearg	978m (3,209ft)	(skoor jerrak = red peak)
Sgurr na Banachdich	965m (3,167ft)	(skoor na ba-nakh-teekh = milkmaid's peak)
Sgurr nan Gobhar	630m (2,067ft)	(skoor nan gow-ar = peak of the goats)

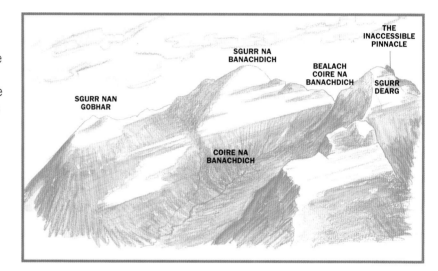

Tourist Information: Bayview Road, Portree (tel. 01478 612137)

Accommodation: Glen Brittle offers limited accommodation including a bookable mountaineering hut, a Youth Hostel, B&B and a campsite. Carbost also has limited facilities, including an inn

Geology: Typically the rock is gabbro, interspersed with basalt dykes. The coarse-grained gabbro is famous for its hard roughness, which gives good friction and makes it an excellent rock on which to climb. It does vary in quality, however, and on this round there are many variations in its texture and colour, which changes from the usual greeny-grey to reddy-brown, brown, and blue. Loose rock and scree will be found on the ledges and paths – take care not to dislodge any stones in case there are climbers below. The basalt is a darker, more compact rock; it becomes extremely slippery when wet

Flora & Fauna: Raven, black cap, snipe and oyster catcher may be seen regularly, also fox, stoat and rabbit. Sea campion and roseroot grow in this area

Comment: This round takes you into the heart of the Black Cuillin without undue difficulty and, traversing between Sgurr Dearg and Sgurr na Banachdich, gives a tremendous taste of the main Cuillin Ridge.

■ Remote, lapped by the sea, overlooked by Sgurr Alasdair (the highest mountain), the head of Glen Brittle seems to encapsulate all the wild character and wonder of the Black Cuillin. On a clear, sunny day, with the mountains shimmering distant blue in the heat, it is heaven; lashed by rain and gale, black in mood and colour, it can feel just the opposite. Perhaps you have to experience the latter in order to appreciate the former – but don't let it worry you, because in a very short space of time, Glen Brittle is capable of providing both.

Above Glen Brittle the Coire na Banachdich round is a wonderful ridge walk into the heart of the Black Cuillin: it takes in two mountains over 3,000ft, it offers good views of several spectacular features including the Inaccessible Pinnacle, it observes the unfolding seascapes, and as a part of it you can savour a portion of the main knife-edge Cuillin Ridge. In all it provides one of the best rounds from Glen Brittle, with the added bonus that it is also one of the most straightforward – a mountain expedition well within the capabilities of most hillwalkers.

A path bears up the hillside diagonally to the right to cross Allt Coire na Banachdich burn by a little footbridge; take care not to foul the burn because it provides the drinking water for Glenbrittle House. Climb directly up the hillside to a green grass notch in the heather overlooking the great ravine of Eas Mor. The sheer scale of the canyon, with its 30m waterfall and woods of rowan, silver birch and ash, comes as a complete surprise as it is hidden from view from below. Within the grass area the circular mounds are

Sgurr Dearg and the Inaccessible Pinnacle viewed from Sgurr Alasdair; this route ascends the ridge rising from the left

undoubtedly ancient burial chambers, indicating the importance of this site many thousands of years ago.

Follow around the rim of the ravine and continue up the hillside until, on passing a gabbro boulder, a smaller path branches off left in the direction of the west ridge of Sgurr Dearg. Already the seascapes extend over nearby Soay to the islands of the Inner Hebrides: Canna, Rhum, Eigg and Muck. Keep going: you will pass a very large boulder and then will reach a relatively level area. From here, the Coire na Banachdich reveals itself to be a world of rock and scree mainly devoid of any vegetation. The path begins in easy zig-zags up the scree, then steepens; a number of minor, but strenuous variations lead to the top of the first pyramidal pinnacle and the start of the west ridge proper. Already the view extends over Coire Lagan to the rocky vastness of the great north face of Sron na Ciche and on over Sgur Sgumain to the cone of Sgurr Alasdair. To the north-west, should you pause and look, stand the intriguing flat-topped hills of Macleod's Tables, with the seastacks of Macleod's Maidens lying off Idrigill Point below.

The stony path leads up the shoulder to reach the foot of a little rock buttress, which looks rather formidable from below; it weaves a line up the front of the buttress through the rocks, and involves a rocky step of Scrambling Grade 0.5 in difficulty. At the top, with the cold blueness of Loch Lagan a long way below to the right, another pinnacle appears ahead. From the gap below this, the easiest, most natural route is to keep right of the crest initially and follow a dyke that threads its way through the steep rocks (Scrambling Grade 0.5). At the end of this, return to the crest of the ridge – from here it is a straightforward climb to the knife-edged summit of Sgurr Dearg, overlooked by the remarkable Inaccessible Pinnacle. This up-ended slab of gabbro, with a little face block balanced precariously on top (this is the usual abseil anchor for those who have ascended its east ridge intent on making the full traverse of the Cuillin Ridge), overlooks the summit of Sgurr Dearg by some 9m.

From the crest just beyond the Inaccessible Pinnacle the path leads down steep scree to the gap of Bealach Coire na Banachdich. This is straightforward until, some 10m above the gap, a rock outcrop necessitates an easy scramble (Scrambling Grade 0.25). From the gap, climb up and out to the left, to the crest of the ridge: it commands a marvellous position with notable exposure. Continue until you reach the top of a broad pinnacle, known as the Third Top, Sgurr na Banachdich; the next top – the Second Top of Sgurr na Banachdich – is most easily bypassed along the path down to the left (Scrambling Grade 0.5, though this depends on the route you take – the higher you go, the harder it is; then climb up and along to the summit crest of Sgurr na Banachdich.

Continue along the crest for a few metres until an easy path breaks down to the left and descends the scree. Views extend across the Sea of the Hebrides to the Outer Hebridean islands of Berneray, Mingulay, Pabbay, Vatersay, Sandray, Barra and South Uist, the last outposts before the Atlantic Ocean and America. As the flanks of Sgurr na Banachdich ease onto the shoulder leading to Sgurr nan Gobhar, a blade of dark rock rises above the ridge; make your way across its crest until it ends in a steep nose. Scramble carefully down this for about 15m (easy Scrambling Grade 1), then follow the path; progress is easy now, left to pass

Left: Eas Mor waterfall, a surprise feature below the hanging corrie of Coire Banachdich

The Inaccessible Pinnacle stands above the narrow rock crest of Sgurr Dearg

shattered rocks, then right, and back to the crest to the cairn marking the end of the shoulder ridge and the top of Sgurr nan Gobhar.

Descend straight down the nose for about 30m to reach the head of a narrow chimney cleft ('death rift') descending steeply through the rock; avoid this to the left and continue descending – you will find another similar, though smaller, rift. Go left again, down a steep, zig-zag path through rock and

scree until you reach a 3m rock step requiring the use of hands as well as feet (Scrambling Grade 0.5). This gains the final scree slope that leads down at an easier angle to the grass and heather below. Head straight down the grassy slopes making directly for the Memorial Hut. From above, the going looks rough and boggy in appearance, though in fact it is quite reasonable, and in pleasant contrast to the stony ground above.

THE TROTTERNISH RIDGE

Unfolding seascapes, views back to Quirang, great cliffs, the Old Man of Storr, views to the Cuillin

Fact Sheet

Location: Trotternish, the northernmost finger of the Isle of Skye, north-west Scotland

Length: 32km (20 miles)

Ascent: 1,385m (4,544ft)

Time: 11 hours

Difficulty: There are no technical difficulties and the going is good underfoot, so a good pace can be set without difficulty. However, the long length of the route and its remoteness are important considerations

Escape Points: There are a number of bealachs (passes) where escape from the ridge is possible and these are worth noting. At Bealach Uige (approx 1½ hours from the start), follow the path to Uig. At Bealach a Mhoramhain (approx 2½ hours from the start), follow the path from Uig. At Bealach Chaiplin (approx 3 hours from the start), descend to the plateau and cross it, then follow the stream to Loch Cuithar; it is possible to leave the car/be collected from this point – the walk out along the road is long. At Bealach Beag (approx 7 hours from the start), descend a ravine by following the stream to a car park by the road; this is an alternative finishing point)

Seasons & Restrictions: Summer conditions may be expected from May to October; winter conditions from November to April. There are no restrictions

Map: OS Landranger 23, North Skye

Start: From the head of the Staffin/Uig Pass (NG 440 680)

Finish: At Portree, or just above, where the A855 makes a right-angle bend and joins the road to Achachock (NG 488 454)

The Tops

Bioda Buidhe	466m (1,530ft)	(bid boo-ya = big yellow pointed peak)
Beinn Edra	611m (2,006ft)	(by-an edra = outer mountain)
Groba nan Each	575m (1,886ft)	(graupa an ee-ak = horse point)
Glasvein	597m (1,959ft)	(glaas-bhy-an = grey mountain)
Creag a' Lain	608m (1,995ft)	(craik a la-en = full crag)
Sgurr a' Mhadaidh Ruaidh	587m (1,926ft)	(skoor va-tee roo-ah = peak of the red fox)
Baca Ruadh	637m (2,091ft)	(bakh roo-ah = red bank)
Hartaval	668m (2,192ft)	(harta-val = rocky fell)
The Storr	719m (2,358ft)	(the staur = the stake)
Ben Dearg	552m (1,812ft)	(ben jerrak = red mountain)
A' Chorra-bheinn	459m (1,506ft)	(a khoora by-an = steep hill)
Beinn a' Chioch	292m (958ft)	(by-an a khee-ook) = hill/mountain of the pap)

Access: The head of the pass is found some 8km (5 miles) above Uig (25km/16 miles north of Portree along the A856 west coast road) and some 4km (2½ miles) above Staffin (28km/17 miles north of Portree along the A855 east coast road)

Tourist Information: Bayview Road, Portree (tel. 01478 612137)

Accommodation: Staffin is served by a campsite, and numerous bed and breakfast and self-catering establishments; the Flodigarry Inn (with bunkhouse behind) lies a couple of miles up the road. Similarly Uig has a campsite, two inns and a Youth Hostel. Portree has all facilities

Geology: The dark rocks are generally volcanic lavas with intrusions of basalt and dolerite; although the lavas are

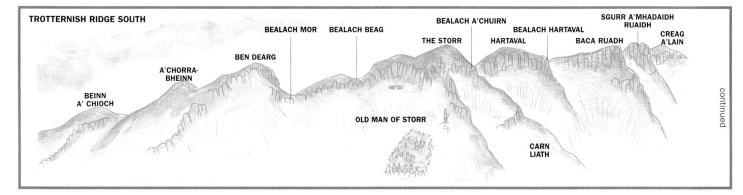

TROTTERNISH RIDGE SOUTH

BEINN A' CHIOCH — A'CHORRA-BHEINN — BEN DEARG — BEALACH MOR — BEALACH BEAG — OLD MAN OF STORR — THE STORR — BEALACH A'CHUIRN — HARTAVAL — BEALACH HARTAVAL — CARN LIATH — BACA RUADH — SGURR A'MHADAIDH RUAIDH — CREAG A'LAIN

continued

The Old Man of Storr with the flat top mountain of The Storr above, seen over the Storr Lochs

mostly rotten in nature, they break down to produce a fine scree which is pleasant to walk over

Flora & Fauna: Golden eagle, white-tailed eagle (or sea eagle), merlin and sparrowhawk may be seen. This region is very rich in arctic and alpine plants; photography is permitted, but on no account touch the plants themselves. These include alpine pearlwort, mossy cyphal, mossy saxifrage, mountain avens and the exceedingly rare koenigia islandica – this has only one other recorded site in Britain. Fox, stoat and rabbit also inhabit this area

Comment: A linear outing of some length, often known as The North Ridge of Skye, this route traverses the rolling grassy spine of Trotternish to pass through a remote and special landscape. The long daylight hours of spring and early summer typical of this northern region (it never really goes dark) may be useful. Bealach Beag (see Escape Points) provides a convenient alternative finish. Huge cliffs lie to the east, and great care should be exercised in poor visibilty. Trotternish often basks in sunshine when the Cuillin are completely covered in cloud.

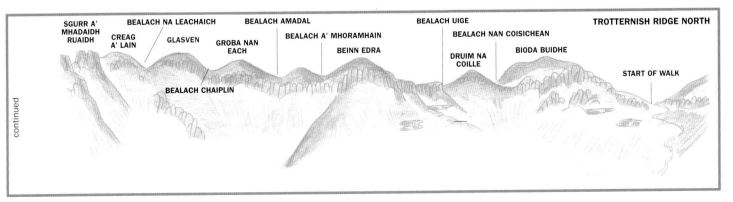

SGURR A' MHADAIDH RUAIDH
BEALACH NA LEACHAICH
CREAG A' LAIN
GLASVEN
BEALACH AMADAL
BEALACH A' MHORAMHAIN
GROBA NAN EACH
BEINN EDRA
BEALACH UIGE
BEALACH NAN COISICHEAN
DRUIM NA COILLE
BIODA BUIDHE
TROTTERNISH RIDGE NORTH
START OF WALK
BEALACH CHAIPLIN

continued

South from the Quirang, the long spine of the great North Ridge of Trotternish can be seen fading into the distance

■ The wild, remote beauty of the Isle of Skye and its dramatic historical connotations have made this island famous the world over. Despite the fact that it has now been linked to the mainland by a bridge, it is still a world apart. For those who love mountains, the Black Cuillin have no equal; for those who love wildness and wet open spaces, the untamable sea and nature in the raw, then Skye has it all, and much more. From a walking/climbing point of view there are six distinctly different regions, each unique, each with its own very special qualities.

The kingdom of Trotternish, the most northerly and the most substantial claw of this lobster/langoustine-shaped island, is in many respects one of the most fascinating. A high spine of gentle mountains runs due north along its length: this is the Trotternish Ridge, its flanks falling to the Sound of Raasay and the Inner Sound to the east, and to Loch Snizort and the Little

Minch to the west. It stretches some 30km from Portree to Rubha Hunish, and is a remote world of mountain, moor, sea cliff and sea which offers a landscape rich in detail.

The acid rocks are underlain by limestone, and these conditions foster rare alpines. The golden eagle and the sea eagle occupy the same air space, and you can watch the merlin, the hen harrier, the rough-legged buzzard and the lapland bunting all in the same day. On the coastline below, wild salmon are still netted between Staffin Island and Staffin Slip. Sea otters play amongst the rocks, and killer whales follow the mackerel around these shores. Tread this ridge lightly and quietly because it is one of the most precious environments in Britain.

These mountains were volcanoes, and although long extinct, what remains of them is impressive enough, namely the 50m high Old Man of Storr and the weird pinnacles of the Quirang. Historically we most readily think of Flora

Macdonald, who lived in a cottage at Flodigarry for a time, sheltering Bonnie Prince Charlie and helping with his escape; and of the awesome retribution which followed, resulting in the break-up of the Highland clans and the Clearances. Cleared crofts and villages are sadly an integral part of this north-western landscape – yet the human interest here covers a much longer period than this. For those with an eye to see, the graphic remains of prehistory in the form of burial mounds, hut circles, earth and stoneworks litter the ground; and recently discovered above the road to Staffin Slip were remains from the mesolithic period – at 8,500 years old, this has proved to be one of Europe's oldest known sites.

The place names here are a fascinating mix of Celt and Norse. Though Gaelic still remains the first language, showing the Celtic origin, interestingly for 400 years Trotternish was a Viking stronghold, and the name itself is of Norse origin. The people speak with a lovely gentle rolling lilt that well conveys their open, hospitable nature. I well remember one of my first climbing trips to Kilt Rock. Taking an unknown course across a farmer's field, and at its perimeter finding myself with a barbed-wire fence in front of me and a cliff beyond, my heart rather sank when I saw the farmer himself bearing down on me. But instead of rebuke and redirection, he actually took his jacket off, laid it over the barbed wire and helped me over! Trotternish is one of those special places.

The Trotternish Ridge, or the North Ridge of

Skye, is a mountain expedition longer than the famous Black Cuillin Ridge; however, it is never too demanding. Conditions underfoot are generally excellent, and could sometimes be mistaken for those typical of a well maintained putting green. Of course, the ridge is isolated, and its position away from most forms of civilization should be carefully noted – it's a long way back to the road!

At 260m, the col at the head of the pass makes a good starting point; from here, follow the path that climbs up and across to the edge of the cliffs overlooking Loch Leum na Luirgin. For the most dramatic scenery and views eastwards across Rona and Raasay to the hills of Torridon and Applecross, the best route is to follow along the rim of the cliffs for the length of the ridge.

It is a gentle climb to the summit of Bioda Buidhe and along to the flat plateau between Bealachs nan Coisichean and Uige; then follow the wire fence to the top of Beinn Edra (about 2 hours out). Next, cross Bealach Mhoramahain and Bealach Chaiplin to reach the summit of Glasven: climb to the top above the great coire of Cuithar, Creag a' Lain, eventually to drop down to a rock table outcrop from which the views across the cliffs of Creag a' Lain are truly impressive. Descend a little further, and if you look carefully, you may find the hidden spring to the west at this point; then ascend to the independent summit of Sgurr a' Mhadaidh Ruaidh.

Continue to Baca Ruadh (4½ hours out) over immaculate greensward; the next summit is Hartaval. After the dip into Bealach a' Chuirn, a steepish slog takes you to the summit of The Storr (6½ hours out), the highest point of this tremendous outing; the cliffs fall vertically some 200m from the summit point, and the amazing pear-shaped pinnacle of the Old Man can be spotted far below. The volcanic rocks/lava flows hereabouts are pretty rotten – on a still day you can even hear stones falling, so take care looking over the edge. Drop down to Bealach Beag (this is a good point to descend to a welcoming car) and along the flats to a very steep rise to Ben Dearg (8 hours out). Then follow the long, gradual slope down to Portree (the Harbour Bar is approximately 11 hours out).

Without any doubt at all, this is one of the great mountain outings.

On Trotternish North Ridge; taking a break by Druim na Coille with Bioda Buidhe and then the Quirang seen beyond to the north

THE TRAVERSE of BEINN ALLIGIN

Fairy knoll, Wolf's lair, rift of the screeching, Corrie of the Beast, over The Horns

Fact Sheet

Location: Torridon, Wester Ross, the Northern Highlands of Scotland

Length: 10km (6¼ miles)

Ascent: 1,255m (4,117ft)

Time: 6½ hours

Difficulty: A little easy scrambling over The Horns (Scrambling Grade 0.3)

Seasons & Restrictions: Summer conditions may be expected from May to October; winter conditions from November to April. This region is under the jurisdiction of the National Trust for Scotland, so there are no restrictions

Map: OS Outdoor Leisure 8, The Cuillin & Torridon Hills

Start & Finish: From the Coire Mhic Nobuil bridge car park below the Torridon to Diabaig road (NG 869 576)

Access: Torridon lies some 100km (62 miles) north-west of Inverness along the A862, A835 and the A896, and some 75km (47 miles) north of Kyle of Lochalsh along the A87, A890 and the A896; these are slow roads, single track in places

Tourist Information: The National Trust for Scotland, The Countryside Centre, by the Diabaig junction in Torridon village (tel. 01445 791221)

Accommodation: Within Torridon village there is a variety of places to stay, including an hotel with a bar and meal facilities; there is a campsite and a Youth Hostel. There is also B&B and an inn at Kinlochewe

Geology: The rock is largely Torridonian sandstone, a delightful rock often including a matrix of quartz pebbles; it is hard and reliable, a little like concrete to walk and scramble on

Flora & Fauna: Golden eagle, buzzard and golden plover may be seen; also pine marten, red deer and pygmy shrew. Mountain sorrel, alpine saw-wort and angelica grow in this region

Comment: This is the most westerly of the three Torridon giants – Beinn Eighe, Liathach and Beinn Alligin – and it is the friendliest and the most amenable. From afar it has a green, grassy appearance, nevertheless it is an excellent outing offering a superb position, delightful scrambling and plenty of excitement.

The Tops

Beinn Alligin (by-an alli-gin = jewelled mountain, or mountain of beauty)

Tom na Gruagaich	922m (3,024ft)	(tom na groo-agikh = fairy knoll)
Sgurr Mhor	986m (3,235ft)	(skoor moar = big peak)
Na Rathanan (north top)	866m (2,841ft)	(na ra-anan = horns/grooved block or pulley)

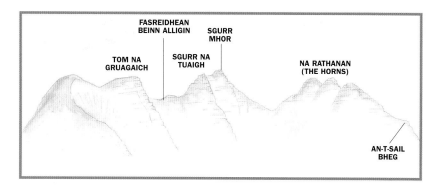

■ High on Scotland's north-west coast, opposite the Isle of Skye, above Applecross and south of Loch Maree, you will find Torridon's loch, glen and mountain, its incandescent brilliance of light and colour unsurpassed in the Scottish Highlands. It is of unique beauty, in character somewhere between the intensity of the Central Highlands – that of Glencoe and Ben Nevis – and the expansiveness of the great north – of Stac Pollaidh and Suilven. And beyond the blueness of Loch Torridon, above the deserted shielings and the heather of the glen, tower upwards three mountains of great individuality and giant stature: the domes and spires of Beinn Alligin, the neck-craning steeps of mighty Liathach, and the naked whiteness of Beinn Eighe.

Beinn Alligin, the 'jewelled mountain', or 'mountain of beauty', is the lesser of the Torridon 'big three', and because the dark red sandstone is clothed in a green garb, it does look the most hospitable. Forming a great horseshoe around Toll a' Mhadaidh Mor (the Wolf's corrie), Alligin comprises three main tops, connected by ridges of considerable exposure: Tom na Gruagaich, which

Beinn Alligin seen from Mullach An Rathain on Liathach; Tom na Gruagaich seen to the left and the highest top, Sgurr Mhor, to the right, followed by The Horns

offers the best view of the whole round; Sgurr Mhor, the highest and the most central; and finally the three dramatic spires known as the Horns of Alligin (An Rathanan).

A rather inauspicious path begins by the bridge, above the west bank of the Abhaim Coire Mhic Nobuil gorge. After only a little way another path branches off up to the left: follow it – the going is rough and bouldery, but as it steepens to climb directly up the hillside, it becomes better defined and climbs through the rocky bluffs via a series of shelves aiming for the nose of Na Fasreidhnean (which has descended from the top known as Meall an Laogh). Before reaching the bottom of the nose, however, it moves diagonally right to ascend the pass of Coir nan Laogh, falling from the central hollow of Alligin's first dome. Generally following the line of the stream, the path steepens and becomes quite bouldery before reaching a col.

Ascend to the right to find the sandstone trig point of Tom na Gruagaich perched on top of a pile of large, flat, circular sandstone slabs. The aspect along the whole horseshoe is quite superb; in

particular it gives a tremendous view of the great rent of Eag Dhubh na h'Eigheachd ('Black Notch of the Outcry') slashing the flank of Sgurr Mhor. Move onto the northern nose; it is a blocky descent to the col below, where a tiny lochan resides in the hollow. Then climb the narrow crest to a small, unnamed cairned top (altitude 858m) – this is a good place for a breather. Descend to the col and from there start the steep, strenuous ascent of Sgurr Mhor over large plates of sandstone that move underfoot. The main path heads diagonally left and zig-zags upwards; more interesting, however, though steeper, is to keep to the right edge and so up to the rocky crest of Sgurr na Tuaigh that flanks the great cauldron rift of Eag Dubh. Move left, taking care not to fall into the bottomless steeps, and make your way round the head of this great rift. Keep climbing the edge above: eventually the gradient relents and the shoulder leads to the circular, beehive-shaped summit cairn, the highest point of Beinn Alligin.

Descend the ridge to the west; this leads to the col beneath the first Horn. Even though the crest is some 10m wide it feels very exposed, with the

A Brocken Spectre seen over Toll nam Biast (corrie of the beast) whilst descending the ridge from Sgurr Mhor

great drop of Toll nam Biast ('Corrie of the Beast') waiting to the left (north). The path is well worn and leads to the top of the first Horn (steeper ways up, of Scrambling Grade 0.5, are possible). This is the most substantial and the highest of the three horns. A narrow (2m wide) rock ridge resembling the top of Hadrian's Wall runs along its summit, then a small rock step of Scrambling Grade 0.25 leads down a short gully and so to the col. The way up the second Horn leads over sandstone blocks – done directly this gives Scrambling Grade 0.5, though it is just a walk to the right – to the pyramidal jumble of sandstone blocks that comprises the summit.

Descend to the right via another small, rocky step down a gully; this constitutes Scrambling Grade 0.3. There are two ways to climb the final little turret/horn: the easy way is to the right, and the harder is to climb the rocks directly (Scrambling Grade 1). The downward path leads out onto a minor ridge, then falls centrally to the platform of An-t Sail Bheg below. Keep to the middle of the platform, and continue to the point where a small cairn marks the way off; the path drops down over the steep sandstone steps, with one little scoop reaching Scrambling Grade 0.3 in difficulty.

Follow the path below, bearing left at a large rock and walled ruins, to cross left over a small footbridge above the Allt a' Bhealach, a smooth, slabby gorge carved from the sandstone. This was once the main route between Torridon and Shieldaig (by Loch Gairloch). Continue, then cross the bridge over the main burn of Abainn Coire Mhic Nobuil, another rock gorge; keep going, down its true left bank, on an excellent sandy path. Before the bridge the gorge deepens, and mixed woods of smooth-leaved holly, rowan, beech, oak, silver birch and Scots pine lead seductively back to the main road bridge.

The beehive summit cairn on Sgurr Mhor (surrounded by cloud)

THE EAST to WEST TRAVERSE of MIGHTY LIATHACH

The old shielings of Coire Liath Mhor, sandstone bluffs, a tremendous view over Beinn Eighe, and great exposure on The Pinnacles

Fact Sheet

Location: Torridon, Wester Ross, the Northern Highlands of Scotland

Length: 11km (6¾ miles)

Ascent: 1,490m (4,888ft)

Time: 8 hours

Difficulty: Long with strenuous ascent, and serious in that there are no simple ways off the 4km (2½ miles)-long spine of the mountain. If tackled directly, The Pinnacles offer interesting and exposed scrambling (Scrambling Grade 1.5), though they can all be bypassed by a path to their south. In winter The Pinnacles are a formidable proposition (Winter Grade II)

Seasons & Restrictions: Summer conditions may be expected from June to September, and winter conditions from October to May. The National Trust for Scotland is responsible for this region, so there are no restrictions

Map: OS Oudoor Leisure 8, The Cuillin & Torridon Hills

Start & Finish: At Glen Torridon, from the lay-by/pull-off south of the A896, 500m east of the trees of Glen Cottage (NG 935 566)

Access: Torridon lies some 100km (62 miles) north-west of Inverness along the A862, A835 and the A896, and some 75km (47 miles) north of Kyle of Lochalsh along the A87, A890 and the A896; note these are slow roads, and single track in places

Tourist Information: The National Trust for Scotland, The Countryside Centre, by the Diabaig junction in Torridon vIlage (tel. 01445 791221)

Accommodation: Within Torridon village there is a variety of places to stay, including an hotel with a bar which provides meals and snacks, also a campsite and a Youth Hostel. At Kinlochewe there are places offering B&B, and an inn

Geology: The Pinnacles and lower rocks are composed of Torridonian sandstone, a delightful rock, often including a matrix of quartz pebbles; hard and reliable, it is a little like concrete to walk and scramble on. The tops and higher rocks are of blocky grey quartzite, granular and sharp-edged, good to walk over and climb on, though more brittle than the sandstone

The Tops

Liathach (lee-ag-akh = greyish one)

Stuc a' Choire Dhuibh Bhig	915m (3,002ft)	(stookh a' kora ghoo bayk = little conical peak of the black corrie)
Bidean Toll a' Mhuic	983m (3,225ft)	(beedyan towl a' vukh = top of the pig's hollow)
Spidean a' Choire Leith	1,055m (3,461ft)	(speedyan a kora nan lay-ha = peak of the grey corrie)
Am Fasarinen	927m (3,042ft)	(am fas-rinnen = the teeth)
Mullach an Rathain	1,023m (3,358ft)	(moolokh an ra-han = summit of the pulley block)

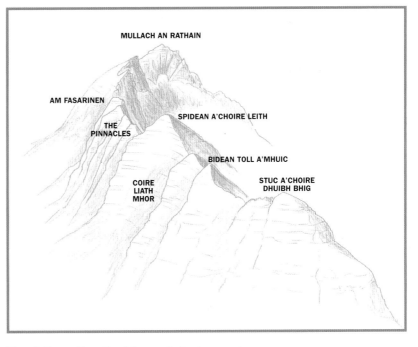

Flora & Fauna: Peregrine falcon and wheatear may be seen, also mountain hare and red fox. Spotted orchid, bog asphodel and dwarf cornel grow in this region

Comment: This is the toughest of the Torridon 'big three', particularly if The Pinnacles are climbed directly. Nevertheless it is a wonderful, powerful, high mountain challenge – the fairest of the fair.

■ From Glen Torridon you can certainly sense the awesome power emanating from Liathac, but you have only a limited visual impression of her immense bulk. Her lower slopes and mid-heights dominate the field of vision, but you can only make out a fraction of her distant heights, and then the effect is softened by the telescoped perspective, where 1,000m of vertical height are crammed into hardly any horizontal. To see the real Liathach – the great pinnacles, the razor-sharp edges, the soaring aretes, the towering cones and spires and the great hanging corries of that 4.5km (3 mile)-long spine, you have to view her from afar, preferably from the heights of the great north – from the mountains rising above the Shieldiag and Flowerdale Forests – or better still, by climbing her steep flanks, and experiencing her great ridge at first hand.

Walk east along the road a little way until you come to a cairn marking a junction with another path: this climbs the heather to reach the Allt an Doire Ghairbh burn. Cross the burn and ascend its east bank. Recent path repairs of pitched sandstone, invisible from below, have much improved the going, and progress up through the steep ground and rock bluffs above the waterfall is much easier.

On entering the heather basin of Coire Liath Mhor, surrounded by blocky sandstone buttresses, the gradient moderates. Here can just be seen the remains of ancient ruined buildings; barely discernible, they are most probably those of a summer shieling traditionally occupied on May Day.

Follow the steepening east bank of the burn to the cliff, then make your way out to the right from the gully. It is a well worn path here, which climbs a series of small sandstone bluffs, offering some easy scrambling (Scrambling Grade 0.5); even so, taken together it makes for a strenuous ascent. Then suddenly you arrive at a knife-edged col of pale pink/chocolate brown sandstone. To make the full traverse of the mountain and for spectacular views east over Beinn Eighe, you must first bear right, round a little pinnacle, and ascend the shoulder, continuing until you reach the final rise to the top of Stuc a' Choire Dhuibh Bhig. In fact the least interrupted view is a little further along on the eastern terminus.

Retrace your steps to the gap, and on along the narrow, switchback ridge until a blocky sandstone crest merges with the first pyramid-shaped summit of two-topped Bidean Toll a' Mhuic. Steep, blocky quartzite leads to the first top, then you run down

into a dip, and up again to the quartzite crest summit of Bidean Toll a' Mhuic. Descend to the next col, and then again there is a steep climb upwards: as you approach the top of the great pyramidal dome of Spidean a' Choire Leith, the summit of Liathac, the steepening blocks of quartzite make interesting scrambling; finally an exposed rock crest leads to the summit cairn.

A whole new perspective now opens up: over Coire na Caime the view west is daunting, over The Pinnacles and along the sharp sloping edge which leads to the final summit of Mullach an Rathain: and it can be appreciated that the most challenging section of the traverse of Liathach is yet to begin.

A faint path weaves very steeply down the quartzite blocks and scree of the west flank of Spidean a' Choire Leith; eventually it traverses left and reaches a col. A narrow, steep-sided rent in the sandstone, the head of a gully, provides a clear view north to the green-edged, dark waters of Loch Coire na Caime far below. Now begins the traverse of The Pinnacles, and there is a choice of route: either you can take the easy path which skirts round to the left – though exposed, this route will avoid all the difficulties. Alternatively you may choose to climb The Pinnacles themselves, in which case you will start by climbing the flat top above the head of the gully – this is the first and easiest pinnacle. There are four major pinnacles in all: the second is interesting; the third towers over the first two and is the most difficult; and the fourth is the highest and grandest. It's a steep climb to the third pinnacle, with tremendous exposure, though the technical difficulties are not too great: overall it probably warrants Scrambling Grade 1.5. Continue then to the fourth, to Am Fasarinen, the highest and the grandest of them all; and finally descend to regain the shoulder at a flat platform. The easier path rejoins the main traverse at this point.

A path leads diagonally down across the southern flank of the ridge. However, before you think of descending, it is well worth climbing up to the right first, to include the unnamed top, and then joining the crest of the ridge and following its exposed edge to the final top and trig point of Mullach an Rathain. This offers a truly awe-inspiring position, with breathtaking views in all directions.

Now descend the southern slopes towards Creag Dubh nam Fuaran, bearing left and descending the broad gully of Toll Ban. As you approach the base of this hollow, bear right above the Allt an Tuill Bhain burn, and make your way down the broad rocky nose, following the path around the rocky bluffs; you will reach the road as it touches the River Torridon between the two plantations (there is a small lay-by/pull-off above the river). Head east back up the road for 2.5km (unless you have been canny enough to have left a car at this point).

Above: Traversing The Pinnacles of Am Fasarinen

Below: Looking west towards Mullach an Rathain from Am Fasarinen with Loch Torridon below left

THE GREAT RIDGE of BEINN EIGHE

Black Carls/Black Men, six tops, six ridges, the Triple Buttress of Coire Mhic Fhearchair

Fact Sheet

Location: Torridon, Wester Ross, the Northern Highlands of Scotland

Length: 19km (11¾ miles)

Ascent: 1,425m (4,675ft)

Time: 10 hours

Difficulty: This is a long expedition: even the approach to the massif involves a considerable distance, as does the way out, and the ridge itself has six sections of ascent. Technically the most difficult part of the whole ridge lies in the negotiation of the shattered quartzite pinnacles of the Bodaich Dubh (the 'Black Men/Pinnacles', also known as 'Black Carls'): if tackled directly they make interesting scrambling (Scrambling Grade 2), though with care the main difficulties can be bypassed

Seasons & Restrictions: Summer conditions may be expected from June to September; winter conditions from October to May. This region is the responsibility of Scottish Natural Heritage, so there are no restrictions

Map: OS Oudoor Leisure 8, The Cuillin & Torridon Hills

Start: From Glen Torridon; there is limited parking on the verge of the A896 just north of the bridge crossing the Allt a' Chuirn burn, some 100m south of Cairn Shiel cottage and 1km south of Kinlochewe (NH 025 609)

Finish: In Glen Torridon, at the small car park above the north side of the A896 just west of the Allt Coire an Amoich (NG 958 568)

Access: Torridon lies some 100km (62 miles) north-west of Inverness along the A862, A835 and the A896, and some 75km (47 miles) north of Kyle of Lochalsh along the A87, A890 and the A896; note these are slow roads, single track in places

Tourist Information: The National Trust for Scotland, The Countryside Centre, by the Diabaig junction in Torridon village (tel. 01445 791221)

Accommodation: Within Torridon village there is a variety of places to stay, including an hotel with a bar offering meals and snacks, also a campsite and a Youth Hostel. There are limited facilities at Kinlochewe, including a barn bunkhouse and petrol station, a 'B&B' and an inn

Geology: The rocks along the ridge are predominantly quartzite, and the going is generally good. The Bodaich Dubh pinnacles are black (mineralised)-skinned, white

The Tops

Beinn Eighe (by-an ay = ice mountain)

Creagh Dhubh	905m (2,969ft)	(craik doo = black cliff)
Sgurr nan Fhir Duibhe	963m (3,160ft)	(skoor nan eer dooya = peak of the black men/pinnacles)
Sgurr Ban	970m (3,182ft)	(skoor baan = white peak)
Spidean Coire nan Clach	993m (3,258ft)	(speedyan kora nan clakh = peak of the stony corrie)
A' Coinneach Mhor (east top)	954m (3,130ft)	(a' chawnyokh voar = the big moss)
Ruadh-stac Mor	1,010m (3,314ft)	(big red stack)

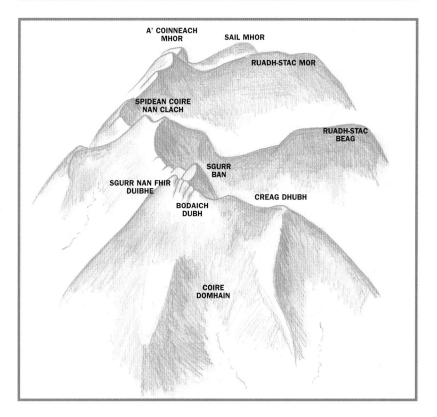

quartzite, and heavily jointed and frost-shattered – so have a care with the hand- and footholds. Underfoot some blocky beds of quartzite contain coral-like fossils. The rocks of the basin of Coire Mhic Fhearchair and the base layer of the Triple Buttress are red Torridonian sandstone

Flora & Fauna: Golden eagle, buzzard and lapwing may be seen; also red deer, wildcat and pine marten. Alpine meadow rue, interrupted club moss, alpine club moss, parsley fern and alpine lady fern grow in this region

Comment: This is a major mountain expedition; moreover it is linear, and requires two cars or pre-arranged transport. Tackling it this way, from east to west, has the advantage of ending in Coire Mhic Fhearchair (corra vik erra-ka), a particularly magical place at sunset and with an excellent, recently reconstructed/paved path leading all the way back to the road.

■ Especially in mid-summer, the long white quartzite scree slopes which fall from the high shoulders of Beinn Eighe are clearly the reason for its Gaelic name of 'ice mountain'. Beinn Eighe is permanently white, apparently always clad in winter garb. The full traverse of its main ridge is the longest of all the Torridon ridge traverses, and despite a somewhat bland appearance from Glen

Torridon, it is undeniably a most magnificent expedition.

In all there are six separate sections of ridge, each with its own particular character, crossing six major summits. Setting off from the east, the traverse begins with the steep climb of the east ridge of Creag Dhubh, and ends with the highest top of all, Ruadh-stac Mor; finally you descend into the hallowed, magical mountain sanctuary of Coire Mhic Fhearchair, to make the long circuitous trek back to Glen Torridon. Each top also signals a change in direction. Thus after a westward ascent to Creag Dhubh, the way swings through 90 degrees, striking a line south over the exciting pinnacles of Bodaich Dubh to ascend Sgurr nan Fhir Duibhe. Subtle changes follow, and we find that the final leg has swung through 90 degrees, this time heading due north.

A track climbs upwards on the west side of Cairn Shiel cottage and joins a good path,

A superlative panorama showing all the main tops of Beinn Eighe seen from Creag Dhubh; from left to right Sgurr Ban, Spidean Coire nan Clach, A' Coinneach Mhor and Ruadh-stac Mor

Above: The Beinn Eighe ridge from Fhir Duibhe with Liathach beyond to the left

occasionally peaty, above the right bank of the Allt a' Chuirn burn. Before you get to the Scots pine, a kissing gate leads through the Beinn Eighe deer fence; this was erected by the Nature Conservancy Council to keep deer out and so allow the natural woods to become re-established. Scramble down the bank to cross the burn and up the far side, which is steep; then follow a heather ridge – also steep – up through the magical little enclave of trees. Follow the broad quartzite spur above, until the steep east ridge of Creag Dhubh lies in front. Start your ascent of the ridge by the path on its right side; it leads diagonally right across the scree towards the head of the burn. After a little way a steep scree path grinds up to the left, to a shoulder on the sharp-edged ridge above. Continue directly up the crest to the summit cairn of Creag Dhubh.

A fine view extends over the vast northern corries to the last and highest top of Ruadh-stac Mor. Make your way along the ridge and over the

Right: Negotiating The Black Carls of Bodaich Dubh

first shattered pinnacle of Bodaich Dubh; the going is relatively easy. Then clamber along the broken crest to another little buttress; if this is climbed directly it provides a short sharp scramble (Scrambling Grade 2), although it can be bypassed more easily to the right (the north-west). A notched col follows, and at this point an easier path may be taken to the left (the south-east): this path bypasses all the difficulties and leads to an easy climb taking you to the top of Sgurr nan Fhir Duibhe. The direct route follows the true crest to ascend the next blocky pinnacle; it then descends to another rift, and up again to the summit (this is Scrambling Grade 2 – take care with the blocky holds).

Descend to the col, then up the steep ascent to the shapely pyramidal top of Sgurr Ban. A lesser descent leads to the flatter ridge which connects with the next top, that of Spidean Coire nan Clach. The ridge itself involves a short section of easy rocky scrambling, then a traverse of flat, slabby blocks of quartzite. The crest of the ridge is around 3m wide at this point and reveals the fascinating fossilised remains of what were probably once ancient corals growing on the sea bed. It seems strange to find them here, and in quartzite. The going steepens to climb the flanks of Spidean nan Clach to gain the highest summit rocks.

The 1998 OS map states the true height of this point, which is so obviously much higher (actually 21m) than the trig point to be found down to the left. It is unusual to find a trig point placed so far off what is evidently the highest point of a top – indeed, until now most sources of reference have quoted the height of the trig point as being that of the highest point, which makes this anomaly even more strange. I can only assume that the good men of the OS, in the days when they used to carry a theodolite to these heights, placed it thus to ensure a clear sight line enabling them to complete their triangulation – or perhaps to see beyond Sgurr Ban to the summit of Sgurr nan Fhir Duibhe.

Beyond the trig point, follow the snaking ridge line; after some way it finally curves to climb greener heights and gain the east top of A' Coinneach Mhor. Descend to a col, and a well used scree path which takes you down into Coire Mhic Fhearchair; then climb again over terraces to the amazing circular cone of white quartzite blocks which constitute the final and highest summit of this superb ridge. However, don't rest for too long, because there is still a considerable distance to go.

If you don't fancy retracing your steps to the col, it is possible to descend directly (south-west) from the summit cone down the steep quartzite screes, rough and bouldery, to the basin of Coire Mhic Fhearchair. If you do, a word of caution: nearing the base of the steep scree there is a line of sandstone bluffs which are best avoided by turning left (south). Cross the tumble of dark red sandstone blocks; you will then pass a long white line where the final glacier melt has deposited its load of quartzite, and pick up a path above the shore of Loch Coire Mhic Fhearchair.

This is one of those special mountain places. As the sun begins to set, these three great citadels of rock become infused with light pink and orange, and gaze, like great faces, over the darkness of loch, wilderness and mountain to the distant sea. Cross the burn issuing from the loch and over the flat sandstone slabs, then make your way down the path to the west of the waterfall. A long, easy walk takes you around Sail Mhor, beneath the eastern nose of Liathach, and back to the road.

The falling sun illuminates the magnificent Triple Buttresses of Coire Mhic Fhearchair

THE GREAT FORGE of AN TEALLACH – by the LOCH TOLL AN LOCHAN HORSESHOE

Marble staircase, alpine peaks, then either high grade scrambling and great exposure or easy path

Fact Sheet

Location: The Northern Highlands of Scotland

Length: 15km (9¼ miles)

Ascent: 1,430m (4,690ft)

Time: 9 hours

Difficulty: This route is very demanding – even without the technical difficulties it is a strenuous outing with steep ascents and descents. The amazing alpine skyline of knife-edged crests and rocky pinnacles above Loch Toll an Lochan offers a superb scramble, and is both technically absorbing and incredibly exposed. The crux section is beyond Corrag Bhuidhe Buttress, over the three tops of Corrag Bhuide followed by Lord Berkeley's Seat, then ascending to the summit of Sgurr Fiona (Scrambling Grade 3, though easier variations can always be found to the south-west). All technical difficulties can be bypassed by following well worn paths off the crest to the south-west (on the Loch na Sealga side). This becomes a major mountaineering expedition in winter (Winter Grade II/III)

Seasons & Restrictions: Summer conditions may be expected from June to September, and winter conditions from October to May. Stalking may be in progress from August to October: apply to the Dundonnell estate (tel. 01854 633219)

Map: OS Landranger 19, Gairloch & Ullapool

Start & Finish: From the Dundonnel glen above the sea inlet of Little Loch Broom; there is limited off-road parking by a little bridge on the west side of the A832 (NH 112 858), or there is a larger car park 1km (¾ mile) south along the A832

Access: Dundonnell can be found some 38km (24 miles) south of Ullapool on the A835 and the A832, and some 95km (59 miles) north-west of Inverness along the A862, A831 and the A835

Tourist Information: Ullapool (tel. 01854 612135)

Accommodation: In the nearby Dundonnell Hotel and bunkhouse. Ullapool has all the facilities, including a campsite and a Youth Hostel. There is also a campsite with excellent facilities at Poolewe

Geology: The meat of the expedition is on wonderfully

The Tops

An Teallach   (an tya-lokh = the forge)

Sail Liath	954m (3,129ft)	(saal lee-a = grey heel)
Stob Cadha Gobhlach	959m (3,145ft)	(stop ca-ha goalakh = peak of the forked pass)
Corrag Bhuidhe Buttress	929m (3,048ft)	(korak a voo-ya buttress = yellow finger buttress)
Corrag Bhuidhe (the highest of three tops)		
	1,036m (3,399ft)	(korak a voo-ya = yellow finger)
Lord Berkeley's Seat	1,027m (3,369ft)	
Sgurr Fiona	1,059m (3,474ft)	(skoor fee-ana = wine peak)
Bidean a' Ghlas Thuill	1,062m (3,484ft)	(beedyan a glas hil = peak of the green hollow)
Glas Mheall Liath	962m (3,156ft)	(glas myowl lee-a = grey mound above the green)

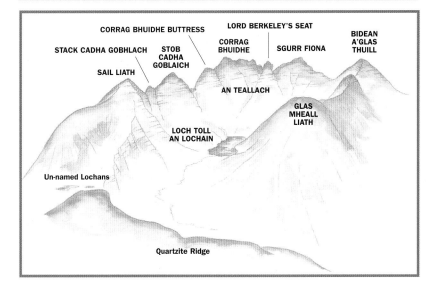

hard and sound Torridonian sandstone, though the 'marble staircase' is ice-polished quartzite, and the white-grey tops of Sail Leath and Glas Mheall Liath are also of blocky quartzite

Flora & Fauna: Golden eagle, buzzard, kestrel, curlew and hooded crow may be seen, also fox and mountain hare. Alpine bistort, willowherb and mountain sedge grow in this region

Comment: An Teallach offers one of the most spectacular skylines in the Scottish Highlands. It is not to be won easily, however, and is best tackled, as described, in a clockwise direction around Coir a' Ghiubhsachain and Toll an Lochan – an immensely fulfilling and satisfying expedition for those fit and competent enough to meet the challenge. Note that the heights given for the tops – and in particular for the slender pinnacles between Corrag Bhuidhe Buttress and Sgurr Fiona – should be taken as an approximate guideline only, certainly until the new series of 1:25,000 scale maps becomes available. Indeed, most other current sources of reference on the subject indicate that the height of Lord Berkeley's Seat is higher than the highest top of Corrag Bhuidhe – although to all those who look down on the former from the latter, it will be obvious that this cannot be so.

■ With its pyramidal spires, jagged pinnacles and knife edges, the skyline of An Teallach is one of the most impressive in the whole of the Scottish Highlands. This route describes a great horseshoe around Toll an Lochan, beginning along the 'marble staircase' of polished quartzite, then ascending Sail Liath, and finally ending down the nose of Glas Mheall Liath: it is undeniably one of the most perfect of high mountain adventures. It is also an outing in the upper stratum of difficulty, where a reasonable degree of physical fitness is a minimum requirement.

There is a stile over the fence to the left of the bridge (the true right bank of the burn), and the path then follows along above the burn; it is well trod, though overgrown by rhododendron at the start. It continues through a section of peat bog, then, with the burn tumbling from a rock gorge, climbs for a while; when the going levels again, strike a route ascending left to gain the end of the long edge of pure white: the Crag of Coir a' Ghiubhsachain. This remarkable natural feature of ice-polished quartzite rises gently for 3km and could be likened to a 'marble staircase'. It provides positively regal conditions to walk in, with a stately view across to the awesome grandeur of An Teallach. After a kilometre or so, however, it becomes somewhat disjointed, a neck of heather and grass, for instance, cutting across the edge, and access to the continuation of the bluff barred by a 20m cliff.

It is a simple scramble, however; climb the central rift, then move out left and up over ledges to reach the top (Scrambling Grade 0.5). Continue along the quartzite edge which becomes ever whiter, with open views over Toll an Lochan revealing the full horseshoe. At its end there is a slight descent, then the route swings round the left (south) end of the unnamed lochans to climb towards the nose of Sail Liath; the going is rough. Just left of the nose an eroded path leads up the steep scree to the gentler shoulder above. Continue to the summit cairn. Descend to a col, past Stack Cadha Gobhlach standing between the head of the two gullies of that name; it is then a steep climb to the summit cone of Stob Cadha Gobhlach.

Before you lies the long, flat-topped Corrag Bhuidhe Buttress (sometimes known as South Buttress), the pinnacles of Corrag Bhuide, and the great pyramidal cone of Sgurr Fiona. This naked sandstone edge, with huge cliffs falling to the right down to Toll an Lochain, presents a somewhat daunting challenge. This is, however, the best direction from which to tackle the obstacles, because all the difficulties lie in front and above, and it is a relatively easy matter to pick the best line (this is not the case the other way round). It is also an easy option to move left and follow one of the easier paths which traverse the south-western flank of the mountain safely below the rocky steeps.

Descend to the col and again cross over the heads of two gullies, then climb upwards to the blocky sandstone top of Corrag Bhuidhe Buttress. The way now ascends to the left of the edge,

On impressive ground – a solitary figure traversing the knife-edge crest of the middle top of Corrag Bhuidhe. Beyond the notch stands the north top and right again over the gap the pinnacle of Lord Berkeley's Seat

Left: An Teallach over Toll an Lochan as seen from the Marble Staircase

picking the easiest line to the south top of Corrag Bhuidhe (Scrambling Grade 2). There are three tops, the far northern one being the highest. Undoubtedly the boldest way to reach the middle top (actually an elongated crest) is to follow along the crest, although this is really knife-edged and fearfully exposed (Scrambling Grade 3) – just a little lower and to the left the route is a lot easier. The northern top is a small, independent spire, and an airy perch (Scrambling Grade 2). It is best to descend via the line of your ascent, then to follow round to the left to descend to the col and the foot of Lord Berkeley's Seat, a lovely independent pyramidal spire and an interesting climb (Scrambling Grade 1.5).

Make your way up from the col beyond to the

crest of Sgurr Fiona – another entertaining climb (Scrambling Grade 2 if the crest is followed, though there are many easier alternatives just to the left); this may not be the highest point, but because of its striking architecture and strategic position, it really does feel like the honorary summit of An Teallach. The descent is steep, and take care because the crest ends in crags lower down; to get down to the col it is safer to follow a path slightly to its left side. On tiring legs it can feel a mighty long way up to the top of Bidean a' Ghlas Thuill, but this is the true summit of the great An Teallach, with a commanding view back over the ridge.

From the trig point descend to the south-east, skirting to the right of the rocky bluffs and keeping

below the false summits guarding the great gullies which drop to the north. The way soon levels, and at a little notch cut through the crest of the ridge the rocks turn dramatically from dark chocolate-red Torridonian sandstone to strikingly white-grey quartzite. Follow the quartzite to the conical final top of Glas Mheall Liath. Descent is steep and bouldery, and care should be taken. It is best to keep to the right – to the south-east of the nose – for this leads more quickly to easier, heathery ground and avoids the sandstone bluffs near the base of the front (east) of the nose.

A little way further down to the right is the path which falls from Loch Toll an Lochan; although it is narrow, it is cairned, and is not too difficult to find. Follow it, traversing left to the valley floor. It takes a roughly central route along Coir a' Ghiubhsachain, tracking the rounded back of the bare, tilting sandstone beds to make good progress to the burn: this is forded as it meanders above the waterfall. Finally it passes beneath the end of the skeletal white quartzite bluff of Crag Coir a' Ghiubhsachain – truly a stairway to heaven – and so takes you home.

The incomparable An Teallach skyline seen from Stack Cadha Gobhlach

Along the heights; the prospect north from the south top of Corrag Bhuidhe, first to the prominent end of the middle top, then over the north top and finally to the peak of Sgurr Fiona

BEN MOR COIGACH

Narrow rock ridge, the nose of Sgurr an Fhidhleir, great openness with a view over the Summer Isles

Fact Sheet

Location: The Coigach 'peninsula' north of Ullapool, the Northern Highlands, north-west Scotland

Length: 10km (6¼ miles)

Ascent: 850m (2,790ft)

Time: 6 hours

Difficulty: There is some mild scrambling to be had up the nose and along the ridge of Garbh Choireachan (Scrambling Grade 0.25), although all difficulties can be easily bypassed. The paths are all in reasonable condition

Seasons & Restrictions: Summer conditions may be expected from April to October, winter conditions from November to March. There are no restrictions

Map: OS Landranger 15, Loch Assynt

Start & Finish: There is a turning/parking point at the end of the surfaced road at Culnacraig (NC 064 041), with enough space for cars to pull off onto the grass verge so as not to interfere with turning requirements

Access: From Ullapool, follow the A835 north and then the Achiltibuie road, passing through Achiltibuie, for some 45km (28 miles)

Tourist Information: Ullapool (tel. 01854 612135)

Accommodation: There are limited facilities at Polbain and Achiltibuie (the latter has a Youth Hostel) and there are inns at both (though at the time of writing the English landlord at Achiltibuie does not appear to care for the custom of hillwalkers). The nearest campsite is at Achnahaird

Geology: Torridonian sandstone predominates

Flora & Fauna: Golden eagle and golden plover may be seen, also fox and wildcat. Heath violet, devil's-bit scabious and alpine lady's mantle grow in this region

Comment: This is a delightful mountain with an outstanding outlook. The area is classed as a Grade 1 SSSI, and is administered by the Scottish Wildlife Trust. It may be worth mentioning that I experienced navigation problems in thick mist on Ben Mor Coigach, both with compass needle deflection and when trying to match the 1:50,000 scale map detail with actual ground detail. It may have been incompetence, though others have reported similar difficulties.

The Tops

Garbh Choireachan	733m (2,405ft)	(garav coor-akhan = rough corries)
Ben Mor Coigach	743m (2,438ft)	(ben moar coe-igakh = big mountain of the fifth portion of land of Ross)
Sgurr an Fhidhleir	703m (2,306ft)	(skoor an eelir = fiddler's peak)

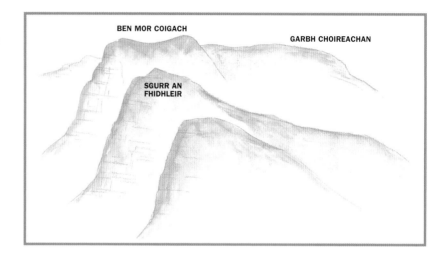

■ Ben Mor Coigach has a wonderful position, with Loch Broom and the Summer Isles to the south and west and the wonderful, unique sandstone mountains and wilds of Sutherland stretching to the north. Yet despite its size – some 10km (6 miles) in length and 6km (4 miles) in width – and its strategic position spread across the base of the fifth finger of land that is Coigach, it somehow manages to draw a veil over its true character. Neither from the A835 Ullapool road nor from the narrow road to Achiltibuie, from where it is largely obscured by Beinn an Eoin, does it reach out and grab your attention: to appreciate this mountain of quiet quality, its remote corries, plunging cliffs and fine ridges have to be experienced at first hand.

Taken in an anticlockwise direction, this round begins at the few scattered crofts of Culnacraig and requires that you drive all the way around Coigach to reach it. It is good that this is so, because it

West towards Sgurr an Fhidhleir from the col beyond Ben Mor Coigach

enables you to savour the special ambience of the area, and enhances the feeling of remoteness. From the end of the road, bear left on the path above the white-washed croft surrounded by lovely rowan and silver birch. The level path traverses the flanks of the hillside; follow it until it begins to descend, at which point strike away from it and up the hill to the left. You will come to the Allt nan Coisiche burn; cross it below the gorge, and climb up the spur to its right (the true left bank of the burn). A well worn path leads to a level shoulder, and then bears right to the steep rocky nose of Garbh Choireachan.

This steep ascent can be made more difficult by scrambling the nose directly, or easier by keeping to its left. Whichever route is taken, both lead to the top of the ridge and along to the cairn marking the top of Garbh Choireachan. The Summer Isles float below, whilst the impressively profiled top of

The nose of Sgurr an Fhidhleir can be seen to the north. The ridge is absolutely delightful, a flat-topped, narrow rock crest on which are balanced little tors and towers of sandstone. Continue along it to gain the broad shoulder of Ben Mor Coigach.

Bear left over the rocky slabs and short grass towards the summit cone. Nestled within pockets or spread across the rocky slabs, where the gravelly matrix of Torridonian sandstone has weathered away with the aeons of time, are clusters of marble-like pebbles of white quartz and blood-red agate, rocks that were old when the 1,000 million-year-old sandstone, one of the oldest sedimentary rocks in the world, hadn't even been born. Locally they are called 'chuckies', a name derived from the children's game for which they are so perfect – that of throwing a handful in the air and seeing how many you can catch on the back of your hand (in the north of England we call it 'jacks' or 'fives').

Right over the head of Loch Bad a' Ghail can be seen the nose of Sgurr an Fhidhleir and the long back of Coigach. (The two peaks in front are those of Beinn an Eoin)

The summit is adorned with a circular shelter and offers a spellbinding panorama. Head north-east to surmount a rocky knoll above the head of the great north-eastern cliffs of the mountain, then follow down their edge to the col beneath the next objective, that of Sgurr an Fhidhleir. The nose of this peak, falling a sheer 300m to Lochan Tuath, is a very impressive sight and a famous rock climb. A little rock peninsula just north from the general line of cliff allows a more detailed examination. In fact it is very difficult to appreciate the sheer scale of the face unless there are rock climbers in action, who appear as little more than pin pricks on this great vertical sea of rock.

The climb to the summit prow of Sgurr an Fhidhleir is very steep indeed: when you get there you will find a slabby rock table and cairn in an impressive position – over Beinn an Eoin and Loch Lurgainn, the great sugar-loaf mountains of Stac Pollaidh (left) and Cul Beag (right) look absolutely magnificent. Descend to the south-west, first over scree and then taking the well worn little path through the heather and grass along the shoulder between Allt a' Choire Reidh and Allt nan Coisiche. With the Summer Isles becoming ever more prominent, continue to make your way back to Culnacraig, along an easy path.

Sgurr an Fhidhleir glimpsed from the north (above); and the Summer Isles seen from the gentle shoulder falling from Sgurr an Fhidhleir

STAC POLLAIDH

Fairy castle, easily accessible, exhilarating scrambling along a ridge of sandstone towers, a supreme panorama

Fact Sheet

Location: Above the Achiltibuie road, the Inverpolly region of Wester Ross, the Northern Highlands, north-west Scotland

Length: 5km (3 miles)

Ascent: 590m (1,936ft)

Time: 4 hours

Difficulty: This walk involves some strenuous climbing, and the route as detailed some absorbing and very exposed scrambling (Scrambling Grade 1.5). There are usually easier alternatives, with the exception of a squat, 5m tower blocking the narrow neck of ridge which guards the western terminus and summit. Climb with care here, because a slip would be disastrous

Seasons & Restrictions: Summer conditions may be expected from April to October; winter conditions from November to March. There are no restrictions

Map: OS Landranger 15, Loch Assynt

Start & Finish: From the car park by the side of the Achiltibuie road directly beneath the mountain (NC 108 095)

Access: Some 25km (15.5 miles) north of Ullapool, follow the A835 north and then the Achiltibuie road

Tourist Information: Ullapool (tel. 01854 612135)

Accommodation: The nearest campsite is at Achnahaird; there is also one at Ardmair and at Ullapool, where you will find a Youth Hostel, too, and all facilities

Geology: The rock is largely Torridonian sandstone, which is generally excellent for walking and scrambling, although there are loose sections of scree on the ledges

Flora & Fauna: Buzzard and peregrine may be seen, also hare, adder and polecat. Heather, blaeberry and starry saxifrage grow in this area

Comment: Positioned immediately above the road, this is one of the most aesthetic and delightful mountains in the whole of Scotland; the open panoramic view, of exceptional mountains and wilderness, is nothing short of stunning. The route described maximises the length and character of the summit ridge by ascending the east nose; it is not the regular path, however, and walkers should take extra care; in particular keep an eye out for stonefall from the 'tourist routes'.

The Top

Stac Pollaidh (west top)   613m (2,011ft)   (stack polly = muddy stack)

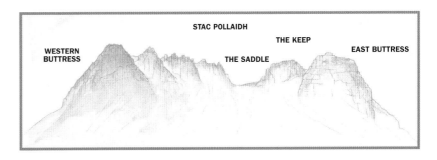

■ If you had to slog through peat bog for hours at a time just to reach the foot of this mountain you would still do it, simply because Stac Pollaidh is of tantalising form and irresistible appeal. Rising in isolation from Loch Lurgainn, its 45-degree flanks are topped by red sandstone buttresses and minaret towers, making it the perfect fairytale castle. And fortuitously, perhaps, it is also one of the most easily accessible mountains in Scotland.

The stickleback profile seen from the car park below is a reasonably true representation of the ridge as it is actually found. To the left stands the Western Buttress, flanked on its right by the deep rift of West Gully. Rock climbers use this in descent, although it involves some tricky climbing down rock slabs near the top (Scrambling Grade 3); in its depths and hidden from below, though seen easily enough from the ridge, is a two-pronged rock pinnacle sometimes referred to as the 'Virgin and Child'. To the right beyond the next prominent buttress (Number Two Buttress) is a wide, deep rift known as the Pinnacle Basin; here stands an even taller pinnacle which I call the Split Totem Pole, though it is more commonly referred to as The Lobster Claw. Again to the right is the distinctive flat break of The Saddle, where most people usually arrive: the most popular (tourist) route climbs straight up to it by the south face – it is steep and quite badly eroded. A similar route on the north si

Stac Pollaidh seen from the west

Left: Virgin and Child pinnacles found on the south flank opposite the Western Buttress

is not quite so steep, and is made even easier by virtue of zigzag paths ascending the scree. To the right of The Saddle stands The Keep, separated by a small rift from the final tower of the East Buttress.

The path climbs steeply to a plateau: it is from here that the hill of the castle rises. Another path bears right from the main drag, then runs beneath the eastern nose to the northern flank of the mountain. Leave the main route and ascend left to tackle the East Buttress to the right of the nose; this provides entertaining and not-too-difficult scrambling. Make your way over the buttress, then across the gap to The Keep; the way down to The Saddle is easy, and the start of a wonderfully entertaining ridge.

After a while you will come to a small crag barring the way. Paths go either side, but the quickest way of regaining the crest is to go right. Then continue following the crest, tackling its many towers, slabs and blocky outcrops in whatever way you feel is best. Towards the end of the ridge the top of Number Two Buttress protrudes to the south: it offers a good view of the ridge as a whole, and of the great cliff which falls from the Western Buttress in particular.

The final tower of this great castle has yet to be won, however. The exposure is considerable, and beyond the head of the West Gully a 5m high block of sandstone bars the way. It is a steep drop on each side, and the only satisfactory route is to climb its face – this requires a little balance work, though good positive handholds can be found, and the way is but short. However, there is no room for error, and the consequences of a slip would be very serious. The route down the other side is straightforward, and now the final obstacle is but a few strides away: the top of the West Buttress and the summit of Stac Pollaidh.

Superlative and uninterrupted views extend in all directions: to Ben Mor Coigach, to Cul Beag and to mighty Cul Mor. To the west lies Enard Bay, the tip of Rubha Coigeach and a blue sea backed by the Outer Hebrides. Best of all is the view north across the great expanse of Sutherland's magical wilderness of moor and loch to Suilven and Canisp. This is undeniably one of the finest landscapes to be seen in this world: the storming of Stac Pollaidh holds great riches indeed.

The most straightforward strategy in descent is to retreat along the ridge the way you came. At The Saddle you can make your way down either of the popular paths.

SUILVEN – THE EAST to WEST TRAVERSE

Sphinx-like head and body, a magnetic personality, and an ancient masonry stone wall spanning the top ridge

Fact Sheet

Location: Above Lochinver (A387), Sutherland, the Northern Highlands, north-west Scotland

Length: 24km (15 miles)

Ascent: 915m (3,002ft)

Time: 10 hours

Difficulty: Suilven is a serious proposition whatever the route you tackle it by. Firstly the formidable nature of the mountain itself must be taken into account: it is a whaleback of sandstone, its flanks steep cliffs, the only natural breach in these defences being the Bealach Mor running north to south over the ridge. Secondly it is extremely remote, a considerable distance of rough terrain separating it from the road, and the length and remoteness of this walk are important considerations. Approaching from the distant west, the route described here then in fact traverses the ridge of the mountain from east to west, and from this direction there are two sections of technical difficulty. The first and most trying of these is the descent from Meall Bheag to the gap below (east of) Meall Mheadhonach: although physically this is not unduly difficult, it is extremely exposed and requires careful route-finding (Scrambling Grade 2). Secondly, the descent from Meall Mheadhonach involves the negotiation of a 12m rock band (Scrambling Grade 2). Of course, in winter conditions the traverse of the mountain is a mountaineering expedition (Winter Mountaineering Grade II)

Seasons: Summer conditions may be expected from June to September; winter conditions from October to May

Map: OS Landranger 15, Loch Assynt

Start & Finish: At Inverkirkaig, the car park by the bridge over the River Kirkaig (NC 085 194)

Access: Some 5km (3 miles) south of Lochinver; the latter is 55km (34 miles) north of Ullapool on the A835 and A837, and 150km (93 miles) north-west of Inverness

Tourist Information: Lochinver (tel. 01571 844330)

Accommodation: There are limited facilities in Lochinver. The nearest campsites are at Clachtoll and Achnahaird, and the nearest Youth Hostel is at Achmelvich

Geology: Typical of this region is Torridonian sandstone

The Tops

Suilven   (sool-ven = pillar mountain)
Meall Bheag	659m (2,162ft)	(meowl vake = little hill)
Meall Mheadhonach	723m (2,372ft)	(meowl vee-anakh = middle hill)
Caisteal Liath	731m (2,398ft)	(kastyal lee-a = grey castle)

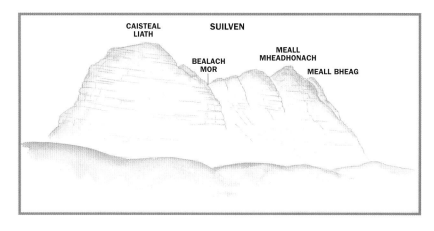

standing on a platform of gneiss; this gives good going where exposed. White quartzite boulders scattered over the top of Caisteal Liath may be mistaken for sheep

Flora & Fauna: Golden eagle, white-tailed eagle, ring ouzel and the great northern diver may be seen, also red deer, mountain hare and wildcat. Heather, northern rock cress, alpine hair grass and mountain sedge grow in this region

Comment: Although there are easier ways to climb Suilven, and shorter routes, this circular outing is one of the finest. It is an outstanding wilderness expedition to a legendary mountain.

The gateway in the remarkable stone wall which runs across the ridge, found beyond Bealach Mor en route to Caisteal Liath

■ Suilven is one of the most beguiling and intriguing of all British mountains. It is also massively impressive, its bulk dominating the wilds of Sutherland, the great flats of interwoven heather, the myriad lochs and the grey, rumple-skinned gneiss. From the west, looking from the sea over Lochinver, the head is a massive, vertical-sided rock dome: this is the aptly named Caisteal Liath. From here a 2km spine runs east, first falling to

Observed from Achnahaird, Suilven's sphinx-like western head, Caisteal Liath, looks to a colourful band of refracted light falling from a stormy sky

the saddle of Bealach Mor, then rising again to the raised rump, the high conical spire of Meall Mheadhonach. Even further to the east, separated by a fearsome rift, is the bobtail of Meall Mheadhonach.

The Vikings had their first impression of Caisteal Liath from the sea, and named it 'sul-r fjall', or pillar mountain. After the Vikings left, the Gaelic speakers referred to it as 'sul-r bheinn' (pronounced 'ven') hence the present name of Suilven ('sool-ven'); it is a famous landmark mountain known to mountaineers and to all who pass this way, from the Celts and the Vikings, to the Travelling People and tourists making their summer migration to the distant north.

This route starts in the distant west: it passes above the Falls of Kirkaig and along the shore of Fionn Loch, then runs beneath the mountain to gain the eastern ridge of Meall Mheadhonach. It then traverses the full length of the ridge from east to west before descending at Bealach Mor. There is then still a further 10km (6 miles) of wilderness to

be crossed, retracing your earlier steps, to return to the starting point. Though the going is generally good, this is a long and demanding hike – the rewards, however, are infinitely worth the effort.

Follow the track above the river until, after a short while, a path bears off to the right. It keeps parallel to and above the great river, eventually rising up the hillside to pass above the rocky gorge and the Falls of Kirkaig which lie hidden below. The path levels, and then begins a gradual descent toward Fionn Loch, with Suilven now standing mightily to the north-east; here a lesser path, with a cairn at the junction, bears off to the left. Follow this; rather boggy, though well trodden, it takes you down to the western wing-tip of Fionn Loch. Cross it by a stone wall bridge, and then follow the path up to the right.

The path descends to cross a peaty hollow known as Coire Mor, and crosses the stream by an ancient clapper bridge of stone slabs. Continue along the path: just before and by a knoll standing to the right it becomes a rather serious peat bog.

The track then steepens and climbs a little canyon to a col; at this point my preferred route is to climb up to the left to gain the level plateau of gneiss and sandstone boulder, then to bear right and continue along this until the flanks of Suilven are passed (the main path continues along the shore of Fionn Loch). The way is rather indeterminate in places, though well cairned and the going easy.

The plateau leads to a tongue of greensward, complete with hidden stream; from here a path climbs up to the right, passing a gneiss outcrop and then bearing right along a higher plateau of sandstone. Pass the path which breaks off to the left and climbs straight up the rocky gully and scree of Bealach Mor, and continue beneath the flanks of Suilven. Keep going, passing beneath the fearsome gap and cliffs of Meall Bheag, until you come to a large boulder with a lochan below: this marks the point at which it is best to begin

ascending towards the east ridge of Meall Bheag. Bear left, then work diagonally right, picking the best way through the rocky bluffs and green terraces – this is not difficult – until you emerge onto the open nose of the east ridge: immediately a tremendous view of Canisp to the north-east, and of myriad lochans entrapped in stony expanse to the east, opens up before your eyes.

Climb the steepening nose through an area of brown, red and white rocks made of pebbles of sandstone and quartz, an attractive mix with a resemblance to an angry swarm of bees. The ascent above begins to look daunting, though if you go to the right of the crest initially, then pick the easiest line, you will find the way is straightforward; it leads to the flat, grass table-top perch of Meall Bheag. A great rift divides this truncated cone from the body of the main mountain, that of Meall Mheadhonach; descending to this rift, and then

The table-top summit of Meall Bheag seen from Meall Mheadhonach. The exposed and demanding line of descent starts

West along Suilven's narrow spine over Bealach Mor to Caisteal Liath, as seen from Meall Mheadhonach. Following the descent of a steep little rock band below the top, the going is perfectly straightforward

crossing it, is the most demanding part of the walk. Finding the correct line of descent is imperative, because steep cliffs lie in all other directions (save that of the east ridge ascent already made).

From the summit cairn go west for a few metres, then down across a lower terrace to the north; you will find the beginning of a reasonably well worn path. Heading east at first, this path, steep and exposed in a number of places, zigzags down the north face until it cuts back left (west) to gain the deep rift at the top of a knife-edged crest (Scrambling Grade 2). Cross this and thankfully ascend the easier zigzags which climb to the high top of Meall Mheadhonach: this position, the comfortably flat top of a high cone perched on the crest of great cliffs, would be hard to better.

An undulating ridge, the cat's spine, now falls eastwards towards Bealach Mor. Descend west: in a few metres you will find a steep band of sandstone cliff barring progress. A little way to the left (south) of centre offers the best route. It is well worn and consists of a series of low walls and flat ledges; it soon reaches – after approximately 12m – easier ground below (Scrambling Grade 2, though it would feel a lot easier in ascent). Descend to the col, then make the short climb to another little top

before continuing down the still undulating, easy grassy ridge. This is broad enough, though knowing that steep cliffs plunge to each side, it would be hard to be totally oblivious of the potential for disaster.

Cross the neck of Bealach Mor – a safe descent can be made to the north or south from this point – then climb to a small, structured gateway gap in the stone wall. This remarkable structure is made from fashioned sandstone blocks, bedded horizontally, to form a cam right over the crest of the ridge. Suilven is a considerable grazing ground – though whether it was built to hold back sheep or deer, who can say? And who built it? Its remarkably pristine state could be because of its superior construction and not necessarily because of its modernity: it could be of recent construction, equally it could be, without evidence to the contrary, very ancient indeed.

Make your way up to a minor top, then down again to a neck before climbing the great dome of Caisteal Liath. Steep rocky outcrops and high exposure make this an entertaining ascent. The summit is wonderfully exposed, like being on the top of a great barrel, and although broad and domed, there is a real feeling that the steep encircling cliffs below are tucking in beneath you. Go forward for the best aspect of Lochinver and the sea.

Return the same way to the bealach; the descent is to the south, and it is steep. Keep to the right initially, and then turn more directly down the steep rough scree; a flood channel washed through the boulders gives some idea of the huge deluge of water that must sometimes flow down the mountainside. The going is rough and strenuous – be thankful that we didn't take this route in ascent. Take the path down to the greensward and sunken stream – if you can find something to push beneath its flow, its cool, clear water will be appreciated on a hot summer's afternoon. After a short, further descent down the greensward, bear right over the heather to regain and follow the gneiss plateau beneath the flanks of the mountain; alternatively it is possible to follow the line of the burn down to the shore of Fionn Loch. In either case, retrace your outward footsteps and make the long journey back to Inverkirkaig.

QUINAG

All the tops, railway siding, tiger rocks, a quick return

Fact Sheet

Location: Between Loch Assynt and Kylesku above the A894, Sutherland, the Northern Highlands, north-west Scotland

Length: 13km (8 miles)

Ascent: 1,200m (3,937ft)

Time: 6 hours

Difficulty: This walk has a few sections of steep ascent and descent, but no technical difficulties

Seasons: Summer conditions may be expected from June to September, and winter conditions from October to May

Map: OS Landranger 15, Loch Assynt

Start & Finish: There is ample parking in an old quarry just over the summit of Skiag Bridge to Kylesku Bridge pass on the east side of the A894 (NC 232 273)

Access: Some 45km (28 miles) north of Ullapool and the A835, A837 and the A894, and some 140km (87 miles) north-west of Inverness

Tourist Information: Lochinver (tel. 01571 844330)

Accommodation: The Inn at Kylesku is most welcoming, with excellent bar meals and restaurant. Lochinver and Scourie are the nearest towns, albeit very small; the nearest campsites are at Scourie and Achmelvich, and the nearest Youth Hostel is at Achmelvich

Geology: The rock is predominantly white-grey quartzite and purple-red Torridonian sandstone, and the going is good throughout

Flora & Fauna: Golden eagle, raven and goosander may be seen; also red deer and red fox. Alpine lady fern, alpine willowherb and alpine lady's mantle grow in this region

Comment: This is a fascinating walk, interesting throughout, with a strategic, elevated position between Kylesku to the north and Loch Assynt to the south. Starting from the top of the pass, at an altitude of 250m, gives you a most thankful advantage, and an excellent stalker's path makes the return route easier.

■ In plan, Quinag takes the form of a mirror image of the letter 'γ'. Looking north over Loch Assynt, above the ruined walls of Ardvreck Castle, along the bottom leg of the 'γ', it looks like a mildly pleasant mountain of no great excitement.

The Tops

Quinag (koonyak = three-legged milking stool)		
Spidean Coinich	764m (2,507ft)	(speetyan kawnyeekh = mossy peak)
Creag na h-Iolaire Ard	713m (2,339ft)	(krayk na hyool-ara aard = high crag of the eagle)
Quinag Central Top	745m (2,444ft)	
Sail Gorm	776m (2,546ft)	(saal go-rom = blue – as in 'distant' – heel)
Sail Gharbh	808m (2,651ft)	(saal garav = rough heel)

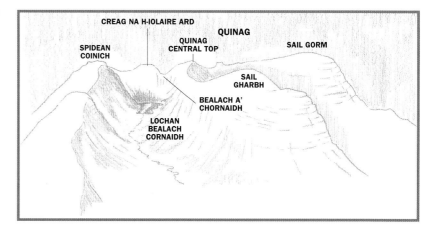

However, as you crest the Skiag Bridge to the Kylesku pass this is an impression that changes rapidly, and suddenly the cliffs and steeps ringing Lochan Bealach Cornaidh, and falling to the barrel buttress nose of Sail Gharbh which forms the right arm of the 'γ', take on dramatic significance. This impression of challenging steepness will only be confirmed should you continue to pass over the Kylesku Bridge and look south into the mouth of the 'γ'. The two tips of the 'γ' are formed by two great plunging noses of rock, separated by the basin of Allt a' Bhathaich.

This delightful round traces a line around the ridges of the 'γ'. The route first takes you along its main leg, over Spidean Coinich, and on to the north-western tip of Sail Gorm, before looping around its head to crest the north-eastern tip of Sail Gharbh. From here it then returns towards the Central Top, and quits the ridge to take a steep path

Quinag seen from the north beside the old road to Kylesku; Spidean Coinich seen to the left, Sail Garbh centrally and Sail Gorm to the right

descending to the path falling from Bealach a' Chornaidh. It returns home by passing the lochan and picking up the afore-mentioned stalker's path, which leads comfortably back to the pass. This is a walk around all three legs of this high milking stool.

From the quarry take the road south for a few metres until a path bears off down to the right to cross a small wooden footbridge. Carry on, and some 50m along it, a lesser path turns off through the squishy peat to gain the bone-hard whiteness of the quartzite shoulder. Follow the shoulder to a minor top, and cross it via a natural rock cleft; then descend to a col. A steep climb leads to the top of Spidean Coinich. Cross the top, and leave it to the south-west; it is now a steep descent down a sandstone ridge to a tiny lochan at the col. Down to the left Loch Assynt and her many jewels are threaded together by the narrow road leading to Lochinver. A short ascent leads to the top of Creag na h-Iolaire Ard; the narrow, grassy crest leads to an even narrower ridge which falls steeply to Bealach a' Chornaidh.

The path now climbs upwards to the Central Top of Quinag, which is located at the junction of the two arms of the 'γ'; out to the west the sea appears to be dotted with many tiny islands, reminiscent of the Summer Isles. Descend in a north-westerly direction to a col with cliffs to the left; a natural, flat-topped ridge of sandstone looks for all the world like a man-made railway track, then you pass a flat table mountain on a good path along its right (easterly) flank. The route now runs down to a col, after which you begin the ascent of the long final shoulder. Pass a rocky spur standing on the edge of the western cliffs (take care here as you make your way down, because a steep-sided rift cuts into the main shoulder) – from now on the path is straightforward all the way to the summit of Sail Gorm. It commands a fine position over sea, mountain and wilderness.

Take the same route back to the Central Top, though when you are partway up, swing left around to the col at the base of the eastern arm of the 'γ'. Cross the col and climb the arm, noting the

position of the small sandstone bluff near the base because this marks your point of departure from the ridge on your return. It is a straightforward, rocky climb to where purple-red sandstone tors become markedly tiger-striped with lighter rocks, and shortly beyond, the rock changes to grey-white blocky quartzite. The top of Sail Gharbh is marked by a concrete trig point surrounded by a low wall of quartzite.

Go down the way you came up, until at the foot of the sandstone edge/bluff, before the col, it is possible to swing left (south) off the ridge. The path falls diagonally to the right before taking a steeper line down the grass to a rough though well defined path that has come down from Bealach a' Chornaidh. Follow this path past the lochan, and on to pass a 3m high sandstone monolith – and so gain the start of the two-lane stalker's path. It is an easy matter to follow this back to the little footbridge.

A view south to the summit of Spidean Coinich and figure

Below: Looking back to the rocky head of Spidean Coinich from Creag na h-Iolaire

ARKLE/FOINAVEN INTEGRAL TRAVERSE

Wilderness challenge, clint and gryke pavement, moonscape quartzite, sensuous ridges

Fact Sheet

Location: Above Laxford Bridge on the A838: it's just a bridge, Reay Forest, Sutherland, the Northern Highlands, in north-west Scotland

Length: 26km (16 miles)

Ascent: 1,775m (5,823ft)

Time: 12 hours

Difficulty: This is a very long and arduous walk, with many sections of strenuous ascent; the going is predominantly over rough and difficult terrain. Add to all this the extreme remoteness, and it will be clear that this walk is a very serious and demanding proposition. There are no technical difficulties

Seasons & Restrictions: Summer conditions may be expected from June to September; winter conditions from October to May. Deer stalking may be in progress from August to October

Map: OS Landranger 9, Cape Wrath

Start: There is a wide verge where you can park on the A838, to the east of the entrance road to Lochstack Lodge (NC 270 435)

Finish: At the parking space by the pumping station on the west side of the A838 (NC 265 529)

Access: Some 90km (56 miles) north of Ullapool on the A894 and the A838, and 185km (115 miles) or so north-west of Inverness

Tourist Information: Durness (tel. 01971 511259)

Accommodation: At the end of the walk the nearby Rhiconoch Hotel has restaurant facilities. Durness has limited facilities, including a campsite and a Youth Hostel; the nearest campsite is at Oldshoremore. Kinlochbervie also has limited facilities

Geology: The rock is predominantly white-grey quartzite capping Lewisian gneiss. Blocky scree and bouldery ground make for very strenuous going

Flora & Fauna: Golden eagle, buzzard, snow bunting, peregrine, cormorant, greylag geese and greenshank may be seen; also red deer and wildcat. Devil's-bit scabious, royal fern and mossy saxifrage grow in this region

Comment: This is a real wilderness challenge and a marvellous ridge walk with sustained interest, particularly along Foinaven's narrow, undulating crest. This is a linear outing, so you should arrange for someone to drop you off,

The Tops

Arkle   (ark fjall = ark mountain)

Sail Mhor (Arkle)	787m (2,582ft)	(saal voar = great heel)
Arkle South Top	758m (2,487ft)	
Meall Aonghais	581m (1,906ft)	(me-owl ungish = rocky lump hill)

Foinaven   (fon-yavin = wart mountain)

Creag Dionard	778m (2,552ft)	(krayk din-aard = crag of the high hill fort)
Cadha na Beucaich Top	808m (2,651ft)	(ca-ha bak-ish = the roaring narrow pass)
A' Cheir Ghorm	869m (2,851ft)	(akeer go-rom = the blue comb)
Ganu Mor	914m (2,999ft)	(ganoo moar = big head)
Ceann Garbh	902m (2,959ft)	(kyown garav = rough end of mountain)

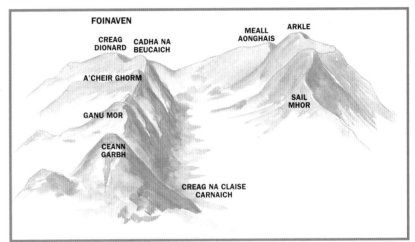

FOINAVEN
CREAG DIONARD
CADHA NA BEUCAICH
MEALL AONGHAIS
ARKLE
A'CHEIR GHORM
GANU MOR
SAIL MHOR
CEANN GARBH
CREAG NA CLAISE CARNAICH

or should pre-arrange transport; nor should this walk be underestimated, because when you have successfully achieved the heights, whichever way you choose to return by, the route back is long.

■ The landscape of these far northern climes is vastly different to any other in Britain. It has an incomparably ancient, timeless feel, of desolate vastness and openness of sky: a world of endless moor and loch, the distant mountains looming upwards like giants of wizened grey, heads bleached white by age and the weather. Lewisian gneiss is the dominant rock, capped by quartzite on the tops. Its great longevity helps put things in perspective, for it

Stalkers path to Arkle

is one of the oldest rocks in the world and has stood here for some three billion years: our fleeting existence by comparison hardly registers.

The long ridge of Foinaven is most remarkable. From the south and west its apparently rounded shoulders belie the reality, because it is in fact sensuously narrow, even knife-edged in places, requiring your constant attention and determined energy. Approaching via Arkle – itself a worthy prize – heightens the feeling of challenge and commitment, and the vast emptiness of this breathtaking region: this is truly a walk on the wild side.

Take the track over the bridge crossing the River Laxford, once much prized for its wild Atlantic salmon (the angling rights owned by the Duke of Westminster) and river pearls (which until recent times were fished for by the Travelling People), to bear right, away from Lochstack Lodge. The well constructed stalker's path provides easy going to the south-western flanks of Arkle; here it bears left, climbing upwards to a col beneath the tip of the north-west nose of Arkle's Sail Mhor. From the highest point of the path keep climbing up to the right, directly up the nose, taking the easiest line through the little rocky bluffs of gneiss to gain the

Looking back from the ascent towards Arkle's South Top in the direction of Sail Mhor

steep quartzite scree, zigzagging upwards and picking a way as best you can through the worst and most blocky section, to reach the summit plateau and beehive cairn of Sail Mhor: Arkle.

A narrow ridge stretches south, sweeping in a symmetrical curve around the great eastern corrie. It is structured from a cracked pavement of flat-topped quartzite blocks which resemble the grykes and clints of a classic limestone plateau; deep in the fissures (grykes) and therefore shielded from the elements, thrives a quite unique microcosm of rich fern and plant life. The pavement ends in a short way at a little square tower, though the knife-edge ridge continues, with Ben Stack to the right and vast openness and myriad lochs ahead. Descend from a flat top to the col, and up again across a remarkable pebble beach to gain the South Top of Arkle.

Cross the flat stones of white quartzite and descend the rocky slopes in a south-easterly direction; the quartzite becomes sharper and more pointed and quite awkward to walk down. A grass col provides just a moment's respite before the rocky protuberance of Meall Aonghais must be tackled – a desolate expanse of white-grey quartzite fills the scene, and you could be on the surface of the moon were it not for the dark basin of Lochan na Faoileige.

It is less stony and bouldery to pass the loch on its right side – its south-eastern shore – because unseen from above, a grassy swathe falls below it and leads to the little burn between the two small, unnamed lochans depicted on the OS map. The alternative route that follows the rocky rib to the left of Lochan na Faoileige is rough, bouldery and arduous, and best avoided. The clear, tumbling waters of the burn and its feeder stream provide a soothing haven of green moss, in pleasant contrast with the harsh moonscape of Arkle – a good place to take a brief rest, for the long, steep ascent and the taxing traverse of the great Foinaven awaits.

Ribs of quartzite run up the hillside, and the best policy is to climb either between, or on one of these ribs until the angle eases and they bring you up onto a peaty shelving plateau (Bealch Horn lies just to the right). Striated slabs of quartzite dip below the peat to form ponds of water, and you will need to pass the boggy sections as best as possible to gain the steeper flanks above; now you must tackle the long, though straightforward ascent to the circular

shelter and broken trig point of Creag Dionard (unnamed on the 1997 OS map).

The way down is steep; then cross the flat, stony hollow and up a sharp gradient again, to a cairn perched on the edge of steep ground: the top above Cadha na Beucaich (altitude 808m; it, too, is unnamed on the 1997 OS map). The next section is steep, rocky and scrambly (though not technically difficult) and requires care. A steep gully drops down to the right, and a path continues down the nose to the col of Cadha na Beucaich. The next climb up is just as sharp, but it leads to easy scrambling over a rocky knoll, Lord Reay's Seat, and on up the crest to the rocky pinnacle top of A' Cheir Ghorm. Strike off down the left ridge; after a while the going levels, then climbs once more to a subsidiary top. The ridge beyond is long, and ascends to the shoulder of Ganu Mor; bear right to gain the summit cairn and the highest top of Foinaven: a whisker beneath the 3,000ft mark at the last survey, depending on the state of the tide, of course (though I wouldn't take this for certain before the new series of 1:25,000 scale OS maps is issued).

The walk's end is probably in sight from here, because the route described here goes between Loch na Claise Carnaich and Lochan Cul na Creige, which can now be seen down to the left (north-west); however, the walk itself is far from over. Go down left to the col, then ascend north to the final top, that of Ceann Garbh. Great boulders of dark gneiss now take over from the quartzite. The way off described here is very interesting, and avoids the huge tracts of unpleasant bog that feature on the

Right: South from Arkle's Sail Mhor to the quartzite pavement of clints and grykes, Loch Stack seen down to the right

more regular route which goes directly north to Gualin House.

Leave the summit in a north-westerly direction, negotiating the boulders of gneiss by the easiest route, and make your way down the middle of the long nose leading first to a plateau, and then between the craglets of Creag na Claise Carnaich towards the shore of Loch na Claise Carnaich. The top section of the nose offers a little mild scrambling through the boulders, though the going soon eases and the route takes a more direct line downwards. Shelves of rock along the plateau hold a fascinating collection of boulders, some quite large ones balanced on stones (usually three) of much smaller size: they stand where the melting ice deposited them 10,000 years ago, and on no account disturb them for they are important natural works of art, providing valuable evidence of the last glacial epoch.

The plateau gives way to the steeper ground of Creag na Claise Carnaich, and now great slabs of gneiss and lesser craglets must be carefully

negotiated to reach the level heather below. With care, however, and a little mild scrambling on sound rock, all the difficulties can be bypassed. Bear right before the loch to cross the Allt na Claise Carnaich burn; in normal conditions, staying dry – with a suitably long jump! – is not a problem.

Follow down the right bank of the burn, then keep on a high route above the loch; at its far perimeter make your way down and cross between the loch to the left and the lochan to the right. A short way beyond this, a natural grassy corridor leads off to the right between the rocky knolls of gneiss; somewhat peaty and rather wet in places, it crosses the little burn and follows the northern shore of Loch an Eas Ghairbh. Finally, a path leads down the narrow, rocky canyon which runs parallel to a path running down the right bank of the burn that issues from the loch. Over the road bridge lies the pumping station. And so we come to the end of a marvellous mountain ridge walk, and a profound wilderness experience.

Foinaven seen looking over Loch na Claise Carnaich from the west

CAIRNGORM – THE FIACAILL RIDGES around COIRE AN T-SNEACHDA

Northern Corries, arctic high mountain environment with ease of access

Fact Sheet

Location: The Northern Corries of the Cairngorms above Aviemore (A9), north-eastern Scotland

Length: 8km (5 miles)

Ascent: 715m (2,346ft)

Time: 4 hours

Difficulty: Despite its close proximity to the Cairngorm Ski Development and even though it is easy to get to, the high plateau of Cairngorm is a serious proposition in anything but perfect conditions – indeed, the weather can be of arctic ferocity. The blocky ridge of Fiacaill Coire an t-Sneachda steepens to provide interesting scrambling (Scrambling Grade 1); in winter it involves easy climbing (Winter Grade I)

Seasons & Restrictions: Summer conditions may be expected from June to September, and winter conditions from October to May. There are no restrictions

Map: OS Outdoor Leisure 3, Aviemore and Glen Avon

Start & Finish: Cairngorm ski-lift car park (NH 989 060), some 15km (9 miles) above Aviemore

Access: Some 50km (30 miles) south of Inverness along the A9

Tourist Information: Aviemore (tel. 01479 810363)

Accommodation: There are all types of accommodation at Aviemore, and a selection of places to stay at nearby Glenmore, including a campsite and a Youth Hostel

Geology: The predominant rock is granite

Flora & Fauna: Osprey, ptarmigan, dunlin and snow bunting may be seen, also mountain hare and reindeer(!). Bell, ling and cross-leaved heather, moss campion and creeping azalea grow in this region

Comment: The rugged cliffs and lochans of the high Northern Corries, topped by the Cairngorm plateau, have a great deal of stark grandeur. The ascent of Fiachaill Coire an t-Sneachda ridge provides an exciting scramble, and returning by Fiacaill a' Choire Chais is straightforward.

■ Despite its brevity, this is a worthy outing on the edge of the great Cairngorm wilderness: it explores the intimacies of the Northern Corries, views the desolation of the Cairngorm plateau, and

The Tops

Cairngorm	(kaarn gorom = blue mountain)	
Cairn Lochan	1,215m (3,986ft)	(cairn lochan = cairn of the lochan)
Stob Coire an t-Sneachda	1,176m (3,658ft)	(stop corra an dreka = peak of the snow corrie)
Stob Coire Chais	1,141m (3,743ft)	(stop corra ca = peak of the steep corrie)

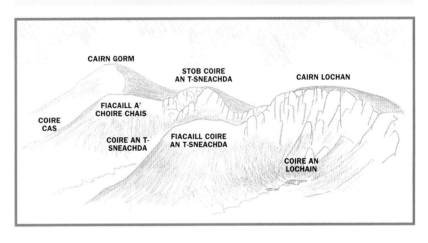

provides an exciting scramble before rounding the rim of cliffs and making a straightforward return. A strong word of caution, however: despite a simple, benign appearance from below, the Cairngorms are anything but this in character, and within a very short space of time the weather can change completely. Thus a winter's day can range, not untypically, from sun and calm, through driving rain to screaming blizzard – and the winds here blow with fearsome strength.

Leave the head of the car park and bear right over the bridge to pick up the constructed path leading to the right across the hillside; it crosses the Allt Coire an t-Sneachda burn, and although in summer you may pass by without a second thought, in winter you must take care not to fall through the covering bridge of snow. More dangerous still, in a rapid snow-melt situation, the burn can quickly become a raging torrent and may be completely uncrossable. Keep on the path for a

A walker pauses at the start of the rock difficulties on the top section of the Fiacaill Coire an t-Sneachda ridge

little way as it climbs, then aim directly for the base of the Fiacaill Coire an t-Sneachda ridge.

Both the basin of 'Sneachda' to the left and 'Lochan' to the right are famous rock and winter mountaineering playgrounds. There are many famous routes, such as the Aladdin's Couloir, first climbed in winter conditions on 24 March 1935; and the Savage Slit, first ascended as a rock climb on 17 July 1945, and as a winter climb, plastered in snow and ice, on 21 April 1957. However, should you look for the once-famous climbing bothy of Jean's Hut, marked on some maps as being on the floor of the basin of 'Lochan' to the right, you won't find it – it has been removed in its entirety, and there is no sign at all of its ever having been there.

Make your way up the ridge: in summer it rises before you as a pleasant, bouldery heather crest, and in winter as a fine arete of snow. You will reach a subsidiary top with excellent vantage over both corries; then at around the 1,120m altitude mark, the going steepens. The final section offers exposed rock scrambling up the blocky granite nose, and leads to the high shoulder plateau of Cairngorm. The wind on the exposed plateau blows very strongly – sometimes, on emerging from the top of the ridge, walkers may find that, although it has been sheltered below, it is blowing with such force that the safest option is to retreat back down the same way they came up.

It is worth walking to the right first of all, to take in the summit of Cairn Lochan (the summit

Heading into Coire an t-Sneachda with Fiacaill Coire an t-Sneachda rising to the right

cairn is located right on the edge of the cliffs, so have a care); then go north-west across the rim of cliffs at the head of 'Corrie Sneachda'. Climb to the top of Stob Coire an t-Sneachda (unnamed on OS maps) and keep going until you reach the final little dome of Stob Coire Chais (unnamed on OS maps) – this marks the top of Fiacaill a' Choire Chais. The way down is straightforward, and leads you back to the original path and the sprawling car park.

This is a worthy, if very small, taste of Cairngorm magic.

Looking around the rim of Coire an t-Sneachda from the Cairn Gorm plateau. The heights of Cairn Lochan are seen centrally with the Fiacaill Coire an t-Sneachda ridge descending to its right

ACKNOWLEDGEMENTS

For holding things together at home and on our travels, very special thanks is due to my wife, Susan.

This book draws on a vast number of guidebooks and reference works that have gone before, particularly the maps of the Ordnance Survey and Harvey Maps, Ambleside's Armitt Library and the Arran Heritage Museum at Brodick.

For their help with the text, and for sharing their knowledge of mountain walking, I would particularly like to thank Dave Bishop, John Hargreaves, Philip Lund, Cameron McNeish, Andrew Sheehan and Noel Williams.

I am indebted to a great number of people for assisting me in this project, those that accompanied me on the walks, became a part of my photographs, shared their knowledge, corrected text and supported me personally:
Dave Allen, Martin Battersby, Dave Birkett, Paul Birr, Marian and Peter Cheung, John Cleare, Paul and Gregg Cornforth, Ann, Heather, Jessica and Jackson Corrie, Brian and June Dodson, Paul Dunkley, Fiona Fraser, Roy Garner, Rick Graham, Tony Greenbank, Dale Huey, Heather Johnson, Alan Hinkes, Andy Hyslop, Mark Murray, Ross Murray, Outdoor Writers Guild, Steve Reid, Mark Smith, Roly Smith, Emma Parkin, John White. For imparting their local knowledge and helping me with pronunciation thanks to Andrew, Ed, George, John and Maureen Birkett, Melly and Marie Dixon, Jackie and Mark Dugdale, and B.A. Morrison. There were many more and I must offer my sincere apologies to those whose names I have missed.

I would also like to thank the publishers for their patience and commitment especially Sue Viccars and the team of Sue Cleave, Les Dominey, Anne Plume and Jane Trollope.

Also great thanks to Martin Bagness for his ridge profiles.

Credit must be given to those who keep a watchful eye over our mountains and do a tremendous job preserving their beauty and character – the Snowdonia National Park Authority, the Lake District National Park Authority, the National Trust for England and Wales, the National Trust for Scotland, the Countryside Commission, the Friends of the Lake District and the various National Nature Reserves; and those who hold the best interests of the hill walker and mountaineer to heart – the Rambler's Association, the British Mountaineering Council, the Mountaineering Council of Scotland, the Scotttish Mountaineering Club, Open Spaces Society, the Climbers' Club and the Fell & Rock Climbing Club.

For those who have helped to supply me with equipment a huge thanks to Sue Reay and Martin Geere of Berghaus – whose superb and constantly reliable gear, particularly boots and waterproofs, has kept me walking and climbing, unfailingly, in all types of extreme conditions.

And also thanks to Dave Brown of DB Mountain Sports and Edelrid.

Mention must also be made of the local mountain people of Wales and Scotland whose hospitality has always made me most welcome when on leave from my native Lake District. In particular, I must thank Glenda Lloyd Davies and Sian Evans of the Welsh Tourist Board who have been absolutely magnificent in their support for this project.

BILL BIRKETT PHOTO LIBRARY

All the photographs that appear in this book are from my own photographic library. The library holds a huge selection of material covering all of Britain's mountains and wild places including one of the most comprehensive collections of photographs of the English Lake District.
Tel. 015394 37420
e-mail: billbirkett@ukstamp.co.uk

INDEX

Index

Entries in *italics* indicate illustrations

INDEX

A DAVID & CHARLES BOOK

Copyright © Bill Birkett 1999
First published in the UK in 1999
First published in paperback 2003

Ridge profiles by Martin Bagness

ISBN 0 7153 1621 4

Printed in Hong Kong by Hong Kong Graphic and Printing Limited
for David & Charles
Brunel House   Newton Abbot   Devon

A catalogue record for this book is available from the British Library.

Bill Birkett has asserted his right to be identified as author of this work in accordance with the Copyright, Designs and Patents Act, 1988.